Αγάπη

VINTAGE CANADA

JAMES CHATTO

THE GREEK FOR LOVE

A MEMOIR OF *Sorrow and Joy*

VINTAGE CANADA EDITION, 2006

Published in Canada by Vintage Canada, a division of Random House of Canada Limited, Toronto, in 2006. Originally published in hardcover in Canada by Random House Canada, a division of Random House of Canada Limited, Toronto, in 2005. Distributed by Random House of Canada Limited, Toronto.

www.randomhouse.ca

Library and Archives Canada Cataloguing in Publication

Chatto, James
The Greek for love : a memoir of sorrow and joy / James Chatto.

ISBN-13: 978-0-679-31314-4
ISBN-10: 0-679-31314-1

1. Chatto, James. 2. Corfu Island (Greece)—Social life and customs—20th century. 3. Corfu Island (Greece)—Description and travel. I. Title.

DF901.C7C53 2005 949.5'5 C2005-905093-4

Book design by CS Richardson

Printed and bound in Canada

2 4 6 8 9 7 5 3

For Wendy

Αγάπη

Prelude

November 1982

The storm reached the island just after nightfall, a monstrous anvil of cloud that came twisting down the Adriatic, lit from within by red and white lightning. For a moment, it towered over the hills that surrounded our high mountain valley, while the tall cypress trees moaned and swayed in panic. A sudden gust of wind sucked the dried brown leaves from the grapevine above the patio. Panes of glass buzzed in the window frame, shutters swung hysterically on their hinges. As the first great peal of thunder shook the house, the electricity gave out. Wendy and I had been doing our accounts in the privacy of the bedroom. We sat motionless in the sudden darkness and watched the glowing red bar of the tiny electric heater fade to black.

Feeling my way along the walls of the corridor, through the parlour with its red plush, Sunday-best sofas, I reached the warmth of the kitchen. Our friend Kostantes was bent over the wood stove, loading another log. "Woo woo woo, Dzimi!" he laughed, his gold tooth flashing piratically in the candlelight. I pointed at the candle on the table, trying to make him understand we too wanted light. He limped across to the old dresser beside the fridge and started to rummage around in a drawer. "Olé, Dzimi!" he called triumphantly, brandishing a half-burned stub. He lit it in the other candle's flame, dripped some wax into a small glass tumbler and stuck the little stump down. "Oreia?" he asked, glancing up at me coyly. *Oreia* was one of the half-dozen Greek words I knew. It meant "beautiful," and Kostantes and I used it with reckless abandon in our long, mimetic conversations. "Oreia," I agreed with genuine enthusiasm, and he chuckled and patted my back. "O Dzimi!"

Back to the bedroom, shielding the precious light. Wendy's eyes were wide with excitement at the imminent adventure. She loved storms. We struggled into our overcoats and made our way to the kitchen, where Kostantes was waiting to shake our hands and wish us luck. With a flourish, he opened the door onto the street. The wind blew the candles out.

By now, the night was as black as fury, the air thick with flying matter. Something that might have been a cardboard box banged against my legs. Farther up the street, a window glowed faintly where Philip had lit his emergency hurricane lamps. The owner of the village kafeneion—a bar that also sold coffee, cigarettes and chocolate—Philip spoke pretty good English and had agreed to act as translator for us tonight.

"What?" shouted Wendy.

"I said, this is the wind the banshees ride, bringing madness and woe!"

Our lives had been just as chaotic for the last three months—the death of my father in England, the deaths of my two grandmothers, my marriage to Wendy, our decision to leave our penurious lives in Toronto and move back to Europe, the delightful, terrifying, totally unexpected discovery that Wendy had become pregnant on our wedding night. And now we were about to take the final step off the clifftop of common sense. We were going to buy a house on the edge of a remote mountain village on a Greek island, a 150-year-old ruin with nothing to recommend it but stone walls that were three feet thick and the most beautiful view in the world.

We knew the owner, Panayotis, only by sight—a farmer and sometime builder with a thick, drooping grey moustache and a docile, dignified manner. The house where he lived stood almost across the road from the kafeneion but we might have missed it if we hadn't seen Panayotis's flashlight bobbing up and down. He was out on his porch in the storm, urgently waving us in. I felt Wendy's hand on my arm, her warm breath against my ear.

"Remember," she whispered. "We have to beat him down to ten thousand pounds. Two million drachmas. No more!"

Too nervous to manage much of a smile, Panayotis led us into the front parlour and gestured that we might like to sit down on the sofa. Then he pointed at the useless electric light in the ceiling and the paraffin lamp on the sideboard, its yellow flame casting melodramatic shadows around the room. He shook his head and murmured something in Greek. We nodded reassuringly, trying to show him we understood. Now his wife, Elpitha, appeared, tall, broad and haughty, carrying a tray of coffee, glasses of water and a small dish of preserved kumquats in heavy syrup. Doilies were spread on the polished coffee table, the treats carefully handed out. Elpitha shot her husband one emphatic glance and glided away into the kitchen.

Rain rattled against the shuttered windows. We sipped the thick, sweet coffee. Panayotis glanced at his watch and began to gnaw a fingernail. "O Philippos," he said, spreading his hands with an expression of despair. At last, we felt a gust of cold air from the front door and heard a man stamping and cursing in the hallway. Panayotis hurried out. He was still talking as he followed Philip back into the parlour.

"Fuckin' hell, man!" growled Philip cheerfully. "I'm thinkin' this is fuckin' crazy to be out in these weathers. Even my dog is staying home. Anyhow, let's do this business."

He turned to Panayotis and a long conversation ensued, our host talking quickly and intently, Philip frequently interrupting, raising his voice.

"Okay, James," he said at last, muttering the words in his gravelly bass in case Panayotis, or Elpitha lurking behind the kitchen door, had suddenly learned to speak English. "He wants to sell you that house. The one on the other side of the hill over Zervou ridge. The one which is having the two rooms upstairs and the one big room downstairs. And with it, also, the other small house which is just one room. And with it, also, the land." He turned to Panayotis. "Posses elies?"

"Endeka elies," said Panayotis.

"With eleven olive trees. That's the house you want?"

"Yes!"

"But . . ." Philip paused for effect. "He has some problems. He wants still to be using that path which is between the house and the small house for him and his family to pass by."

"Absolutely. Their right-of-way. That's fine."

Philip grunted in surprise.

"And with him, his donkey will also pass by."

"Sure!"

"And . . . There are still some certain things, I can say, inside the house, that are belonging to him until he can take thems away."

"What things?"

"Some almonds and some wools."

We smiled and nodded at Panayotis. "No problem! Please ask Panayotis if he has decided on a price."

A brief conference. The silence from the kitchen was palpable.

"He says one million two hundred thousand. In cash. In sterling pounds that he can turn around into drachmas when the rate is improving in May."

"One million two hundred thousand?"

"Yes, man."

I looked at Wendy.

"Okay."

Philip seemed slightly disappointed. He shrugged, leaned back in his chair and pulled a packet of cigarettes from his pocket. Panayotis stood up, suddenly relaxed and genial, almost giggling, shaking our hands. Elpitha entered, beaming with approval, and kissed Wendy on the cheeks. Outside, the storm raged on, though whether in fanfare or warning I really couldn't say.

And that was it. Days followed with lawyers, surveyors and notaries public, bank managers and vice-consuls, mornings going from office to office in Corfu Town, trudging through steady rain to spend hours in a dozen badly furnished anterooms. So many laborious wheels to set in motion, but they were mere details, *ex post facto*. The handshake with Panayotis had been the irrevocable moment. Then we were on the plane, flying back to England to close up our lives there, to sell my flat in South London and figure out how to bring our belongings to Greece. We sat in exhausted silence until the seat-belt sign went out. Wendy was looking at me.

"What are you thinking about?" she asked.

"The house, down there in the rain. I think this is when we're supposed to pause in sober reflection upon the magnitude of our folly."

"Or we could play poker." And she reached into her carpet bag for the deck of cards.

Chapter One

Sometimes, on nights like this, when I've been working late and the house is quiet, my mind skims away through the years to the time when we lived on Corfu. Our life there floats in the darkness of the past like a tiny island of green and yellow light, growing closer and closer until I can almost make out its shape, the narrative map of its coastline, the ordered sequence of events. But I'm moving towards it too swiftly, getting too close. The magnesium glare of its sun envelops me and I find myself free-falling into some random moment of memory.

At the time, so long ago, we were too young and too busy to take note of the details, the feelings, the kisses and quarrels, and store them neatly away for future retrieval. Now I want to remember them all—to find my way back and make sense of what happened, arranging those innumerable, luminous memories into a story my children can read. The night when we bought our house, twenty-three years ago, seems just one of several beginnings. So does the afternoon two years earlier when we first set foot in the village, hungry and hot and hardly speaking. The huge blue Mercedes bus roared away in a billow of dust and diesel fumes, leaving us standing beside our suitcases. We watched it climb on through the village, almost as wide as the street and as tall as some of the houses, until a bend in the road hid it from view.

"We made it!" I grinned. Wendy tipped back her head so she could glare at me more effectively from under the brim of her new straw hat. It was becoming clear that she regretted leaving the organization of our summer to me. What I saw as blithe and carefree trusting-to-luck seemed to her to be mere inefficiency, or worse—a kind of arrogance.

"You know what really drives me crazy?" she asked. "It's the way the English always think they know best."

"I know."

"And then the refusal to admit they've done anything wrong."

"Well, I . . ."

"Or to offer even a single word of apology."

"Sorry."

The idea of spending our second summer together on a Greek island instead of in my drab little London flat had been suggested some months before. We had known that her old friend Dee would be over from Canada and could share her last weeks in Europe with us. I had been to Corfu as a child, for a fortnight's holiday my mother had organized, and had vague but vivid memories of mountains and storms and a dolphin glimpsed in the warm blue sea. The first brief flurry of enthusiasm had sent us combing through glossy brochures, ogling villas and apartments that were far beyond our budget until we found one listing we could afford—two lines tucked away at the back of the *Sunday Times:* Villa Parginos, traditional, Loutses, Corfu. There was no photograph, no description beyond that single "traditional," an epithet that runs the gamut from enchantment to squalor, and can even encompass both.

Weeks passed before we received confirmation of our three-month booking. After that, the scramble for charter flights had distracted me from more detailed research, and when we finally landed at Corfu airport, I realized I had no very clear idea where to go next. A brief conversation with the bored English tour guides who stood at the gate waiting for their groups of holidaymakers proved fruitless. None of them had ever heard of Loutses. Not a good sign. Outside the terminal, the three taxi drivers who lounged against their cabs, smoking competitively, were more helpful. They knew the village, but none of them wanted to go there—it was too far away, the roads were too bad, and there would be no chance of finding a fare to bring back to town.

"Take a bus," shrugged the ringleader. So we rode into Corfu Town in his cab, suffocated by tobacco fumes and crushed by the luggage that wouldn't fit into the trunk. The bus station was squeezed into a square behind the new harbour, where the blue leviathans bellowed and growled as they backed and turned, scattering the milling crowds of tourists and shoppers. I pointed out how lucky we were to have caught the midday bus—no doubt we would be able to find seats sooner or later—and as soon as we got to Loutses we'd head for the nearest restaurant and have lunch. Dee mustered the ghost of a smile. Wendy didn't.

An hour and a half later, we were still standing in the aisle, crushed and jostled and trodden upon. The road north along Corfu's mountainous eastern coast was an endless series of tight bends, steep climbs and sudden descents, which the driver attacked at breakneck speed. It was also stunningly beautiful, if the tourists in the seats were to be believed. They pointed out every perfect bay, every noble cape and immaculate beach far below the serpentine corniche. "That must be the house where the Durrells lived," they cooed. Wedged upright, we could see nothing but a blur of potholed tarmac.

Kassiopi, on the island's northeastern point, was the last resort on the route. We could finally sit, scrutinized by the few remaining passengers, elderly men in short-sleeved shirts with bulging plastic bags at their feet, elderly women dressed in many layers of black—the local chapter of the Queen Victoria impersonation society. Now we were heading westwards along the northern coast of the island, bare yellow hills rising to our left, grey and white cliffs plunging down to the right, carving the sea into placid, turquoise bays. Across the straits, the mountains of Albania were blurred and distanced by the heat. Then we turned inland along a straight flat road bordered by orchards and olive groves and came to a halt in a village.

"Peritheia," said the bus conductor. All eyes were on us.

"Peritheia," agreed one of the old ladies, nodding encouragingly.

"Loutses," I ventured. Their eyebrows shot up in surprise, as if the notion of foreigners wishing to carry on to that particular destination were somehow bizarre.

The bus began its final ascent, leaving the houses behind, climbing now up a narrow and rutted track that grew increasingly steep. Olive trees scraped the roof and flanks of the vehicle; the wheels on Wendy's side seemed to stray beyond the crumbling verge, spinning in space over vertiginous ravines. Each hairpin bend necessitated a three-point turn, the conductor leaning out of the open door, shouting instructions to the driver. Sometimes the trees thinned or vanished altogether and then we were rewarded with an astonishing view—the whole northern coast of the island, dark green hills and scattered villages, a plain beyond them, long promontories like sleeping crocodiles jutting out into the glittering Ionian. At last the road squeezed through an opening in the hills and entered a broad valley rimmed by steep, olive-covered slopes. There were houses again, some with gardens or allotments, a pink church on a distant outcrop surrounded by tall, dark cypresses, and a taverna, its plastic-topped wooden tables and wooden chairs set in the shade of five little trees. The bus stopped.

"Loutses," barked one of the ladies, leaning forward to push Wendy's arm, and we tumbled out into the heat while the conductor lifted our suitcases onto the roadside. He climbed back in and the bus pulled away.

"So? What now?" asked Wendy.

"I'll ask at the taverna."

But the taverna was closed, the windows shuttered, the door bolted and padlocked. It was two o'clock in the afternoon and there was no one to be seen, no sound except the shrill, ceaseless rasp of the cicadas in the trees, a vibration that seemed to fill the whole valley, like the sound of heat itself. Already prickling with sweat, we carried our suitcases into the shade of some olive trees and sat down on a low white wall. Behind us was a chicken run where a gang of dishevelled hens picked through a litter of plastic bags, watermelon rinds and rusting paint pots. From the faint but unmistakable smell in the air, a whitewashed cement-block construction the size of a sentry box could only be some kind of outhouse.

"If that's the Villa Parginos, I'm going back to London," said Wendy.

Time passed. A small, furtive black cat loped across the road, a lizard's tail dangling obscenely from the side of its mouth.

"I'll try to find someone."

As far as I could see, Loutses was essentially a single road that climbed gently as it wound on up the valley. A number of footpaths and tracks led off it in various directions, disappearing into the olive groves or into some fold of the hills. I had pictured something more closely knit, a maze of buildings and alleys all painted white like the postcard images of villages in the Cyclades, but these houses were detached, set back from the road behind unkempt gardens and vineyards. A couple of them were modern bungalows, but most were older and larger, made of stone, with two storeys, porches and balconies. Many of them had a cement patio shaded by dusty vines. Pots of red and pink geraniums added gaudy splashes of colour. Pressing in behind the buildings, the olive groves provided a backdrop of green.

I passed a shop with three or four rickety tables set out in a small courtyard—no sign of life. Then a proud two-storey building with a limp, sun-faded Greek flag hanging from a flagpole—the village police station—but the door did not open and nobody answered my tentative knocking. Farther along the street, a steep flight of concrete steps led up to what might be a bar. I peered through the glass of the front door into a long, bare room full of tables and chairs with a counter at one end and a makeshift wooden telephone booth at the other. All dark, all empty. The entire village was asleep, deep in its afternoon siesta. Either that or we were dealing with a landlocked Corfiote version of the *Marie Celeste.*

Walking back down the street, I could feel the heat from the tarmac through my shoes. I stopped again by the taverna, squinting into the white glare of the sun. Wendy and Dee had disappeared, taking their luggage with them, but the door of the little pink one-storey house across the road from the chicken run was open and there were familiar voices from within, the sound of laughter.

"Here he is," said Dee.

I stepped inside. A couple in their early fifties stood there, the man dressed in crumpled grey flannel trousers and an old white shirt over a string vest. He had a grizzled stubble and several missing teeth, and from the way his hair stuck out to one side it looked as if he had just woken up. Beside him was a short, sturdily built woman with jet-black hair pulled back tightly into a bun. She wore a black dress, brown slippers and a wary smile.

The man stepped forward with a cheerful cry of greeting and gripped my hand, shaking it vigorously. His callused hand felt like tree bark.

"Kostantes!" he said, slapping his chest delightedly.

Wendy held up a piece of cardboard on which someone had written VILLA PARGINOS in black felt-tipped pen. "Look, Jimmy," she said, meeting my eye. "They'd made a sign but hadn't actually put it up outside . . ."

"Dzimi?" asked Kostantes, quizzically.

"Dmitri," murmured his wife.

"Dmitri! Dzimi!" And from that day forth I was Dmitri.

The introductions continued. Kostantes's wife, Alexandra, seemed to approve of Dee's name—short and to the point. But neither of them were able to master the initial *W* of *Wendy.* She was therefore christened Goo-endy. Kostantes was still laughing as he threw an arm around my shoulders and led me back outside and around the house to a small patio, separated from the street by a low wire fence. Wasps thronged overhead, busy at a straggly vine that broke up the sunshine without providing any real shade. Kostantes noisily dragged three plastic chairs across the cement and positioned them among the geraniums that grew profusely from old rectangular metal cans. Then he opened a door that led into a sort of lean-to shed and pulled out a fourth chair, much older, wooden and decidedly wobbly. The three of us sat down opposite him, feeling as if we were about to be examined and wondering how on earth we could answer. Kostantes was evidently having the same linguistic problems. He rubbed his stubbly chin, scratched his head, raised his eyebrows, made a comical face like a man deep in thought, and then started to chuckle. We chuckled too. From his shirt pocket he fished out a flat cardboard box of untipped, oval-shaped cigarettes and offered them to each of us. Wendy and Dee smiled and shook their heads but I felt obliged to accept. Then another idea occurred to him.

"Loutses!" he said, with a look of pride and a magnificent sweep of his arm that encompassed the whole village.

"Loutses," we agreed.

"Oreia!" ventured Wendy, the only word we had yet prised from our phrase book, apart from please and thank you. Kostantes roared with laughter, and when Alexandra appeared round the corner of the house carrying a tray with four glasses of water on it he reprised the entire conversation for her benefit. She answered something in her shy way, refused my offer of a chair and hurried back into the house. Kostantes handed round the water.

"Oreia?" he asked when we had all sipped.

We assured him that it was. He pointed across the road at the outhouse in the chicken run and then at the water in his glass, repeating the gesture until we all understood where the water had come from.

"Oh . . ."

"Dzimi . . . Inglis?"

"Yes! English!"

"Inglis. Oreia." He twisted on his chair, reaching into his trouser pocket, and drew out the stub of a pencil. Beckoning me to look, he started to write, laboriously, on the back of his cigarette packet. He showed us his handiwork. A date: 1944.

"Kerkyra. Yirmanes." He tapped the box.

"Germans were here in 1944?"

"Inglis." He pointed up at the yellow mountaintops that rose above the village to the south. "Boom boom boom. Yirmanes . . ." Then he mimed a kick, slapped his hands together twice, horizontally, and tapped one eyelid. "Inglis. Sithero."

World War Two in five seconds flat.

"Yirmanes?" A scowl. "Italiani?" He mimed a man playing a concertina. "Americani?" He blew out his cheeks and slapped his stomach. "Inglis!" And he flexed his biceps like a strongman.

"What about Canadians?" asked Dee.

"Kanadesi, Inglis; Inglis, Kanadesi."

"He says we're the same," I translated.

"Hm," said Wendy.

Kostantes looked at each of us in turn, clearly mulling over a question. Then he drew another number on the cigarette packet: 55. "Kostantes," he said, showing us the box.

I wrote down our ages. Me, twenty-five. Wendy and Dee, twenty-three.

Alexandra was standing at the edge of the patio. She said something to Kostantes. He stood up and led us back into the house.

The Villa Parginos was a most unspectacular bungalow. The front door opened straight into the kitchen, the largest room in the house and the centre of life. The walls had been newly painted a pretty shade of pale blue that matched the linoleum floor; the light on the ceiling was a fluorescent tube that buzzed like a distant bee. In one corner stood an ancient wooden dresser with lace doilies on the empty shelves and a drawer full of useful things like candle ends, corks and pieces of wire. The tall refrigerator, we would learn, was the appliance equivalent of a DeSoto automobile, far bigger outside than in, noisy, expensive to run and apt to break down unexpectedly. Only the cold tap worked in the little sink—we would have to boil a kettle to clean the dishes—and the two-ring gas stove looked as if it had been built for a doll's house. In the winter, we later discovered, Kostantes moved in a beautiful wood-burning range with two ovens that kept the kitchen warm and aromatic with the scent of almond wood. For the rest of the year, it was stored away in the apothiki, the little room that opened off the patio.

Behind the kitchen, on the other side of a frosted-glass door, was a bedroom with two single beds and a wardrobe. From the bundle of sheets thrust into a corner and the newly made look of the beds, we guessed that Kostantes and Alexandra had been fast asleep when we arrived. Another door led from the kitchen into a narrow front parlour. Two ugly modern sofas, hard as board and upholstered in vivid red plush, faced each other across a glossy coffee table. The outside shutters were closed and only a narrow line of sunlight filtered through the net curtain, illuminating dancing motes of dust. Beyond the parlour, a corridor turned right for the second, more formal front door (which was never used) or left to the master bedroom, containing a double bed, a small bedside table and a wardrobe. Beside it was Kostantes's pride and joy, a modern bathroom so new it still smelled of fresh paint and grouting. High on the wall, opposite the lavatory and washbasin, a shower faucet protruded beneath a tiny white cylindrical immersion heater with a dial near its base. Kostantes showed us a switch in the hallway that would start the long process of warming the water and explained in elaborate mime how the red needle pointed right when it was hot, left when it was cold. There was no shower stall or curtain, just a small round drain in the middle of the floor.

"Oreia?" he asked with an expression of comic anxiety.

We nodded enthusiastically and he beamed.

Back in the kitchen, Alexandra stood holding carrier bags full of bed linen, green leaves like spinach and a litre bottle of olive oil. She looked around her, saying a silent farewell to her home, then she and Kostantes walked outside and stood by the side of the road to wait for the bus.

"Should we shut the door?" I wondered. "They're bound to see. They might think it rude."

But it was our house now, and for the next three months. I closed the door very slowly and silently, shutting out the heat and the street and the village. Dee had dragged her backpack into the room off the kitchen. Wendy and I carried our suitcases through to the master bedroom and began to unpack.

Kostantes did not leave on the four o'clock bus with Alexandra. They rented a two-room apartment in Corfu Town, up on the fifth floor of an ancient tenement in the old Jewish quarter, where Alexandra lived from Monday to Friday. Nikolas, their son, went to high school in town and needed his meals cooked. Kostantes's work was here in the north of the island, building villas down on the coast for tourists to rent or taking odd jobs that were more or less to do with construction. We had barely finished unpacking when he appeared at the kitchen window. With his shirt buttoned up and tucked into his trousers, and his hair wet and combed back, he looked like a different, younger man, but the roguish grin was the same. In his hands was a gift, a recycled wine bottle full of thick, golden olive oil. I started to take it from him, but he shook his head.

"Goo-endy," he said, nodding at her and then at the stove.

"He thinks you must be the one who does the cooking, darling."

"Well maybe I'll learn . . ."

We thanked him profusely and he waved goodbye but was back again five minutes later with a plate of apricots, perfectly ripe, swollen with juice, some with twigs and leaves still attached. He watched while I bit into one, enjoying my expression of amazement at the delicate, perfumed flavour, the sweetness of the flesh. Then he beckoned me to the window and pointed across the street at a tree still heavy with fruit.

"He stole them from the neighbour's garden," I explained to Wendy and Dee.

"God, they're good."

None of us had eaten a thing since the vile, foil-steamed omelette breakfast on the plane that morning, and the apricots never stood a chance. We had barely finished wiping the juice from our chins when Kostantes returned yet again, this time knocking discreetly at the kitchen door. A tall young man stood beside him—in his early twenties, perhaps—with tousled, curly black hair, a face like a teenaged Omar Sharif and a soccer player's body.

"Hello, hello," he said, laughing. "My name is Ilias. My uncle has asked me to find out if you need anything."

Introductions. Another chair found. A palpable sense of excitement as the barrage of questions began. Ilias did his best to answer them all, glancing often at Dee, while Kostantes sat waiting for occasional rapid translations from his nephew. Ilias had a few questions of his own.

"My uncle asks if you like the house?"

"Oh yes! Oreia!"

"And the bathroom? It's very new. A new idea to have the bathroom inside the house."

"It's wonderful."

"You are the first tourists who ever stayed in Loutses, I think."

"Do you live here?"

"I go to university in Athens, studying economics, but I'm home for the summer. I live next door."

"Could you ask your uncle where we can buy food?"

"And when the taverna opens?"

"And the best way to get to the beach?"

Kostantes stood up.

"My uncle wants to show you the way."

"Now?"

"Of course!" said Ilias with a dazzling smile.

"You go," said Wendy. "We'll stay here."

I followed Kostantes as he sauntered out into the street. The heat was less intense now and the village was stirring, slowly regaining consciousness after the long afternoon sleep. The door of the taverna stood open. Farther up the road a woman shouted after two small boys who had raced away into the olive groves. A badly bruised pick-up truck went by with three men squeezed into the cab and three more crouched in the open back. They called to Kostantes and he answered with a joke that set them all chuckling. Across the street, he pulled open a gate in the chicken run and wheeled out an ancient white Vespa scooter, climbed on carefully, then patted the seat behind him. As soon as I was settled, feet on the narrow running boards, he heaved away with his legs and we began to freewheel down the street, picking up speed as we passed the last of the houses.

So this is how it ends, I thought, gripping the back of the worn plastic seat behind me. A quick plunge over a cliff, no helmet, body impaled on the pointed crown of a cypress tree . . . As the tarmac petered out into a rutted track, Kostantes showed no sign of slowing down. He avoided the deeper potholes and patches of loose gravel with instinctive ease, just a twitch of the handlebars. Might as well enjoy the view, the warm breeze, the sudden sharp scent of oregano or the musty perfume of Jerusalem sage. Looking down to the left or up to the right, I could see beneath the leaf canopy of the olive groves. Gnarled trunks flickered by, rising from the steeply sloping hillside in a dwindling perspective of twisted pillars. The dim light beneath the trees had an extraordinary quality, the gold of the afternoon sun fragmented and diffused by the innumerable leaves. It was like a pointillist picture, a three-dimensional mosaic, a cathedral. At our backs, the yellow mountain peaks rose up above the olive tree line; below us, the unbroken blanket of the olive groves smoothed the contours of the hills until they reached the sea.

Swooping around every curve, we finally reached the place where the road recovered some semblance of a surface. There were houses and gardens now, a pink church, people. As we came off the hill, Kostantes put the scooter in gear and its small motor spat into life, puttering us along the main street of Peritheia at a walking pace so that Kostantes could exchange pleasantries with passing friends. Everyone knew him and smiled when they saw him. Then we were through the village, accelerating onto the coast road, briefly out of sight of the sea. We passed a small shrine, a pair of heavy wrought-iron gates surmounted by an iron cross.

"Monasterios," shouted Kostantes over his shoulder, taking his hand off the bike to indicate a great stretch of land,

and turning down the corners of his mouth in an expression of grave sobriety that immediately dissolved into loud laughter. Now we could see the sea again below us on our left, the sere yellow mountains of Albania suddenly much closer across the straits. Kostantes drove a little farther, then pulled off the road into the shade of some trees, turning off the engine. We both climbed stiffly off the scooter. The hiss of cicadas echoed from the surrounding hills; the sun was hot on my back. There was no signpost or marker to indicate where a track might descend through the olive groves, but Kostantes clambered off the edge of the road onto a smooth boulder and set off through the trees down a steep path. The hard, yellow soil was slippery in places—my jeans were soon covered in dust. There were more boulders to negotiate at the bottom and then we stepped out from the shadow of the grove and onto the beach.

Kostantes stood beside me, his hand on my shoulder. A quarter of a mile of white powder sand stretched away on either side, silent and pristine, sloping gracefully down to the sea. There it flattened into the warm shallows, stained the colour of caramel by the water. No intimation of humanity, not so much as a footstep corrupted its perfection. Far to the left and right, twin promontories sheltered the bay. Thickets of tall bamboo provided a natural backdrop, and from between them a small stream emerged, growing ever more shallow as it crossed the beach, finally disappearing into the parched sand a few yards from the sea. A squadron of swallows darted and turned above us, flickering off over the sandbars, wheeling back, flashing navy blue wings. Kostantes picked up a length of green bamboo.

"Kalamaki," he said, tapping it with his hand. Then he pointed at the beach, the bay, the encircling hills. "Kalamaki."

I followed him back up the path through the olive groves. Halfway to the road he stopped, not to catch his breath but to show me another treasure. Reaching above his head, he took hold of the end of a slender olive branch, pulling it gently down for my inspection. Against his callused, nicotine-stained fingers, the tiny, embryonic fruit of next winter's crop looked no bigger than bright green grape pips.

"Eh, Dzimi?" he murmured reverently, giving me a piercing look. "Oreia . . . ?"

I nodded. "Oreia."

ILIAS HAD GONE by the time we returned. Wendy and Dee were giddy with hunger, and at six o'clock we strolled next door to the taverna and sat down at a table under the trees. Eventually a woman appeared in the doorway, wiping her hands on her apron. Her mouth fell open when she saw us and she hurried back inside. It was a while before she returned, followed by a gaunt, dishevelled man who scuttled into the tiny, glass-fronted lean-to at the side of the building. The woman tucked a wisp of yellow hair behind her ear and smiled at us. We smiled back.

"Are you open for dinner?" I asked. She answered in Greek. A linguistic impasse. Then she beckoned for us to follow her into the building. The room was dark, and empty except for an old blue-and-chrome jukebox in the corner and a refrigerator filled with bottles of Amstel lager and Kourtaki retsina.

We mimed a need for beer and then someone eating with a knife and fork. She nodded and led us back outside to the lean-to. In that cramped little space, the man was bending over a large charcoal brazier, fanning the coals with a folded newspaper until aromatic sparks crackled and leapt. He barely had room to turn around, and we could feel the heat streaming out through the open window. No wonder the guy was so thin. He gave a beaming, toothless grin and showed us a plate of uncooked pork kebabs. We nodded vigorously, and he shooed us back to the table.

Six in the evening was clearly the hour for socializing in Loutses. Villagers passed in a slow parade, pausing to talk to each other, often bidding us a friendly good evening. A blond-haired youth, slender as a wand, posed briefly by the low wall that separated us from the street, pretending not to look at Wendy and Dee. Then he sauntered away, eerily reminiscent of an early Clint Eastwood. A horse clopped by with a man sitting sidesaddle, a great bundle of foliage tied behind him.

We were no longer the only customers at the taverna. A very old man had wandered in and sat down in a chair with his back to the wall. He had white hair and a beautiful face and he gazed at us unaffectedly through sky-blue eyes. Every time one of us glanced his way he nodded slowly and smiled.

The food arrived: a side plate with some olives, two thin slices of feta cheese and a dozen french fries (we counted them), each one transfixed by a toothpick. Dismay! Then Dee spotted Ilias. He was on his way to our table when the man in the lean-to called him over and handed him three small kebabs, about six inches long, each bamboo spear topped with a hunk of soft white bread. Ilias brought them over.

"Hello! Georgie asked me to give you these. But you already have mezethes. That's good—very traditional."

"We're starving, Ilias, but we don't know how to order!"

"Oh . . . What do you want to eat? More souvlakia?"

"Anything!"

"I will arrange this."

The souvlakia were delicious, the tender cubes of pork cooked through, slightly charred, then lifted straight off the grill and dipped into a wet marinade of lemon juice, olive oil and oregano, where they hissed for a second before Georgie stuck the hunk of bread on the end and handed them out through the window. By now a line of small boys was queuing patiently at the lean-to, each one clutching a handful of coins. Georgie charged fifteen drachmas for a souvlaki, about fifteen cents, and business was brisk.

Ilias rejoined us, and I told him how beautiful the beach was.

"Of course. But it's only June. I think the sea may still be too cold to swim."

The barrage of questions began again, Ilias fielding them with grace and good humour. He had learned his English at school, doing his homework by lamplight until the momentous day in 1973 when the village acquired electricity. Working down on the coast as a waiter during the summers had improved his skills.

"How old is Loutses?"

Ilias didn't know. He had a distant relative down in Peritheia who was something of a scholar and who might have an answer, but all he knew were stories he had heard from his father, Petros, and from Kostantes. "And my uncle's crazy," he added, laughing, "so they may not be true. But the village was once much bigger and more important than it is now."

We begged him to tell us anything, and after rubbing his head for a while he began. In the 1930s, when Petros and Kostantes were boys, the house we were staying in had been the village store, owned and run by a distant relative of theirs. Loutses was the centre for a sizable chunk of the northeastern corner of Corfu, and all the farmers and shepherds for many miles around did their shopping there. It was also their trading post, the place to which they brought their lambs, cockerels, wool, timber and anything else they wished to sell to the storekeeper. He in turn sold them in Corfu Town. There was no coast road in those days, so the goods were carried by donkey down to a beach and then taken by boat to the island's capital. The only other road to town lay over the mountains—a man on a donkey could just get there and back in a day if he set off before dawn.

The store prospered, but Kostantes's relative took to spending the profits on liquor and women. He died just before the Second World War, at the climax of a week-long wedding party, leaving his family with crippling debts.

The war, Ilias thought, had changed everything. The rural economy was ruined during the years of occupation, first by the Italians, then by the Germans. The population of Loutses, once around five hundred souls, began its long decline. When Petros and Kostantes went to school, in the old stone building beside the bar, there had been seventy students. Once a month, they were turfed out of their classroom and the place was transformed into the regional courthouse. In

Ilias's day, there were only twenty children there, aged from six to thirteen, and it was difficult finding a teacher.

"Where did the people go?"

"Look. Some went to Athens or West Germany, to work. Some moved to the coast."

"Are you going to move when you graduate?" asked Dee.

"I don't know. I want to work in a bank. But if I can't find such a job, I may become a dentist. Either way, I still have to join the army."

"National service?"

"Yes . . . Eighteen months." He looked suddenly stricken, and we all sipped our beers in silent sympathy.

More food arrived. Three souvlakia each, a tower of thickly hewn bread and two plates of fried potatoes, golden, salty and piping hot. We made space on the table for a salad bowl filled with cool, moist chunks of cucumber, crunchy green peppers and crimson tomatoes so ripe that their sweet juice became a dressing that we soon enhanced with mellow, coral-coloured vinegar and yellow oil from the two small bottles that Georgie's wife brought. On separate dishes were more slices of feta dressed with oil and dried oregano flowers, and very small, firm black olives, slightly pointed at one end and without much flesh on their pits, that tasted sweeter and nuttier than any olives I had ever eaten.

"This is so delicious," I gasped between bites.

"Of course," confirmed Ilias. "Georgie's wife grows everything herself. It's much easier."

We urged him to share the food but he said he was expected home for dinner.

"You have to go?"

"Not yet!" The idea made him smile. "We eat around eleven o'clock in the summer."

Our dinner was unfashionably early, but it was also our lunch, which mitigated our embarrassment. A lean yellow dog with a tail like a whip appeared beside the table. Ilias tried to shoo it away, but Wendy rubbed its gritty head, then dropped a piece of souvlaki onto the dust in front of it. The pork vanished in seconds.

As the daylight faded, a string of light bulbs threaded among the lower branches of the trees were switched on, and the jukebox started to play a bouzouki ballad. Men began to wander in from the street. Most of them greeted Ilias, smiled and nodded at us. It was clear that we were the objects of a gentle but pervasive curiosity, and even those people who usually preferred to drink at the village's other two watering holes, the shop a little way farther up the street or the kafeneion beyond that, were taking the evening's first ouzo at Georgie's in order to check us out.

We were curious, too, and while Ilias's natural good manners prohibited him from mentioning anyone's name while they were still within earshot, he tried to tell us who people were and what they did for a living. Almost everyone was either a farmer or a builder, though the builders also had land, of course, that needed working, and the farmers were all perfectly capable of mending a roof or putting up a shed if they had to. But the builders worked down on the coast, taking advantage of the construction boom that tourism had brought in recent years. Life on the island was changing quickly, explained Ilias. Anyone who owned land down there was thinking of selling it, if they hadn't already done so, or else uprooting some of their olives and building a villa to rent out. Tourism had not yet reached Loutses, and he doubted it ever would—everybody knew foreigners weren't interested in venturing inland—but the money that could be earned on the coast was irresistible. Even the teenaged boys cashed in, working as waiters in the restaurants and bars. A season's tips could buy you an old scooter or a stereo system.

The policeman sauntered in and sat down at a table, very burly and dignified, with two stripes on the sleeve of his pale blue shirt. Georgie's wife arrived with more beers for us and a plateful of tender, juicy grilled pork, its crackling crisp and tangy with salt and oregano.

"It's from my uncle," explained Ilias. I twisted round, and there was Kostantes grinning and waving from the road. We beckoned him in but he shook his head and set off up the street, turning into the little store.

"He likes to drink at Stamati's."

"Where will he sleep while we're in the house?" asked Dee. Ilias didn't know. We found out that night when we finally left the taverna and heard deep rhythmic snores from the little apothiki behind the patio.

I dare say we slept as soundly. It seemed as if only minutes had passed before we awoke to the sound of a cock crowing and the patter of raindrops outside our bedroom window.

"It can't be raining!" I crawled out of bed and swung the shutters open. Dazzling sunshine. An attractive woman in dark glasses and a black dress was standing about ten feet away with a chicken under her arm. She had cut its throat. The sound of rain had been its blood hitting the stones at her feet. She smiled and called a greeting.

"Something tells me we're not in Kansas any more," said Wendy from under the sheets.

NOTHING ABOUT THAT first summer was quite the way we had imagined it would be. Wendy, with her art history degree, had hoped for classical clifftop temples, for a way of life enriched by an ancient and instinctive cultural wisdom. I wanted magic—silent, throbbing sunsets and nights on a mountainside under the stars, some kind of direct and preferably mystical communication with the landscape. It soon became clear that Loutses was unlikely to serve either fantasy. Set in its bowl-shaped valley, watched over by the yellow peaks of the island's massif, the village offered its own reality. We had pictured a private terrace where we could sit at dusk and sip wine and look out over the Ionian. Instead we had Kostantes's very public patio with its chicken-wire fence between us and the street. Inside the house we could hear whenever a car or truck or broken-mufflered motorbike passed by, the late-night arguments of the neighbours (odd to hear infuriated sarcasm screamed in a foreign language by a lady we were soon referring to as the Loudest Woman in Loutses), the early-morning sinus-clearing snorting and gobbing of the man who lived next door but one. We were dismayed by the occasional plastic bag of garbage dumped at the curb or dropped down a hillside. Even the road itself was marred by crudely painted political graffiti—the green rising sun of socialist Pasok, the red KKK of the local Communist Party, the blue ND of the conservatives.

We asked ourselves why people had no interest in cleaning up the village, or at least doing something about the untidy bare earth yards around their homes. It wouldn't take much to grow things in this climate, but only the widow Maro, the woman who had killed the chicken that memorable morning, had an actual garden. The problem, Ilias told us, was water. There were no springs or wells in the valley. Never had been. Every drop was collected in winter when it rained for months on end, gathered from the roof by guttering and drained into the family sterna, the big underground cistern upon which each household relied. In summer, the supply had to be eked out carefully, for there was little chance of rain between May and October. It would be profligate in the extreme to pour good water onto flowers. Kostantes's sterna was up the hillside opposite his house, well beyond the small white outhouse. Wendy and I looked at each other and thought of the two showers a day we had been taking.

"It's okay," said Ilias. "There's a man in Peritheia, Diomedes Parginos, who has a water truck. He can refill my uncle's sterna."

We asked him if everyone on the mountain was called Parginos. That was the name above the little shop and on the outside of the bar. Were they all related? Some were, some weren't, he replied. He didn't know why it was such a common name.

Years later, I found out the answer in an old book. After Napoleon conquered Venice, its Ionian possessions, including Corfu, six other islands and a number of enclaves on the mainland, had changed hands frequently, according to the fortunes of war. The Republican French had been superseded by the Russians, who were soon ousted by the Imperial French, until Waterloo and the Congress of Vienna gave Corfu and the islands to the British.

The territories on the mainland, however, were claimed by the local Turkish leader, Ali Pasha of Iannina, and the British were obliged by treaty to hand them over. Of these, the most important was the impregnable port of Parga. The citizens were understandably nervous at this arrangement, but the British, to their credit, devised a compromise. In 1817, they invited the Parganauts to move, en masse, to Corfu, and 2,700 of them, all but two families, accepted the offer. Many changed their surname to Parginos in memory of their heritage, and while some settled in the suburbs of Corfu Town, the British encouraged others to move on into the countryside, to farm the olive groves that had been planted centuries earlier by the Venetians. Three families called Parginos came over the mountains to Loutses and built homes on the rocky ridge that sheltered the valley on the northeastern, seaward side. Its name was Zervou, for it had once been the property of an absentee Venetian landowner called Zervos who had donated it to the church. The land was too poor even for olives, so the church had agreed to sell it to the Parginos families.

Ilias had inherited some land up on Zervou; his aunt owned a house. Indeed, a good many families who now lived down in the centre of the village had another home on the ridge—a place to store large things like grape-treading vats and barrels of wine. Ilias knew one man who kept an old mattress in an upstairs room of his Zervou property and when the weather grew unbearably hot in August he would spend the night there, with the windows thrown open, for a breeze always came off the sea after dark. I thought that a fine, romantic thing to do.

The village looked its best at night. There were no street lights, which gave the moon an importance and personality it lacked in London or Toronto, and turned the taverna into a small oasis of light and conviviality. I didn't feel like cooking in the relentless heat so we spent every evening there, nibbling on souvlakia, salad and french fries, stretching out dinner for hours, for there was little for us to do after dark except sit in the kitchen and play cards. We were soon very familiar with the jukebox's repertoire, bouzouki ballads that had been hits when the machine was installed, years earlier. We could date the collection by the only two recordings in English, "American Woman" by the Guess Who and "Don't Go Down to Reno" by Tony Christie. Once in a while we checked out the other watering holes, but Stamati's shop seemed reserved for a handful of his cronies and the kafeneion was as much a community centre as a bar, full of men playing poker under baleful fluorescent lighting. Only the taverna offered anything to eat.

The weeks of our summer began to glide by. Wendy and Dee said their tearful goodbyes the morning Dee left to go home to Canada, taking advantage of a free ride to Corfu Town in the back of a pick-up truck. Ilias stood mournfully by, looking as if he wished he could go with her. After that, Wendy and I slipped easily into a hedonistic routine, setting off each morning for the beach at Kalamaki, sometimes catching the seven o'clock bus but more often on foot, hitching a lift down the mountain. With Dee gone, Ilias rarely joined us, and we had the beach entirely to ourselves, running naked, swimming, sunbathing, quarrelling, making love. We never discussed the future but we sometimes talked of the past.

We had met two years earlier, when I was a would-be actor of twenty-three and Wendy, still at university, was twenty-one. All through my teens, I had sung with a rock band and occasionally played saxophone as a session musician—one single had got to number two in Britain's Northern Soul charts—but I had never been sure if that was the career for me. I also wanted to be a writer and had a drawer full of short stories and plays that bore unpublished witness to the fact. The stage was our family business. My father was an actor and my mother a theatrical agent, and I had performed in occasional television commercials and as an extra in movies for as long as I could remember. Until my writing became readable, therefore, I was making a living in the theatre, starting again at the bottom, in the traditional way, by working as an assistant stage manager. The play that took me to Canada was a farce called *A Picture of Innocence,* written by and starring my godfather, Robert Morley. We were touring England's provincial theatres, ironing out the kinks before opening—it was hoped—in London's West End, and somewhere between Birmingham, Brighton and Bath the management had organized a month in Toronto at the Royal Alexandra Theatre. Wendy had taken a summer job as a cocktail waitress in a bar down the street from the theatre. I soon began to hang out there after the show, but it took me three weeks to pluck up the courage to ask her out. We spent the last seven days together before the play went back to

England, and though the parting was painful we both knew we would meet again.

We wrote to each other once or twice—romantic, self-conscious letters. Then, a year later, she left a message for me at the stage door of the theatre in London where I was playing Annas the priest in *Jesus Christ Superstar.* She had interrupted her degree and set off to see the world. We took up where we had left off, lovers but virtual strangers, barely understanding ourselves, let alone each other. We lived together in my London flat for six emotionally tumultuous months, then she went back to Canada at Christmastime to finish her degree. It was my turn to follow her, and we met up in June in San Francisco, travelling for a while through California and Arizona before she agreed to return with me to London. Another year had rumbled by, during which time I wrote a whimsical cookbook and acquired a literary agent who saw some promise in my prose—and now here we were on Corfu, neutral territory, where neither of us had the cultural advantage, on a beach that seemed conjured from fantasy, disengaged from the world.

One morning we followed the cold freshwater stream into the bamboo thickets and discovered a garden that had run wild—figs and damsons, melons, tomato vines that sprawled up over a pomegranate bush, a lemon tree heavy with fruits so ripe we could eat them like oranges, the juice sweet and refreshing in our salty mouths. We raided Eden daily and rinsed our hands in the shallows where the sea was as warm as bathwater. Occasionally, a fisherman called Yanni came into sight, rowing his boat around the distant point, knocking on the wooden gunwales to drive the fish into his net. Wendy and I would put on our swimsuits and wade out to meet him. He spoke no English but was willing to sell us half a dozen of the small, turquoise-and-gold-striped fish he caught. We carried them back to the beach, cleaned them and wrapped them in vine leaves and baked them slowly in the embers of our campfire among the rocks. No fish ever tasted so good.

Around three every afternoon a northerly breeze sprang up, stirring the blue glass sea into ripples and tossing the tall, soft plumes of the bamboo spears. That was our sign that it was time to climb back to the road and walk the furnace-hot mile to Peritheia. Salty and sandy, we would buy a few groceries from the store run by cheerful Spiro, have a beer in Sotiris's bar and wait for the four o'clock bus up the mountain, a bus that was already becoming a *cause célèbre.*

The road was the official problem. Drivers had complained about the unpaved surface, the fact that it was a dead-end route, that the number of passengers did not justify the effort of going up to Loutses at all. The villagers, on the other hand, had spent years petitioning authorities to provide the service in the first place, and their prayers had been answered only six months before we got here. It was an endless topic of conversation in the taverna. With Ilias translating, we gathered that the state of the road was merely a camouflage for far more sinister issues. There was almost certainly a political conspiracy behind it all, possibly involving certain influential men in Corfu Town who were determined to withhold the reins of power from the Loutsiotes. Cancelling the bus route was a blow aimed at the working man. Twice, now, we had climbed onto the bus in Peritheia, laden with shopping and beach towels, only to learn that the final leg of the journey would not be attempted that day. There were always tantrums, long, melodramatic tirades from the men who were stranded at the foot of the mountain, heard in grim silence by the driver and conductor until some line was crossed and honour demanded an equally hysterical response. Such scenes ended when the driver switched off the engine, jumped down into the street and stalked into Sotiris's bar. Then the elderly women would gather their shopping bags and set off in single file to walk home. They rarely had to trudge far. There were always good Samaritans with pick-up trucks to give them (and us) a lift.

But that wasn't the point. Such cancellations set a dangerous precedent and necessitated a great deal of debate in the kafeneion that night, followed by accusatory phone calls and a formal letter of complaint to the bus company from the mayor of Loutses himself.

The third incident occurred on a particularly scorching afternoon in July, about a month after our arrival. Again we climbed onto the bus in Peritheia, hot, salt-crusted, sandy and eager for a shower.

"Hold it," said Wendy as we sat down. "The driver's turned off the engine."

"And yet he's still here . . ."

About twenty Loutsiotes were in the bus. Without the engine running, the air conditioning did not work, but in spite of the rapidly soaring temperature, no one was shouting. No one had left the vehicle. Old women sat stoically, fanning themselves; children peered over the backs of seats, staring at other, smaller children. The conductor came by to take our money.

"Loutses?" we asked.

He shrugged and answered in English. "The inspector will decide."

We looked around. There were only three other men on the bus, and we recognized their faces. None of them was a bus inspector. A baby started to cry and was instantly soothed by an impromptu committee of women.

That he was twenty minutes late was a measure of the inspector's authority. He arrived at last by car, parking it outside the bar, and strolled across to the bus. The engine started as he stepped on board and stood surveying the passengers with arrogant self-assurance. His black hair was greased back tightly, his skin the orange-brown of a sunbather rather than a workman. He wore impenetrable dark glasses and a beige safari jacket with no fewer than five ballpoint pens in the breast pocket.

"Okay," he said in English. Then he sat down in the front seat and the bus pulled away up the road. It was not a normal ride. Instead of the usual breakneck speed along the straight and the sudden jolting deceleration as a bend loomed, the driver crawled along, changing gears often with elaborate precision and swerving to avoid even the smallest ruts and potholes. The first hairpin bend was a classic three-point turn, though sometimes a skilful pilot could negotiate it in one. Today, it took minutes of backing and turning, inch by inch, before we were off again, the driver sighing and mopping his brow.

The next bend was even more theatrical. The inspector felt compelled to alight and watch the proceedings from the roadside while the driver put on a dazzling show with the conductor pressed up against the rear window, yelling an endless series of instructions. The inspector climbed back in, pausing to smile at Wendy, and we continued—until the road curved again.

The journey took thirty minutes instead of fifteen. The villagers who disembarked with us outside Kostantes's house stood and talked, shaking their heads and looking grim before they scattered to their homes. And next day, the bus did not come.

"The service is cancelled," said Ilias with a shrug. "Don't worry. It will start again."

"When?"

"A week, maybe two or three. Certainly before the winter when the tourists are gone."

So we went to the beach less often, spending our mornings reading or writing or exploring parts of Loutses we had never seen. Often we went up to the kafeneion (which was always deserted at lunchtime) and sat outside under the vines, drinking coffee and idly watching this tiny corner of the world go by. One of the maps of the island sold in the tourist boutiques on the coast showed the road up to Loutses as a bold red line that continued through the village, over the mountains and down the other side towards Corfu Town. It was touching to see a carful of lobster-coloured holidaymakers pass by, the map spread out on a lap. They were always smiling, having negotiated the unpaved hairpins from Peritheia and then found proper tarmac again as they entered the village. "It's all plain sailing now, Mother! I told you they wouldn't print it if it wasn't true!"

Alas! The tarmac ended just above Loutses, where the

road had been widened to let the bus turn around and where the driver and conductor took a half-hour nap before returning down the mountain. After that, there was gravel, pitted and potholed, often strewn with boulders where a miniature landslide had brought down a fragment of the mountain. The track did climb on, winding above the olive tree line into the high wild places, coming at last to the abandoned town of Ano Peritheia beneath Mount Pantokrator, Corfu's conical summit. We had yet to venture that far, but we knew that the track went no farther, for we saw the same rental cars creeping back down the road an hour later, dusty and battered, the passengers sitting in tight-lipped silence.

The local traffic was almost as entertaining. Several farmers still rode horses, sitting sideways on crude wooden saddles; others used donkeys as beasts of burden. Most, however, had motorized vehicles that defied categorization but might once have been a motorcycle, a flatbed wagon and a set of iron banisters before their identities were merged by the welding torch. Then there were the gypsies. We heard them coming from half a mile away, the jaunty, Turkish-sounding music and come-hither announcements echoing around the valley from the loudspeaker on the roof of their truck. The truck appeared, painted in outlandish colours and laden with a teetering stack of whatever the driver was selling—plastic chairs and buckets and bowls or brightly coloured fabrics and ladies' underwear or crates of turkey chicks cheeping in the heat. The truck would stop every few hundred yards, and sometimes a housewife would emerge from her doorway to haggle with the driver while the gypsy women and children waited impassively in the cab.

We never bought from the gypsies—they had nothing we needed to buy—but we learned to look forward to the arrival of the sardine man. He drove an ancient blue three-wheeled van with a hooped canopy over the back like an old covered wagon. Beneath it were open crates of fresh silver sardines and a set of weigh scales that swung out on a hinge when they were needed. We watched him measure our half kilo of sardines and then tip them into a cone of newspaper, folding over the top so that it looked like a tiny wrapped bunch of flowers, flecked with fragments of seaweed and fish scales like glittering mica. I grinned like a fool the first time I bought some, carrying my purchase back up the steep stone steps to the kafeneion where Wendy was finishing her coffee. Philip did a double take when he came to take away our cups.

"How are you cooking thems, man?" he asked.

"Rinse them, roll them whole in flour and deep-fry them in olive oil."

He grunted, grudgingly I thought, and sauntered off with our cups. A moment later he reappeared with two lemons.

"You'll need these."

Philip Parginos owned and ran the kafeneion with his father, Leonidas. He was eight or nine years older than me and had seen more of the world, working as a chief steward in the merchant navy. In his twenties, he spent several years travelling through Europe and Scandinavia in an old Volkswagen van, falling into and out of relationships, living the life of a hippie. That was where he had learned to speak his unique, oath-peppered version of English. Though he was balding, he had a bristling beard and looked immensely strong, with a barrel of a chest and a slow-moving, easy masculinity that a good many local and foreign women found most compelling. Philip's mother had died long ago, and he and Leonidas lived as two bachelors in a house behind the kafeneion. The telephone in the little wooden booth beside the poker tables was the only one in the village, and though Philip was usually prepared to take messages for his neighbours he sometimes preferred a more direct approach, striding outside to the edge of his patio and bellowing "Stavros!" or "Maro!" or "Panayotis!" down the road until the recipient of the call came panting up the hill.

A couple of times I had gone to use the telephone late at night when the hit-or-miss, static-infested line to England was open, and had found Philip and his father alone in the bar, eating something complex and deliciously aromatic that Philip had made—octopus stewed in red wine, if he had been diving that morning, or a pilaf of razor clams that Leonidas had dug from the sandbars at dawn. He was a good cook, and I took his advice about the sardines seriously.

Now he put the lemons down on the table. "Put some paprika in the flour when you are covering the sardines, man," he growled, "and squeeze the lemon after."

As we were thanking him, a lean yellow dog trotted around the corner of the building, saw him and instantly darted under a table.

"Whose dog is that?" I asked.

"He's my dog, the blastard! He knows he's in big trouble. Someone down at the taverna is feeding him souvlakia every night and he's so fat and lazy he's no good for hunting any more." Wendy blushed deeply beneath her tan.

The kafeneion closed at around two every afternoon, when the white heat of the day was at its most relentless. The whole village went to sleep for a three-hour siesta, and Wendy and I had the valley to ourselves. Our favourite walk was to climb the unpaved track that began opposite Kostantes's house, past the outhouse in the chicken run, past the great cement cistern behind it, and up towards Zervou. To our right, a paddock dotted with almond and pear trees sloped down into the olive groves; to the left, elaborate fences of wood, piled stones and chicken wire enclosed small allotments, most of them filled with artichoke plants. They flourished unkempt in the well-manured soil, thrusting up stalks at the parching sun, their ugly, flaccid grey-green leaves hanging like limp rags. The villagers harvested the crop in April when the artichokes were still young, before the fibrous heart had developed, but some were left to mature, for the bees to pollinate. In flower, the spiny petals folded back to reveal a dazzling royal blue explosion of colour.

Above the allotments, the track split into two paths. The right fork led up to the top of the broad ridge; the left disappeared into a cluster of twenty or thirty stone buildings like a small, self-contained village of its own—the houses of old Zervou that Ilias had described. We had no idea of their age, but they had been well made, two storeys high, some terraced, others detached, connected by narrow lanes, flights of stone steps and unexpected courtyards. Peering through grimy ground-floor windows, we could make out curious objects. In one house, bundles of wool and a carved wooden saddle stood on the unswept flagstone floor. In another loomed an enormous open-topped wooden tub for treading grapes, with smaller barrels lined up against the cool darkness at the back of the room. The handsome old building at the end of the row contained the almost-intact machinery of an olive press—huge wooden beams and a circular stone mill about three feet high and six feet across, for crushing the olives. A great round quern stone sculpted of Cephalonian granite stood on its side in the mill, but its twin was missing and the wooden axle that would once have threaded them together, to be pulled round and round by a tethered horse, was no more than a splintered stump.

The houses were interesting, but more often than not we took the other path, climbing over the ridge and following the track as it swung to the right. Loutses and its valley were out of sight, but before us lay a view of breathtaking grandeur. The best place from which to appreciate it was a flat grey rock that Dee had discovered a few days before she went home to Canada. Perched on the warm stone, legs dangling, we could look to the left and see the entire northern coast of the island stretching westwards into the open Ionian. Facing us, the mountains of Albania emerged out of the blue, coming ever closer as we turned our heads to the right, squeezing the sea into the narrow Straits of Corfu, fifteen hundred feet below. There was always a breeze stirring the leaves of the stunted arbutus bushes on the hillside, and sometimes a flock of a dozen sheep grazed amongst them, chewing to the accompaniment of the sweet-sounding bells at their throats.

Past Dee's rock, the path slipped a little way down the ridge as it curved on towards the northeast. A house stood beside the path, built into the slope, so that we could have jumped onto its red-tiled roof. The family who owned it seemed prosperous, for the building was well looked after, surrounded on three sides by a broad patio. A new Volkswagen minivan was often pulled into the driveway, shaded by a magnificent mulberry tree.

Beyond that, the track sloped suddenly down, turning right, away from the sea, into an olive-filled valley before it ended at a low stone wall and a row of four derelict houses. Ilias had told Wendy that the local name for this particular fold of the hills was Koulouri, which meant something like "peace and quiet," and it was easy to see why. Behind the hiss of the cicadas in the olive trees, the murmur of bees and the throaty chatter of the swallows that flitted in and out through the missing upstairs windows, a pervasive silence hung over the valley. Not a brooding silence, but a generous, beneficent, satisfied hush. It emanated as much from the ruined houses as from the olive groves and orchards that smothered the hillside below. Here a wall had collapsed or a roof had caved in; there a courtyard was choked by a bramble thicket, but enough remained to convey a sense of what life here had once been like.

The first of the four houses was in the best condition. It was very tall and square, and its stone walls were easily three feet thick. Chiselled blocks of white marble, as thick as my thigh, framed the small windows; the lintel was a single slab of pink limestone. Across a narrow courtyard, a one-room stone house looked like a tiny chapel, and because the hillside was so steep this smaller building had another room beneath it, accessible from the land below—a windowless, ripe-smelling byre with a ceiling so low we had to duck when we went in.

"I wish we could get into the big house," sighed Wendy one afternoon. It proved easier than it looked. The front doors were rotten and crumbling at the bottom, a haphazard array of planks held together by metal bands and a hefty iron bolt, but on one side the hinges had rusted to powder and the entire construction could be lifted inwards enough to squeeze through. Our eyes slowly grew accustomed to the darkness. The floor was mostly compacted dirt and rubble, but the ceiling looked sturdy enough—eighteen feet high, beams of rough cypress trunks slotted into holes in the wall with thick cypress floorboards laid across them. Here and there, great black nails had been driven into the wood, and growing like tree fungus from the side of the beams were swallows' nests made of mud. The roughly plastered walls were stippled and crusted with generations of guano. We both thought it was beautiful.

In the corner, a wooden staircase led up through a gap in the ceiling. The stairs were firm enough. Gingerly, we climbed to the upper floor. Sunshine and light! Up here were two small bedrooms, one leading into the other. The farther room had a ceiling of cypress beams and boards almost as high as the ceiling downstairs. The room where we stood had no ceiling at all, and a number of gaping holes in the roof.

"Oh, but look at the view," said Wendy. She stood by the window gazing eastwards over the roof tiles of the smaller house at a landscape of olive-covered hills dropping away in a series of valleys, then climbing to a distant ridge. It was like looking down on clouds from an airplane, but the clouds were the billowing, unbroken green of the olive groves. Kalamaki and our own coastline were hidden, but beyond them the sea stretched away to the gaunt peaks of Albania, marching inland into the Balkans.

"And look from here!" called Wendy, who had now made her way into the inner bedroom. This window faced north—the same view we saw from Dee's rock. Wendy slipped her arm through mine.

"How much do you think it would cost to buy this place and fix it up?" she asked. It seemed such an idle question, forgotten as soon as spoken, but somewhere the Fates were smirking.

CHAPTER TWO

THE SUMMER MEANDERED ON, JULY drifting into August, though neither Wendy nor I thought much about it. To be honest, the only thing we did think about in those days was each other. We might have been Corfu's sole inhabitants, so profound was our self-involvement and so all-embracing our irresponsibility. By then, we felt we had discovered the best and most beautiful parts of our small corner of the island and we instinctively returned to them, walking in the hills and olive groves, swimming and playing on the deserted beach, climbing Zervou in the evenings to sit on Dee's rock and watch the long, silent melodrama of the sunset. I was more than content to dream on in our lovers' solitude.

It was Wendy who first glanced up and looked ahead beyond the summer's end, though at first her vision of the future terrified me. One early morning, we were ankle deep in the shallows at Kalamaki, slowly working the half mile of the beach, looking for empty seashells.

"You know," she remarked, completely casually, "this would be even more fun if we had a baby to do it with.

"Aren't you going to say anything?" she added, after a while.

"It's just a bit of a conversation stopper."

Somehow this remark developed into a quarrel that lasted for the rest of the morning and scudded far from the point, until we were able to beat back against the emotional wind and start the conversation again. I still felt that we had skipped certain major steps in our relationship by jumping from a shared summer holiday to having a baby together. Then again, if everything we whispered to each other while in the throes of passion or sentiment was true, the idea did not seem so far-fetched. In fact, it was the most natural thing in the world. I simply needed a little time to get used to the idea.

Time, to be sure, was one thing we had in abundance. When we had organized the rental of the Villa Parginos, we had blithely assumed that dozens of my friends would leap at the opportunity to spend a week or two with us, paying their share and turning our summer into one long party. Nobody came. After Dee's departure, I commandeered the second bedroom as a study, a place where I could go for a number of hours every day in order to write a dazzlingly brilliant novel. Wendy lay on the bed in our room, writing an equally marvellous play. Neither project ever came to much. The arguments against sitting motionless, indoors, alone, were clear and compelling.

But the notion of parenthood had broken the spell of our introversion. It was as if our tiny world had received an injection of subject matter, virulent with implications. A future of one kind or another would soon be upon us and there would be choices to be made. Instead of gazing into each other's eyes, I was looking over Wendy's shoulder and she over mine. We began to be a little more attentive to the world around us.

On the other side of the street from Georgie's taverna and three houses farther on stood the Loutses shop, opened thirty-five years earlier by a former shoemaker called Stamati. A low wall and a very small courtyard distanced it slightly from the road, giving just enough room for four rickety, tin-topped tables and a ramshackle assortment of wooden chairs; overhead, a grapevine provided impenetrable shade. Someone had once planted an ornamental gourd beside the vine, and the plants had become inextricably woven—odd, knobbly little orange-and-green gourds dangling like Christmas decorations beside the stunted bunches of grapes. Along the wall an extraordinary array of plastic buckets, old tin cans, recycled pots and jam jars sprouted pink and scarlet geraniums, punctuated by flint balls, geodes and other eccentrically shaped pieces of rock that Stamati's grown-up son, Babis, had collected over the years. From behind this formidable barrier, Stamati—small, fastidious, his milk-white hair swept neatly back—and his matronly wife, Maria, observed the litany of passersby.

It had taken us some time to understand the rhythms and purposes of the store. The door opened every morning at seven o'clock, when Maria came back from milking the ewes she kept on a patch of land farther up the village. Builders on their way to work down on the coast would park their scooters outside and nip in for a coffee and a cognac. Around ten, some of the regular clientele, men and women of Stamati's generation who found the pace of Philip's kafeneion a little too vigorous, made their slow way into the courtyard to wait for the postman on his scarlet moped. Wonderful aromas of chicken and garlic roasting slowly in the wood oven inside Maria's miniature kitchen drifted among them, but food was never offered. At lunchtime, the gate in the wall was carefully closed and Maria, Stamati and his elderly sister, Eleni, gathered around the table inside the shop to eat. The door was locked, of course, during the afternoon, but reopened sometime before five o'clock and stayed open until Stamati went to bed.

Even on the hottest mornings, the interior of the store was as cool and dark as a cave. We would have liked to do all our shopping there, to show support for the village, but the inventory discouraged such attempts: tins of Spam and tomato paste, packets of dried pasta, bottles of cherry syrup, toilet paper, biscuits, an impressively comprehensive range of Greek candies and Greek cigarettes—useful essentials, but scarcely a cornucopia of earthly delights. On the floor, an open box of salt cod from Halifax, Nova Scotia, added pungently to the atmosphere, as did a few ancient but still palatable salamis hanging on strings from the ceiling. Sometimes there was Maria's own wonderful feta cheese for sale, brought from the larder in its tin of brine. Stamati would cut off a slice and lift it, dripping, onto a square of wax paper, fold up the parcel, tape it and tie it with string as slowly and meticulously as if he were wrapping a Christmas present, before weighing it in the ancient pair of brass scales and writing the price down on a scrap of paper. Partly because he was hard of hearing and partly because he knew we were foreign, Stamati never responded to our attempts at Greek. We would point at the things we wanted to buy and then wait while he assembled them into a neat pile at the end of the counter. He wrote the price down carefully on a strip of cardboard cut from a cigarette carton and slid it across to us, discreetly averting his eyes while we read the numbers.

In the evening, the shop was busier. Long ago, in a daring but brilliant move, Stamati had bought a black-and-white television set and mounted it on a shelf above the cigarette counter. It was the first TV in the village and a source of quiet fascination to Stamati's clientele, especially during the nightly weather report. Only Stamati's sister, Eleni, was uninterested in the machine. She preferred to sit outside in the courtyard as evening fell, a tiny, upright figure in a green dress, a black cotton scarf tied neatly over her white hair, staring down the road to where the sun set orange behind the hills. Well into her seventies, Eleni did very little in the shop. We had seen her occasionally in the early mornings feeding the chickens that scratched and fretted under the olive trees behind the building, but mostly she liked to sit, keeping an eye on her bad-tempered ginger cat.

Then, one evening, she was gone. Maria had been in the kitchen, putting the finishing touches to a bianco of small fish, potatoes and onions that had been slowly simmering all afternoon. Stamati was in the shop wrapping a packet of cigarettes for the new policeman, who was standing in front of the counter, legs apart and hands in his pockets, watching the television. The policeman did his grocery shopping down in Peritheia but he bought his cigarettes from Stamati, on credit, and in the three months since he had come to the village had shown no sign of settling up. Perhaps he felt that would undermine his position in the village.

Stamati completed the little parcel, cutting the string with his penknife, and put it down quietly beside the constable. Then he came round the counter and stood next to him, gazing up at the screen with a thoughtful smile on his lips. When Maria came in with the stew and half a loaf of bread, Eleni's cat was nosing about the box of salt cod and she shooed it away with her foot. The policeman strolled down the street to Georgie's taverna and Stamati sat down at the table.

"Where's Eleni?" he asked.

"Outside," said Maria. "She knows it's dinnertime."

Ten minutes later, Eleni had still not come in.

"Go and call her," said Maria. Stamati went out into the courtyard and then out onto the road. The dusk was settling, colour fading from the sky. There were people up at the kafeneion and lights on down at the taverna, but no one out on the road. He made his way up the rocky little path beside the building. It was darker under the olive trees.

"Eleni?" he called. "'Leni?" There was no answer.

Coming back, he saw one of the young men heading up to the bar.

"Did you see Eleni?" he asked. The man shook his head.

After dinner, Stamati and Maria began to get worried. The policeman and two of his cronies were at the table by now, drinking brandy and watching a soap opera. Stamati asked their advice. "She's got a goddaughter down in Peritheia," added Maria. "She may have decided to go and visit her. She's done it before."

"Perhaps she fell down on the road and hit her head," suggested one of the men.

Stamati went back outside with a torch, searching the edge of the olive grove more thoroughly now and shining its beam into the little fenced-off allotment where Maria grew her zucchinis.

By ten o'clock half a dozen people were looking for the old lady. Someone had been down to Peritheia on a scooter but had seen nothing. Stamati made coffee and brought drinks for the men as they returned. The consensus was that although the night was dark it was also warm and Eleni was still strong for her age. She had lived most of her life looking after sheep with a man from higher up in the mountains. As a girl of twenty she had fallen in love with him and ran away when he asked her, leaving one Sunday with her belongings on the back of his donkey. When they had reached his croft she was introduced to his wife. Despite this surprise, she lived with the couple for thirty years, out on the hills with the flock and doing most of the housework, until the man died. Even then she stayed—for another twenty-five years—until the wife died too and left the property to a distant relative on the mainland. Then Eleni came back to live with Stamati, seventy-five years old and a little too dreamy to be of much use in the shop.

"Oh yes," sighed Maria. "She's done this before."

The search resumed at first light. We watched the men and boys striding purposefully up the street and disappearing into the shop, where the policeman organized them into groups. Two of the men had brought shotguns in case they saw any woodcock in the olive groves. Everyone was talking noisily except for one old man who stood by the door, a puzzled frown on his face. He was not from the village, and

Maria made her way through the throng to thank him for volunteering to help.

"I haven't come for that," he said. "I've come for Eleni's things. We're getting married next week."

The policeman called for order and asked the old man to say it again. The visitor looked slowly around at the faces. He had passed the shop the evening before, on his way back up to the mountains for the summer, and had seen Eleni sitting with her cat. He had known her in the past and always liked her. He asked her if she'd like to live with him and she had said yes. Eleni had lifted the cat from her lap and put it gently down on the ground, straightened her scarf, and set off with him up the road.

"She's all right, is she?" demanded Maria.

The old man frowned. "As far as I know."

The policeman threw out his chest and waved the people away from his favourite chair. "Get everyone a beer, Stamati," he announced. "You can put them on my account."

ILIAS FILLED IN the details of the saga for us that evening, with Kostantes leaning in through the kitchen window providing colour commentary. He found the whole affair amusing, but for once he refrained from endlessly repeating the highlights of the tale. There was bigger, more important news he wished to communicate.

"My uncle also asks if you've heard about the bus."

Kostantes had an impish look, as if he knew a joke that we had not yet heard.

"He asks how you have been getting to the beach this week," continued Ilias.

"Well, we've had to walk," said Wendy, "or hitch a lift. The bus doesn't come any more."

"He says if you go with him tomorrow you can see him make the bus come. You will have to be ready at half past six in the morning."

We wanted to know more, but Kostantes was enjoying the mystery too much to divulge any further information. We promised we would be ready.

At the top of the village, just beyond the last house but one, the road crossed a broad, deep ditch. In winter, presumably, it was a stream, draining the rain from the steep valleys, but during the summer there was no sense of moisture at all, just a jumble of dirty rocks and brightly coloured plastic bags full of garbage. A grove of cypress trees grew beside it, their innate elegance pointing up the lost potential of the place. Elsewhere in the world, someone would have built a charming little stone bridge over the gully; here, they had filled the stream bed with boulders, piling them around a metal pipe that let the water through, and iced the construction with cement to carry the road on into the mountains. Not that it went very far. A hundred yards farther on, the hillside had been blasted away to make the broad circular area where the bus turned around. Beyond that, the road and the landscape abruptly changed. The grey tarmac turned into a rutted track studded with rocks; the olive groves gave way to a more ancient *maquis* of yellowed grasses and stunted bushes.

The bus drivers took no issue with the turning point; it was the viaduct over the gully that lay at the root of the latest impasse. For once we could sympathize. The cement was never intended for anything bigger or heavier than a pick-up truck, and the viaduct's fringes had cracked and crumbled until crossing its dwindling breadth became an act of real courage. Now the drivers had refused to attempt it, and since there was nowhere else to turn between here and the coast, the entire mountainside was without public transportation. At a noisy meeting held in the kafeneion, one group of village fathers proposed sending another letter to the bus company, but the majority were all for action. Fix the bridge, then send the bill to the government!

Kostantes was punctual the following morning, but so were we, and the three of us walked up the street together, enjoying the relative cool of the air. The yellow hilltops above the village glowed gold against a cloudless, forget-me-not sky, but the sun was still below Zervou and the valley luxuriated in dewy shadow. Stamati's shop was already open. Indeed, most of the village seemed to have risen early, and we soon became aware of other determined men stepping out into the street and striding along behind us. Kostantes carried a triangular trowel in his belt. He could have been a gunfighter, heading for the OK Corral.

Not far from the bridge, he paused to light a cigarette. We were close to the junction with the road that led up to Loutses's other significant cluster of houses, a part of the village that Wendy and I had never explored. Another man was walking down the road towards us, followed by his own small posse. He too carried a trowel. He greeted Kostantes as an equal and they walked on together while we fell back a pace or two, mingling with the retinue. Other men were waiting by the bridge, among them a small, portly individual with a green plastic hose looped twenty times around his shoulder. He glanced at the two master builders but did not step forward. As owner of the house closest to the bridge, his place in the hierarchy was almost as exalted as theirs, for he would provide the water for the cement. A huge pile of dusty grey gravel blocked the driveway behind him. Kostantes and his colleague, whose name was Tomas, approached the hose bearer and muttered a few comments. One of them said something funny and those within earshot allowed themselves a low, manly chuckle. The hose bearer hitched up his trousers, adjusted his stance and nodded.

Now Kostantes and Tomas climbed slowly down into the gully and inspected the damage to the bridge. It was a side of Kostantes we had never seen. His gestures were authoritative, confident, even with a cigarette hanging out of the side of his mouth and one eye squinting in the smoke. The other men stood about on the road or on the bridge, chatting and smoking while two or three small boys darted between them, playing some game of their own.

Wendy and I sat on the low wall in front of the hose bearer's house, happy to be up so early. We watched the sunlight creep down the hillside until it filled the valley, suddenly aware that the cicadas had started their endless rasping song.

At the sound of a distant vehicle all heads turned as one. It was a red pick-up truck carrying three more men and eighteen sacks of cement. Half an hour later, another, deeper engine was heard and a tractor came into sight, pulling a cement mixer from Peritheia. The owner rode it in majestic isolation, acknowledging the greetings of friends as it came to a halt beside the red truck.

Now the day's work could begin. Kostantes and Tomas remained in the ditch to direct operations, while trusted assistants drove in six strong poles and hammered planks between them to form a wall across the gully, about three feet away from the bridge. The man with the mixer was having some trouble starting its motor. When it finally burst into life, the scattered applause was only half ironic. One of the small boys was caught pretending to cut through the hose with a penknife and was driven off by two grizzled elders. By now most of the men were busy, some mixing cement and ferrying it in wheelbarrows to the edge of the road, tipping it into the space between the damaged structure and the wall of planks. Others brought stones up from the ditch and dropped them in after the cement. They worked instinctive shifts, one man stopping when he was tired, another jokingly calling for the boys to haul him to his feet while his friends jeered and laughed. It was the first time we had seen the village working together, and I was impressed by the efficiency behind the casual attitude.

By eleven o'clock there was no more to be done. The cement mixer was turned off, its last gout of reeking exhaust drifting away across a valley that seemed suddenly very quiet. Kostantes and Tomas surveyed the work, occasionally bending down to smooth the surface of the cement with a trowel. The road was three feet wider. In a couple of days the bus could come again.

That night, Kostantes was in a particularly jocular mood. He joined us at our table at the taverna for a while, twisting around in his chair to conduct two or three simultaneous conversations with various cronies. All of them hung on his every word, and though we understood nothing of the repartee it was clear that our friend was in the best of form, timing his punchlines like a professional comedian. Even the village priest chuckled away at the jokes, his bushy beard bobbing up and down as he laughed.

A short man who wore his long grey hair tied into a neat bun and whose ankle-length blue-grey robe was always immaculately ironed, the papas was relatively new to Loutses, though Kostantes had known him for years. Before his call to the priesthood he had been a builder, and the two men had worked together on several villas down on the coast. One season he was gone—no one knew where—but a year or two later, he appeared in Loutses to take up his duties as guardian of souls. Kostantes had shown us in mime the elaborate double take he did at the sight of his former colleague pulling up to the shop on the pillion of the church warden's moped. The priest lived down on the coast, in the town of Karousades, a thirty-minute drive away, and had to be brought up to Loutses every Saturday night by a devout volunteer so that he could be ready for the Sunday-morning service.

Next weekend was an especially important occasion—the Panayiri, a feast day devoted to the saints. For once, the regular congregation of about forty people would swell to include almost everyone in the village, and more, for relatives could be counted upon to arrive from across the island. But the ceremony would not take place in Loutses. On this one day in the year, the original Loutses church, up in the mountains in the abandoned town of Ano Peritheia, would be pressed into service.

It sounded interesting, but when we asked Philip about it he just shrugged and scowled. Philip had not been to church since he was a child and, as a committed socialist, he had waged a decade-long war against organized religion through the letters pages of local and national newspapers.

Ilias was more forthcoming. "Look," he began. "It's like a big party. Everyone goes. People have been making the road better for weeks, filling holes and moving big stones. That's another reason why they fixed the road over the little bridge. But it's hard to explain about Ano Peritheia. It's very old. Some people say the eighth-oldest town in Europe. You have to see it yourself."

"Can we walk there?"

"Of course! But go early in the day when it isn't too hot."

He wished he could come with us, but his vacation was almost up. On Wednesday, he had to return to Athens, to get ready for the next university term. He would miss the Panayiri.

The following day, we did as Ilias suggested, laden with camera, notebook, straw hats and a water bottle. A few yards beyond the place where the bus turned round, we passed the last house in the village, sending its tethered dog into an ecstasy of barking, then set off up the track, leaving the olive trees behind. To our left, the land fell steeply into a deep green valley marked in places by a rudimentary stone sheep pen or a grove of trees. To our right rose the hillside, smothered in an impenetrable tangle of tall yellow grasses and spiky plants—withered thistles, brambles and big bushes of Jerusalem sage with its musty herbal smell and pale grey-green leaves. Beside the track grew some kind of broom that looked like corn cobs stuck on the end of poles, each kernel a tiny yellow flower. We thought about picking a bunch for the house but on closer inspection found every one of them to be infested with small black insects. We walked on, startling crickets that leapt from the track with a flash of scarlet wings, our footsteps scrunching on stones in the silence of the morning.

At the head of the valley, where the opposite hills were so close we could hear our voices echo, the track began to zigzag, climbing steeply in a series of hairpins. Wendy spotted the shed skin of a snake that must have been five feet long, a sheath like brittle cellophane with every scale incised upon it. We passed between two towering outcrops of rock, perfect vantage points for an ambush, and then the track flattened out, running for a while beside a great sea of blackberry bushes. From here, we could see the sea far below us and the mountains of Albania, blue and indistinct in the heat haze. We inhaled the silence, the faint breeze deliciously cool on our sweat-streaked faces. Our legs ached pleasantly from the climb.

Now the track crept around the flank of the mountain, and slowly the valley of Ano Peritheia opened out before us. Smooth green and yellow hillsides surrounded it on every side, some marked with horizontal grey lines, the last vestiges of manmade terraces. There were trees again—no olives this high, but elegant cypresses, oleasters and mulberries, some protected by ramparts of bramble. We saw a well, a small church faced with faded pink stucco, another church—and then the houses began.

The town had clearly been conceived on a far grander scale than ramshackle Loutses. The buildings had been constructed of stone that had weathered to a lichen-freckled grey colour—two-storey houses with arched porticoes and balconies that showed the elegant influence of Venetian architects. The lanes and streets were also finished with cobbles or slabs of stone, sometimes broadening into a small piazza where a massive mulberry or cherry tree had been planted to provide shade and fruit. And everywhere we looked we seemed to see a church.

Wendy and I strolled along the deserted streets, enchanted by the silence and the beauty of the buildings. Through a massive stone archway carved with the lion of Venice we found the schoolhouse and climbed the outside staircase to peer in through the doorframe of the second storey. A couple of old wooden desks still stood beneath a window. In the town's main square, under a huge poplar tree that spread out to offer deep shade, two cafés faced each other. Both were boarded up and padlocked, but someone had fenced in an area behind one of them, as if for chickens.

Now the lanes converged on a single path that snaked down into a deep valley, no more than thirty yards across and full of vegetation, then up again to more houses, as if the town were folded along a central seam. Here the streets were almost roofed by trees, and as we walked up one narrow lane a cloud of butterflies fluttered and rose around us. Farther on was a vineyard, clearly still well tended, and beyond that a small paddock full of beehives, also very much in operation. We began to feel that we were trespassing and followed the lane upwards to the last church, a fine building with a free-standing bell tower and a number of graves around it. The most recent ones were from the 1950s, and each bore a small black-and-white photograph of the deceased dressed in his or her Sunday best. Beside the church was a stand of cypresses with forty or fifty sheep lying in the dappled shadows, like an illustration from a book of Bible stories. Occasionally one would stir and the bell around its neck gave a metallic clank, a sharp sound in the drowsy, bee-murmuring air.

We wandered for hours, never seeing a soul, pausing to eat white mulberries from a fruit-burdened tree or to admire a particularly pleasing detail of architecture. Some of the buildings were ruins, but many looked habitable, as if the owners had only recently closed the door behind them and might return at any time. Once, we were startled by a flock of sheep pouring through a gap in a hedge, a woollen waterfall, their bells jangling like a child's musical box. I expected a dog or a shepherd, but none appeared, and the sheep seemed to need no guidance, trotting into a yard through an open gate.

The walk back down the mountain was uncomfortably hot, but we reached Philip's kafeneion just before he closed up for the afternoon and a series of lemonades quenched our burning thirst. Men were coming home from work for their afternoon siesta. After the unearthly serenity of Ano Peritheia, Loutses felt as bustling as Manhattan.

While Philip cleaned and tidied, we sat on the bar stools and listened to him talk about the ghost town. In the sixteenth and seventeenth centuries, he explained, wealthy Venetian families from Corfu Town favoured the valley with their presence during the hot summer months—there was ample water there and the altitude was too high for the malarial mosquitoes that plagued the coast. For the inhabitants of the lower villages, the town was a spiritual centre, out of reach of Albanian pirates and raiding parties. Each of a dozen or so villages built its own church in Ano Peritheia and most were still in use, some of them merely chapels on the hillsides at the edge of the town, others tucked in among the houses, maintained and padlocked until the annual rite of the Panayiri. The inhabitants—most of them self-sufficient farmers and shepherds—left at the end of the 1950s, moving out of the mountains to easier, more accessible places where there were more jobs. At that time, with Greece's economy ruined by the war and then the civil war, olive farming was the principal source of income, and olives could not grow in Ano Peritheia. These days, only one couple and one old lady remained, keeping themselves to themselves. Many families still owned houses up there and some of the buildings were looked after, but in the winter it was no place to be, wet and cold and foggy. The track—barely passable in summer—was frequently washed out by landslides.

"But it's a really very interesting place, man," concluded Philip, "and last year, some Italians have been thinking to buy the whole town and turn it into a resort for tourists."

"That would be an absolute disaster!"

"Come on! It would mean a fucking lot of money, man. But the peoples and their relates who own the houses never could agree on a price."

For days after that, Wendy and I talked of little but Ano Peritheia. We fantasized about owning the old schoolhouse, about living up there like lighthouse keepers or hermits, cocooned in silence and solitude. Meanwhile, there was Sunday's Panayiri to look forward to.

On Friday night, well after midnight, we were startled from sleep by the ringing of the Loutses church bells. As I stumbled out of bed in the darkness, I noticed a diagonal line of orange through the window, an unnatural slash of colour. I opened the window. The steep hillside that formed the western side of Loutses's valley was on fire.

The light switch didn't work—the electricity was down again—but Wendy kept a pocket flashlight by the bed. Trying not to panic, we scrambled into our jeans. What if we hadn't heard the bells? Kostantes was away in Corfu Town. No one would have thought to wake us. We could have burned in our beds! We stuffed wallets and passports into Wendy's big canvas shoulderbag and felt our way to the kitchen and out onto the street.

The first person we saw was the village policeman, strolling slowly along in the moonlight, an idiotic grin on his face. He gestured towards the fire and said something, then chuckled at his own joke. The church bells had stopped ringing. On the patio of a house a few doors down, someone had lit a hurricane lamp. An elderly man stood there in long red flannel underpants that reached down to his knees, his face and forearms darkly tanned, the rest of his body lily white in the lamplight. He too seemed to find the situation amusing. We became aware of other people sitting on their porches or patios, none of them remotely anxious, occasionally calling things out to their neighbours, who laughed and answered in the darkness. The adrenalin in our muscles gradually dissipated.

A small girl approached us. "My grandmother asks do you want to see the fire better?"

That she spoke in English seemed part of the night's increasingly surreal sequence of events.

"Is it all right, then, the fire?"

"Oh yes," said the child.

She led us down the moonlit street to a group of four women, each of whom solemnly shook our hands. We followed them along a track behind the houses to a rocky outcrop. Two men sat there, smoking and watching the fire. We could hear it crackle in the distance, like the noise a car makes pulling into a gravel driveway. A faint night breeze could be felt on the hill, blowing the fire away from the village and up towards the top of the mountain. We could actually see the line of orange flame moving, leaving a myriad of winking red sparks in its wake. Sometimes the flames grew higher and illuminated the billowing grey smoke from below. Then we could see the tiny silhouettes of men beating out smouldering undergrowth with boughs cut from trees.

Wendy and the little girl were talking quietly. She had come to Loutses for the Panayiri. Normally she lived in Corfu Town, where she learned English in school. She was remarkably fluent, though some of her remarks were puzzling: "My grandmother is pleased with the fire because she kills birds in the winter."

With a sharp detonation and a whoosh of flame, a wild olive tree near the distant top of the ridge ignited like a firework and began to burn merrily. I tried to imagine the effect a fire like this might have in an olive grove: the villagers would be more actively concerned then, presumably. Now the fire had reached the crest of the mountainside. It hung there for a while then faded, though the smoke still rose into the moon-washed night sky.

"What about Ano Peritheia?" I asked the girl. She asked her grandmother. The old lady cackled a reply.

"It's safe."

"How can you be sure?"

The girl giggled shyly. "My grandmother says it is about a book. I don't know . . ."

One of the men chimed in to say that the old town was safe. Whoever had started this fire knew which way the wind was blowing. So it was arson! Probably shepherds, said the man. Burning off the dead ground cover would let the sheep reach the new green grass more easily when it grew again in October.

The old lady was speaking.

"My grandmother says she knew there would be a fire tonight because there was one across the sea in Albania last night."

No one scoffed at the suggestion, and I wondered what the connection could possibly be. Soon the conversation faded and we all just sat there, enjoying the moonlight and the cool night air until those who had been fighting the fire passed by in the darkness, talking loudly and laughing with the confidence of men whose virility had been tested and found to be up to the task. We followed them back to the village.

Next morning, we were up at the kafeneion, drinking coffee and discussing the events of the night when Wendy mentioned the grandmother's curious remark about a book.

Philip growled an obscenity and began to roll one of his tiny, thin cigarettes.

There was a book, he explained, owned by a family in Ano Peritheia and cherished and preserved over the centuries. It was a remarkable book, in handwriting, not printing, maybe a Bible, though some people said it was the bound manuscripts of the apostle James. In 1537, when the Turks swept over the island, taking twenty thousand of the inhabitants away as slaves but failing to conquer the Venetian citadel in Corfu Town, the head of the family had been caught unawares and threw the book into the bushes. The Turks did not discover it, and later, when a fire burned the mountainside, the flames stopped short of the bush. Obviously a miracle, if you believed in that sort of thing. Eventually, the family returned, found the book in the bushes, and looked after it for another four hundred years.

It seemed impossible that a fifth Gospel could exist—the implications were staggering—but Philip just shrugged. The book was well known in the area, the great relic of Ano Peritheia. After the Second World War it had been given to the clergy in Corfu Town for safekeeping and was presumably still in their private library.

"Have you ever seen it, Philip?"

"No, man. But everyone knows about that book."

On Sunday morning the village was busier than we had ever seen it. Knots of people talked excitedly in the street, the men wearing their most formal shirts and trousers, the women in demure dresses. It seemed as if every vehicle in Loutses had been commandeered for the procession into the mountains. Wendy and I rode in the back of a pick-up truck with a woman we did not know and her three young daughters, who stared at us while she fussed with the ribbons in their hair. Progress was slow and extremely bumpy, the discomfort exacerbated by young men on mopeds and scooters swerving in and out between the cars, whooping with delight and sending up clouds of dust.

We passed close to the hillside that had burned two nights earlier. It looked as if some giant had smothered the landscape in powdery grey ash. From it protruded curiously twisted shapes like sculptures of black wire—the tough mountain plants turned to charcoal. But the wild trees, the little stunted ilex and laurel and oleaster, seemed undamaged, just smudged with black around the base of their trunks. The fire had indeed stopped well short of Ano Peritheia's broad valley—evidence, perhaps, of the lingering protection of the book.

We parked at the end of a long line of trucks and cars that were clogging the road and walked the remaining quarter mile into the old town. Volunteers from the villages had clearly been busy. The hedges and trees that overhung the lanes had been trimmed and the worn flagstones along the broader streets were all strewn with sweet straw. The grassy area in front of the schoolhouse had been newly mown. Down in the main square, both bars were open and busy, with tables set out under the vast poplar tree. People were laughing and talking and greeting each other, and the ancient stone walls of the houses echoed with their voices.

We joined the straggling line of the faithful who were making their way down the path that linked the two sides of Ano Peritheia, up the other side and along butterfly alley. The churches we passed had opened their doors and from each came the sound of the liturgy, a priest intoning, the sung responses of a cantor, his voice joined in impromptu harmony by other men. At the largest and most distant church, where we had seen the sheep asleep under the cypresses, the crowd had spilled out into the churchyard, for there was no room for everyone inside.

Wendy and I recognized no one. This was not the Loutses church, the place where loyalty suggested we should be. We made our way back through the lanes, and there at the bar in the square was Kostantes. He wanted us to join him for a beer or a little retsina but eventually understood we were interested in seeing the service and pointed the way.

We had passed the Loutses church on the way into town; it was set back from the track, slightly above the first outlying houses. A path had been newly hacked through the blackberry bushes, and we scrambled up it, emerging onto a grassy area in front of the old building. It was one of the humbler edifices, and the once pink plaster walls had been bleached into a dozen pastel colours by years of sun and rain. There was no glass in the small round window above the doorway and no bell tower—the bell was hung from a convenient branch of a dead apple tree. A handful of men sat on the low wall beneath it, smoking and talking, and they smiled and nodded when they saw us.

We stood outside the open door, too shy to go inside, nervous of committing some faux pas in the incomprehensible Orthodox order of service. We could see that the women were crowded together at the back of the church, the men at the front, while the children played a surreptitious game of tag. Candles burned in an ornate brass stand, and the smaller boys and girls were given long, pencil-thin tapers of caramel-coloured wax to light from the flame. They were supposed to set them on the stand, but the more mischievous children were blowing their tapers out and then relighting them over and over again. The two Loutses altar boys, angelic in white cassocks, each holding a silver censer, frowned at them sternly.

The priest, no taller than the children, was unconcerned. Looking positively imperial in robes of embroidered pale blue silk, his glasses perched on the end of his nose, he read out loud from the order of prayer, swiftly and with no attempt at dramatization. The men in the congregation murmured their responses with obvious satisfaction. At one point, everyone began to leave the church, and we fell back and watched as a procession formed in the doorway. Four men lifted the tabernacle like a litter and carried it out into the sunshine. Followed by a man with a crosier and another who held up a fifteen-foot banner of purple silk embroidered with gold stars and tassels and a painted medallion of the Virgin, they began to walk slowly around the church, the priest in their wake, still intoning from the book, the congregation following. The air was filled with the sharp scent of wild mint and oregano crushed by their feet. There was no sense of pomp to the ceremony but it had a profound dignity. Bringing the procession into the open made it somehow universal, as if the hillsides and the herbs and the sky above us were involved in the villagers' worship. Then everyone went back into the church to kiss the icon of the Virgin and Child and receive Communion. As they left the church, the priest handed each one a little piece of the holiday bread, a sweet, dark-crusted loaf covered with sesame seeds, and a sprig of basil, the small-leafed Mediterranean species that is said to have grown beneath the cross on Calvary.

Kostantes had long since gone back to the bar, but Alexandra was among the congregation, with her fifteen-year-old son, Nikolas, a soft, slow-moving lad who was big for his age. We had met him several times but had yet to forge much of a bond since he knew no English beyond "hello" and did not seem to understand our rudimentary attempts at Greek. Alexandra came over to us and kissed us shyly, her smile serene, then nudged Nikolas and murmured to him to shake our hands. But he was distracted, tugging at his mother's arm and pointing down into the valley. Another, larger procession was winding through the lanes, passing by every church. We hurried back into the town in time to glimpse the bishop, gorgeous in gold, the seven ballpoint pens in his breast pocket providing an incongruous sartorial touch. The devout pressed forward to kiss his ring.

We found ourselves at the bar, where Kostantes immediately gathered us under his wing. Room was made for us at a table, and we drank some wine and ate some notably delicious mezethes—olives and fried potatoes, tiny pieces of fried liver, morsels of thinly sliced beef that had been cooked in wine and garlic, a salad of beets and parsley. Later, we wandered out of the town to where the trucks and cars stretched away down the road and hitched a lift back to Loutses.

We debated about going down to the beach, but we had learned to avoid our pristine Kalamaki on Sundays. That was the day when the Greeks used it, entire families picking their way down the steep path and setting up camp in the shade of the olive trees. From there, occasional forays were made to the water. Grandmothers in baggy black one-piece bathing suits stood knee-deep in the warm shallows, sometimes calling shrill warnings to children who paddled too far away. Teenaged boys played soccer on the sand, making elaborate diving saves and generally showing off for the benefit of the teenaged girls. Fathers poked about the rock pools along the edge of the bay, half-heartedly looking for edible shellfish, while their wives organized a family picnic under the trees—usually bread and fruit, a kind of breakfast sausage like Spam, olives and hard-boiled eggs. And when lunch was over, the whole family would stretch out in the shade and doze, lying this way and that, like figures from a Breughel painting.

Up in the village, Saturdays and Sundays meant the return of Alexandra and Nikolas from Corfu Town. They all slept in one makeshift bed in the little apothiki beside the patio, and Alexandra did their cooking on a Primus stove propped up between the tools and the four-foot-high drum that contained their year's supply of olive oil. The arrangement left Wendy and me feeling uncomfortable, but we reasoned it was their decision, part and parcel of letting their house for the summer. We ceded the patio to them, and it became a gathering place for their friends and relatives in the early evening.

One Saturday afternoon, a week after the Panayiri, we came back from the beach desperate for a shower and were clattering about in the kitchen when the door of the second bedroom slowly opened and out came an elderly man and his wife, still groggy and blinking from sleep. They said not a word, though the man shook my hand. Then they wandered outside to the patio.

Ten minutes later, Kostantes appeared in the kitchen, tentatively offering us a gift of some eggs and a litre of olive oil. When there was no tirade in reaction to the earlier surprise, he pointed at the stove. "Avrio . . . Alexandra . . . Cusina. Oreia?" Tomorrow Alexandra would cook for us. We could think of no better response than to nod and agree it would be oreia. Kostantes looked pleased with himself.

"You know it's a trick," said Wendy, after he had gone. "A way for them to entertain their visitors."

"Oh well. At least we'll taste some genuine Greek domestic cooking."

We spent Sunday morning up at Philip's kafeneion trying to telephone my mother in London and also feeling Alexandra might need some time alone in her kitchen. It was almost noon when we returned. Alexandra was at the stove, stirring a big pot of boiling water.

"What are you cooking?" I asked.

She stuck a fork into the pot and drew out a great slab of grey meat that glistened and trembled. Veins of transparent gristle ran through it; on the edge, pale as the white of a poached egg, was a fringe of fat.

"Gosh!" I tried to look enthusiastic. Desperate for something to say, I showed her my watch. "When will it be ready? When shall we eat?"

She looked nonplussed for a moment, then she fished out a smaller piece of meat and plopped it onto a plate. She set it down in front of Wendy.

"She thought you meant we were hungry!" said Wendy, pretending to laugh.

"What do we do now?"

"*You* eat it."

I sat down and drew the plate towards me. The meat had the texture I had always imagined whale blubber might have, slippery, sleek and soft but endlessly chewy. It tasted vaguely of fat. Alexandra stood with her hands on her hips, waiting for a reaction.

"Oreia!"

She raised one eyebrow in doubt, then said something long and fast and unintelligible.

I pushed the plate back across to Wendy. "Here, darling, you have some, too!"

Not missing a beat, Wendy flashed her most dazzling smile at Alexandra, pointed to my watch and shook her head as if to say that although the meat looked irresistibly delicious, it was simply too early for her to eat and she would wait until the meal was ready. Alexandra nodded in approval.

We hid in our room for the next two hours, until Kostantes called us to the kitchen. The table had been set for seven, and the others were already seated—Kostantes and Nikolas and the two elderly friends from Corfu Town. Alexandra was busy stirring pots, looking hot and tired. Kostantes patted her affectionately on the bottom, then made the introductions and poured everyone a tumbler of the thick, inky, violet wine that his brother Petros made every year. It had the metallic, bittersweet flavour of blood.

At this point, the overriding question in my mind concerned the fate of the meat: what had she done with it? Had she transformed it, by some culinary alchemy, into something edible? Or even delectable? Perhaps there would be a fairy-tale ending, a rustic gastronomic epiphany.

Alexandra had added tomatoes, tomato paste, onions, olive oil, salt, pepper and cinnamon to the pot, simmering it until at last the sinews and tissue slackened. All the flavour of the beef had suffused the sauce, and into that she had lifted a great tangle of partially cooked spaghetti that ended up absorbing most of the liquid. We were served the spaghetti first, with grated kephalotyri cheese, while the meat was lifted onto a platter and set down in the middle of the table, to cool and congeal while we ate the pasta. Its presence cast a blight over the spaghetti and distracted me from Wendy's valiant attempts at polite conversation with the other guests. She had picked up far more Greek than I had, but neither of us understood a word the others said. After a while, Kostantes perceived the problem and translated their mumbled comments into the pidgin he used with us, a grammarless mishmash of simple Greek and Italian nouns and adjectives. He was in a playful mood.

"Makaronia," he said, scowling down at the pasta on our plates. "Ochi kalos!" No good. We protested, of course, that it was oreia, and everyone chuckled. The joke lost its all-important element of surprise as he repeated it every couple of minutes, but he and his son continued to find it funny. The hilarity redoubled after Alexandra served the meat, spearing hefty pieces and shaking them onto our plates. "Ochi kalos?" asked Kostantes.

The meat was certainly better than it had been earlier in the day—still stringy but more tender. It tasted slightly of the sauce.

"Oreia!"

The finale, a giant, chilled watermelon that Alexandra swiftly cut into crisp, juicy chunks, truly was oreia, and we ate it with unfeigned pleasure and genuine relief.

Then it was time for the siesta. The friends asked Kostantes a question that clearly had to do with the availability of the second bedroom. Wendy invited them to use it and met no argument. We went for a walk, eager for the privacy of the olive groves.

From then on, we felt ourselves gradually losing any sense of proprietorship where the house was concerned. If we had said anything or made the smallest fuss, I'm sure that matters would have reverted to the earlier status quo, but there seemed no point. We would be leaving in a couple of weeks, and to be honest, we had never spent much time on the patio. Alexandra and Nikolas moved back from Corfu Town, and they and Kostantes took over the second bedroom. They were fairly quiet when they used the kitchen very early in the morning; at night, after they had gone to bed, we had our own room in which to talk and play cards or Scrabble.

Increasingly, our conversation turned to London and Toronto. We missed our friends and families and there were even times, strangely enough, when I missed having a job to go to and a purpose in life beyond pleasure and half-hearted attempts at writing. Wendy and I had put the idea of starting a family on hold. But both of us knew our relationship had evolved and at some deep level we were curious to see how it might fare in the real world, away from the island of the lotus eaters.

September 7, 1981

Hey, little Dee!
This is the last letter you'll get from Loutses. We leave tomorrow at dawn, scraping our few remaining drachmas together to pay for a taxi to the airport. Philip has organized it for us and he swears the guy is reliable, but who knows? At least we don't have to trust the bus. Of course, we're sorry to be leaving—I'm sure we'll wish we were back here the moment the plane touches down—but Jim and I agree it's time. The reoccupation of the house by K and A makes me feel as if we've been painted into a corner. They're welcome to the patio. Now that the straggly grapes are ripe, the wasps are a real threat. K snores all night long—we can hear him through the wall.

It feels as if summer has gone on long enough. It's not quite so hot, but it feels hotter because there's a new weight and humidity in the air. You know how we could sometimes faintly hear the blasting from the quarry over in Albania and we always thought it was thunder though there wasn't a cloud in the sky? Last week it was thunder. It didn't rain here and I don't think it rained there, but there was distant lightning flickering all night long. The villagers all wanted rain of course—not a drop has fallen since May.

There have been some arguments up at the bar—Philip says it's the weather, a hot wind from the Sahara that drives people crazy—and we've noticed people getting edgy with each other. Even Georgie at the taverna isn't his usual grinning self—not surprising after four months of grilling himself every night in the lean-to. I never thought I'd say this, but I'm really really tired of souvlakia and the rest of Georgie's tiny repertoire. We had been doing much more cooking ourselves—at least, Jim had been—partly to save money but mostly because we were so desperate for a change. But now that the kitchen is no longer our own, we've been relying on bread and feta and fruit and eating out. Still forage a picnic at Kalamaki when we need to. We've spent a couple of nights down there, spreading a rug and building a fire with driftwood from the rocks. Romantic, but strangely damp around three in the morning.

Kalamaki has changed. One morning there was a line of brown seaweed along the entire beach. Jim was outraged that his pristine sand had been defiled. It's been drying out ever since, turning to beige powder that the wind blows away so the next layer can dry. It's almost gone now. And the stream has dwindled to a fairly stagnant and stinky pond back among the bamboo thickets—full of little green terrapins. The beach is still incredibly beautiful and our great escape.

Felt we needed an outing the other day. We waited for the bus (on time!!!) to Kassiopi and spent the morning window shopping. We ended up buying two of those huge heavy white woollen sweaters from the woman nearest the harbour. It's the end of the season and she gave us a great price. Her daughter-in-law was helping in the store and she turns out to be English—came here on holiday, fell for a guy who worked in a restaurant and married him, had kids. She seemed so miserable. Didn't have a good word to say about the Greeks. All they think about is money, she said. Then we went to a bar and had a pizza (oh God I miss real pizza!!) but there was a beautiful African grey parrot in a cage and it had pecked away some of its own feathers out of boredom and despair. Like the English girl. We came back to Loutses in a cynical mood to find a load of K and A's dishes in the sink. The phone wasn't working up at the bar—Philip got mad at it one day and hit it. I did the math for the rest of the money and found it's going to be touch and go. Now those sweaters look like gross extravagance.

But then last night . . . There was obviously something happening at the taverna. Georgie had not fired up the grill and someone had brought extra chairs and lined them up sideways in the front garden, with all the tables moved inside. They had hung a sheet from the two trees at the other end. Just before it got dark a man from Corfu Town set up a movie projector on a table behind the chairs. We went to have a look. I wish I could speak Greek! I wish Ilias was still here! We couldn't understand what he said, but he asked for fifty drachs each. It was a travelling cinema and he'd been coming for years and years. Half the village arrived and paid and sat down. The Loudest Woman in Loutses (remember her?) saw us and beckoned us over frantically, then made her grandchildren sit on the ground so we could have better seats. There was some problem with the projector but eventually all the lights in the bar were turned out and the movie show began. It was in black and white and it was silent, but it wasn't a silent movie—there just wasn't a sound system. Very surreal. People didn't talk much. They were all leaning forward, staring at the screen like fascinated children while the full moon shone down and the breeze stirred the sheet a little and the owls in the valley peeped and answered each other. It was as if we were all extras in a Fellini movie. Magical. All these people who a few hours ago had been bitching at each other, suddenly wide-eyed and quiet and on their best behaviour. And when it was over there was a sort of sigh of satisfaction. Then people started to come to, and Georgie turned on the lights in the taverna and everyone looked at their watches as if they thought five minutes had gone by but it was really an hour and a half. Jim and I couldn't stop smiling either. All the frustrations and annoyances and hassles we'd endured in the last few weeks, the growing disillusionment with the villagers, had drifted away in the darkness like the smoke from the cigarettes the men chain-smoked during the show. We wanted to stay for ever.

But we can't, and it's probably for the best. We'll stay in London for a bit, but I think we'll come to T.O. in the fall if we can rent out Jim's flat, and try our luck there for a while. Who knows! Either way, what heaven it will be to be COLD again. K and A are full of hugs for us now and you can sense that they're pretty amazed they survived renting out their house for the very first time. Now the end is so close, they're wondering about next summer. They were ripped off by the relative who was acting as their agent—he kept almost half of what we paid at the beginning of the summer—and K knows it. He says we could pay less next year and give it all to him. Will we come back? I don't know—maybe we should all go to China next time—are you up for that, Dee-Dee?

Must go. Jim wants to drag me up to your rock for a last look at the stars and the lights of Albania across the water. He wants to stay up all night until the taxi comes.

See you soon!

Much love,

Wendy

CHAPTER THREE

ALL MY LIFE, AS FAR AS I COULD remember, the sunshine of England had seemed perfectly adequate—fitful, admittedly, but at times intense enough to make a man take off his jacket and loosen his tie. Not any more. That summer, the light of Greece had flooded our minds with such intensity that the northern sun could never again be anything but wimpish and wan. It was the same with the fruit and vegetables in Tooting market—now juiceless and insipid to our Mediterranean palates—and with the muggy, polluted air of South London. Oh, we gorged on things we had missed—the theatre, movies and art galleries, television, Indian restaurants—but while our minds found compensation, our bodies ached for dry heat, sand and salt water. As autumn crept towards winter, we watched our tans yellow and fade.

And there were more serious causes for concern. Under Mrs. Thatcher, the expression on the face of contemporary English society had grown increasingly ugly, the inner cities fetid with racial violence. Coming home on the underground one evening, Wendy saw two skinheads beat up a Pakistani man. No one tried to intervene. She arrived at the flat with clenched fists.

"I want to go back to Canada," she said as she took off her coat. "As soon as possible."

I had no arguments to offer. We talked late into the night, making plans with a speed and efficiency that astonished us both. Wendy would leave first, staying with her mother and stepfather in Muskoka while she looked for somewhere to live in Toronto. I had a week's work in a film at the beginning of November—the last acting I would ever do, as it turned out. We needed the money, and I would follow her as soon as the job was over.

The look of determination was still in her eye when I kissed her goodbye at the airport. It was still there three weeks later when she kissed me hello in Toronto. "I wasn't sure if you'd actually go through with this," she admitted. "I thought you might change your mind and stay in England after all."

A friend of Wendy's stepfather had found us somewhere to live—a one-bedroom apartment on the sixteenth floor of a high-rise block in St. James Town. "That's a bad part of the city," the cab driver muttered when we gave him the address. "Lots of crime after dark."

"Well, it's the best we can do right now," said Wendy icily.

Wendy's parents had divorced four years earlier, almost as soon as Wendy had left home to start university in Ottawa. It took her completely by surprise but the separation was amicable. The three of them simply went their separate ways, flying apart like shrapnel. Her father, Dennis, fulfilled his long-held ambition of moving to a small desert town in Arizona. He had hoped Wendy's mother, Audy, would go with him but she chose to remain in Canada. Dennis eventually met and married a delightful young woman called Roberta. Audy also married again, and she and her new husband, Weldon, bought a substantial old property by a lake in Muskoka, where they lived year-round.

Audy and Weldon were waiting for us in the car park of the apartment block. They had rented a trailer and brought down a generous collection of second-hand furniture from Muskoka, virtually everything we would need, from frying pans to a double bed. There was even a beautiful grey carpet that Wendy had bought when she was a teenager; it all but filled the living room of the apartment. By mid-afternoon, we were moved in and life in Toronto began.

In spite of the cab driver's warnings, we never saw any sign of trouble. The greatest danger was monotony. We looked out at stained concrete buildings identical to our own, or down at the concrete playground far below, where children from a nearby school came to play in their lunch hour. The physical ugliness of our surroundings was unredeemed by any eccentricity or excess, the great blocks as bland and utilitarian as the washing machines in the basement laundry room. Inevitably there were cockroaches in the apartment that no amount of cleaning or pesticides could deter. More obvious was the smell that hung perpetually in the corridors and reached a gagging intensity in the elevators, an aroma of junk food, garlic and body odour to which we never became accustomed. But the rent was a feasible $216 a month, and for the first few weeks the late-autumn sun poured onto our narrow, vertiginous balcony all day long. We bought plants and played house and went for long walks in the neighbourhood, wading through fallen leaves in the sprawling old cemetery on the opposite side of Parliament Street, discovering a string of small cafés, marking out our territory.

Wendy thought about Corfu more than I did. For me, life in Toronto still had an interesting novelty, but she was back on home turf, harnessed to the routine of a nine-to-five job, and, as December set in, her restless soul was already fretting. The work itself was enjoyable—as assistant to the curator of modern sculpture at the Art Gallery of Ontario, she was in a world she loved and understood—but battling the subway and the cold, wet, crowded streets was no fun at all. She would arrive home in the evening stressed and moody, run a hot, fragrant bath and soak in it for a good half-hour while I sat and listened to the events of her day and told her the tiny happenings of mine—two more pages of the short story written, the discovery that chicken livers were on sale at the supermarket. As the weeks went by, far-fetched notions of travel and adventure began to creep into her conversation. If we could save enough to buy a car, we could drive all the way to the tip of Tierra del Fuego, writing a book about the experience. Or we could acquire a boat ("How?" I would ask. "Never mind," she'd reply, "we'll think about that later"), learn to sail it and head for blue water. Maybe anchor off Kalamaki and live in it there, free to do exactly as we pleased. In my literal, masculine way, I would carefully point out the difficulties inherent in such schemes, imagining I represented the voice of reason and maturity, too stupid to know she needed enthusiastic endorsement and a companion in what were only fantasies of freedom.

On Christmas Eve we took a Greyhound bus up north and spent a week with Audy and Weldon in Muskoka. I remember deep cold and deeper silence, especially at night, when we could hear wolves howling far away beyond the ridge. Snow creaked under our boots. Above us, the northern sky glimmered with the shifting luminescence of the aurora borealis.

"Why the hell do we live in a city?" we asked each other on the bus ride home.

"Why the hell do we live here at all?" added Wendy after a while. "We could go back to Greece. We could. Do you really want to spend another winter in St. James Town? You always said it would be so much better being flat broke there than here."

"Yes, but—"

"I mean it! We could sell your flat and buy an old house in Loutses. Or Ano Peritheia, even. Fix it up."

"Just like that?"

"Why not? You could write just as easily there. I could, too. If we were really careful we could live very cheaply indeed."

As the weeks passed, I thought so, too. Toronto would have been a fine place to live if we had had money, but it was miserable being so poor. And the winter seemed interminable. For every enchanting snowfall (the fascination of leaning over our balcony to watch snowflakes *recede* as they fell the last sixteen stories), there was a week of grimy, car-stained slush and bitter wind that made even the smallest exodus from the overheated apartment an endless chore of overcoats and boots. My grandmother wrote to me every week, often enclosing a precious pound note from her slender pension, and described how the first daffodils of March were already out in Chelsea. In Toronto, the trees were bare, the lawns and parks still a barren grey. Winter's last snowfall had barely turned to slush as the Falklands War erupted in April, keeping me glued to the radio. When I looked up, May was almost over and the breathlessly short Canadian spring had been and gone.

So had the last of my money. Before leaving London, I had sold my most valued possession, a Selmer Mark VI tenor saxophone, making sure it went to a good r & b home where it would be treated with love and respect. But that was my last contribution to the communal kitty. I had no work permit, and the short stories I wrote and sent to my agent in England fell upon stony ground.

Being a kept man carried certain responsibilities where cooking, laundry and housekeeping were concerned, but it meant we had only one work timetable to worry about when planning the few excursions we could afford, spending every other weekend up at Audy and Weldon's, two precious days of canoeing, fishing or hiking through the bush. One cloudless July afternoon, after a swim in the cool, tea-coloured lake at the end of the lawn, we were lying prone on the dock, drying off in the sun. The wooden planks felt hot against my skin.

"I can't tell her," murmured Wendy. "I can't. She was so happy when we came back to Canada."

"You have to."

We could postpone it no longer. Somehow or other, we had to tell Audy that we had decided to go back to Corfu and make our home there. Not that there had been a precise moment of decision. The idea had grown slowly, taking up more and more room in our minds until we accepted it as an inevitability. On August the first, Wendy would give a month's notice at the art gallery. Come September, we would move back to England and thence to Greece. But we still had to tell her mother.

Water plopped lazily under the dock.

"I've been thinking." Wendy rolled over and looked at me. "We could soften the blow by getting married before we leave. She'd be so happy, she wouldn't mind where we live."

"Get married?"

"Where's your sense of adventure? I know we've only got sixty dollars in the bank, but think of the fun we'd have—the adventure of it all."

"Married?"

"Why not? You and I don't give a damn, but she'll be thrilled. And people will give us wedding presents . . ."

"I guess . . ."

Wendy jumped to her feet. "I'll go and tell her. You stay here."

I watched her walk up the lawn, turn the corner of the house, heard the screen door bang. Married? There came a scream from the kitchen. Two minutes later, Wendy appeared again, almost dancing across the grass.

"August seventeenth. She's so thrilled! She went straight to the calendar. I think she's afraid we'll change our minds. That gives us six weeks."

"Right . . . Wow! Married!" We sat and looked at each other for a while, wide-eyed. "And did you tell her about Greece?"

Wendy frowned out at the lake. "Not yet. I just couldn't. I didn't want to spoil it. I'm going to put it in a letter."

Back in Toronto, I phoned my father in London with the news. He was delighted, in his calm, rather detached way. "You know, I don't have any money to get you a decent wedding present, but I'd like to give you the stamp collection. It's time you had it, anyway." A vision of sitting as a boy with him at the dining-room table, licking stamp hinges and watching him stick the stamps onto a page . . . The older albums had belonged to my grandfather when he was a child in Australia at the turn of the last century. No gift could have meant more to me. I could feel my dad smiling on the other end of the phone, could imagine him sitting there with the *Guardian* crossword puzzle, a whisky and water, the inevitable cigarette.

Now my grandmother took the receiver. Her voice sounded frail, but at ninety-five that was only to be expected. My mother's mother, she had moved into the small house in Chelsea the week I was born and had looked after us all ever since. She too was overjoyed at the news, especially when I told her Wendy and I would be coming back to England in September.

Then I phoned my mother at her office. More excitement. I heard myself tell her it was just going to be a tiny wedding, in a registry office with Audy and Weldon and a handful of Wendy's closest friends, news that carried the implicit suggestion that there was no need for her to be there.

"We'll have a proper party when you come back, then," she said. "And Corfu is much closer than Canada, isn't it, darling. We'll be able to come and visit you there."

"Absolutely."

Audy and Weldon had themselves only recently married, and it seemed easiest to use their wedding as a template for our own. A civil ceremony in North York City Hall, afternoon photographs on a picturesque bridge in Edwards Gardens, a Japanese dinner for the party of eight. In lieu of a honeymoon we booked a suite for the wedding night in the small but debonair Windsor Arms Hotel.

Nine days before the wedding, soon after sunrise, the telephone woke us up. I staggered groggily into the living room to answer it. When I didn't come back, Wendy followed me and found me sobbing. The previous evening, my father had suffered an aortic aneurism. He never regained consciousness.

I flew to England the next day, feeling numb and stricken, vaguely aware of fire doors closing in my mind, sealing off pain and regret, containing it until some future time when I could attempt to deal more effectively with my emotions. In London, there was nothing to be done: my younger brother, Daniel, had made all the arrangements.

The day after the funeral, I drove out to see my father's mother. At ninety-five, she lived alone in a large house in the country, still in full control of her faculties and ever ready to criticize the "devils and fools" in government or in the village grocer's shop. My uncle Bob and his family lived ten minutes away and looked after her with unstinting devotion, but this morning she was on her own. We stood in the sunshine that streamed in through the kitchen window while I cooked her some lunch. My father was the eldest of her three sons, and she had adored him.

"He always used to joke that nothing would ever happen to me until either he or Bob died first," she sighed, "so there'd be someone up there to mix me a pink gin and help with the *Sunday Telegraph* crossword. Do make sure that's hot enough, dear. I can't bear tepid food."

A week later, after I had returned to Toronto, my mother phoned to say she had died peacefully in her sleep.

MANY MEN, I suspect, find themselves emotionally dazed, not to mention hungover, as they stand at the altar. My soul had taken a bruising, and I was grateful for the intimacy and simplicity of our wedding. It seemed to be over as soon as it was begun.

At the hotel, our friends had been busy, filling the bed with confetti and rose petals and leaving beautiful little gifts and hand-drawn cards in unexpected places. Next morning, a knock on the door ushered in an unexpected trolley of eggs Benedict, blueberries and cream, coffee and orange juice. We felt like millionaires until the moment came to check out and we walked back to St. James Town.

There had been no time to mourn my father or grandmother. Now we were far too busy to explore any subtle changes in our relationship that getting married might have inspired. We passed on the lease of the apartment to a friend who agreed to look after our furniture and plants in perpetuity—all except Wendy's grey carpet. That was coming with us to Greece.

"But how will we get it there?" I had asked her. "How will we even get it to the airport?"

Wendy's gift for lateral thinking kicked in. "Hire a stretch limo. It's only ten dollars more than a taxi."

And then we were back in London, standing in my flat, jet-lagged and confused, aware, as we opened our suitcases, that we would soon have to pack it all up again and move on. It was one year to the day since we had left Corfu.

The great wedding party that my mother had planned before my father died was to go ahead. It was certainly what he would have wanted—he loved any excuse to put on evening dress. My mother had rented the grandest of the three-decked pleasure boats that cruised the Thames from Greenwich to Battersea, large enough for the hundred friends who were to attend. She booked a jazz band, organized an extraordinarily elaborate dinner and even hired a renowned barman to create a custom cocktail for the occasion. We called it an Ancient Mariner, because it was potent enough to stop one in three wedding guests, and I seem to remember it resembled a Manhattan, though I drank too many that evening to be entirely sure.

Wendy looked ravishingly beautiful in a vintage skin-tight white evening gown, borrowed for the occasion. After dinner, when everyone had moved up to the dance floor on the main deck, we sought out my godfather, Robert Morley. He loved Wendy. She had worked as his secretary for a while when she first came to stay with me in England and the two of them soon found they shared a socialist conscience coupled with an irrepressibly irreverent view of the world. He put his hand on Wendy's arm.

"You're pregnant, darling, aren't you? I can always tell."

Wendy turned as red as her lips.

"Yes, I am," she murmured. "But how did you know? We only found out ourselves two days ago. We had no idea, but just to be on the safe side I bought one of those tests and it turned blue. Jimmy ran out and got two more and they turned blue, too. We've figured out it could only have happened on our wedding night."

"And you're still determined to move to Corfu?"

"Yes."

"Then you'd better hurry up, dear. James, have you spoken to Bully?"

The actor, writer and renowned teddy bear enthusiast Peter Bull was another old friend of my parents. Almost forty years earlier, he had bought and renovated a house on Paxos, the island just south of Corfu, and he still spent his summers there. The rest of the year he lived a short walk from my mother's house, above a punk-bondage boutique called Oh Boy.

A day or two after the party, I went round to see him. He talked about my father while he made tea, remembering times when they had acted together and describing my dad as the wittiest man in Chelsea. Then we sat down amidst his collection of antique bears and he reached for a pencil and paper.

"Do you speak Greek?" he asked.

"No, I'm afraid not. We've forgotten anything we picked up."

"Oh well, never mind. There are only three words you need. *Etsi-k'etsi,* which means 'so-so,' *po po po,* which means something like 'ooh la la,' and *malaka,* which means 'wanker' but must be used with caution. I've always found I can get by with them. And you must find a trustworthy Greek friend. Corfu is on the frontier, so to buy a house you must first create a company with a Greek as majority shareholder."

"Oh."

"So you will need a lawyer. Do you remember George Kaloudis?"

"No, I don't think so."

"His father was my great friend and George is a little like my godson. You met him years ago, when your mother took you to Corfu on holiday. He took you out on his father's caique."

"Oh yes!" I remembered him vividly now—a boy of twelve with a flop of straw-coloured hair who handled the heavy boat like a veteran, anchoring in pristine, inaccessible bays so we could swim, cutting up lemons to suck when we emerged from the sea (they seemed improbably sweet after so much salt water), cooking us a lunch of fried sardines and potatoes in the cabin. A year or two younger and immersed in the Swallows and Amazons books, I had envied his abilities and lifestyle to the point of hero-worship.

"Well, he's a lawyer now. Speaks perfect English. I think you're going to have great fun. And remember, if you want to get something done in a hurry—with a notary or even a neighbour—a bottle of single malt whisky is always a very effective gift."

November 30, 1982

Dear Mom,

So much to tell you. First some very sad news. James's other grandmother (Ros's mother) passed away. She had been bedridden for weeks and just got weaker and weaker. She was so sweet and kind to everyone. Ros's house seems very empty now. I think she and Jim and his brother have had enough funerals for a while. At least my pregnancy has given her something positive to concentrate on—until we leave. I still feel great, by the way. No more morning sickness. I'm hardly even showing yet, though my belly's hard as a drum. Ros made me go and see a Harley Street gynecologist and he turned out to be one of those typical old English doctors who drive me nuts! He asked me why I was there and I said because I was pregnant, then he gave me a lecture about pregnancy not being a disease and I was a perfectly healthy young woman, and on and on. I said that in Canada it was customary for a woman to tell a doctor when she got pregnant but he just faffed on until I wanted to slap him.

But the BIG news: we bought a house!! We flew out there a week ago. On the plane we tried to put together some sentences from a modern Greek dictionary we bought. Jim studied ancient Greek at school, so he knows the alphabet at least, but the language and pronunciation is totally different. We looked up "I want" and "to buy" and "your house" and practised saying them until a woman who was sitting next to me begged us to stop. She was Greek and she wrote down the sentence with the correct grammar and taught us how to say it properly. I think she thought we were crazy, doing all this. But that hardly makes her unique.

It was damp and cold in Corfu, and so quiet and deserted. We spent the night at the only hotel that stays open in the winter—the Cavalieri. You could tell it was once rather grand but the charms have seriously faded. Our room had certainly seen better days. We thought we'd rent a car, but all the rental offices were also closed until next summer, so we ended up taking the bus to Loutses—just like old times.

Jim had sent a telegram to Kostantes telling him we were coming and we eventually found him. He looked pretty dishevelled and he was limping badly. He had an accident on his scooter months ago and broke a leg and it hasn't mended properly. He hugged us when he saw us and we all got tearful. Then we went up to the bar and Philip, the owner, translated for K and us. After about THREE HOURS we were finally all on the same page! At that point, K started to act strangely. Philip kept asking him something and he would just close his eyes and lift his eyebrows, trying to look holy. I think Philip was trying to get him to say which house he thought we should buy—apparently there are several for sale, but K had one particular place in mind.

Loutses is so different in winter! Everyone goes around in sweaters and jackets and complains about the cold. The taverna's closed but luckily the little shop is open so we were able to buy some food to cook in K's kitchen. Alexandra (his wife) is in Corfu Town with their son so we have our old room back. In the shop—you'll never believe this—I met an English woman who lives here. Her name is Michelle, she's married to the son of the shopkeeper and she just had a baby, a little girl called Louisa. She said that when the time comes I mustn't go near the hospital but to this modern clinic that has just been built by a young obstetrician/gynecologist called Dr. Babalis. She seemed a bit wary at first but we talked for hours and I think she's happy there'll be another English-speaking young mother in the village, though she also speaks Greek, of course.

The house! Kostantes took us up there and the closer we got the more certain we became that it was going to be the house we saw that summer, the one with the amazing view. It was. We kept asking how much it would cost to buy, but he wouldn't say. Just "poli ligo," which means "very little." Jim was convinced we were going to be ripped off, that everyone thinks we're loaded. Obviously it's going to need a lot of work, but Kostantes says he can do it. He kept telling us there were eleven olive trees and that we would have our own oil, as if that made up for everything else. Later, we tried to get Philip to give us advice but he wouldn't. I talked about it with Michelle, too, but she just said, "Yeah, well, they close ranks, don't they." She said her husband, Babis, also owns a ruin up on Zervou and she's hoping he'll fix it up so they can live there instead of in the little apartment over the shop. Anyway. We spent the next day up at the house, dreaming and making plans, and then we just went ahead and bought it. The price would make you laugh, though of course it's going to cost a lot to fix it up. We have borrowed from Jim's mom until we sell his flat and can pay her back (typically, she says there is no hurry, but I'm determined to), and there is also the money he inherited from his other grandmother—enough to make this possible, so there's no need for you to worry.

We have our own lawyer and he's started to get all the paperwork together. Could take months, maybe years. We had to think of a name for the company we formed and decided on Niapos Publications with Kostantes as the main shareholder. It's all an act of faith but everybody has to do it. George, the lawyer, wouldn't believe K's name was Kostantes, though we told him a hundred times. "It must be Konstantinos," he kept saying. You also have to have the person's father's name to make it legal, so J became James tou Tomas, James son of Tom. So medieval. The first time we met the lawyer, Jim insisted on bringing him a bottle of Scotch!! I was so embarrassed, but he accepted it graciously, with an odd sort of smile as if he thought we were quaint. I tried to find out how much his services would cost but he just prevaricated and said it didn't matter and he'd send us a bill someday. We just said okay. It's been an ordeal and we've been so exhausted we haven't even had time to talk about it all properly. When one of us wants to be serious and responsible, the other one wants to fantasize, and vice versa.

Jim sends his love and I'll call you on Christmas Day.

Love from Wendy

ONLY ONCE in my life have I felt the infatuation that can exist between a man and his vehicle. I have fallen for many a house and garden over the years, but where cars are concerned I have loved only once and never will again. It was a twenty-year-old short-wheelbase diesel Land Rover, army green with a white roof, and I saw it first in a muddy field in Wiltshire, in the January rain, as the twilight was fading.

Even then, it was obsolete. Four-wheel-drive vehicles had not yet become the desirable objects of fashion they are today, and this one offered no concessions to comfort. It was designed for hard work under extreme conditions, with component parts that could be repaired thousands of miles from the nearest garage. The heater was a free-standing steel box, a virtual stove, bolted to the floor on the passenger side. Each windshield wiper had its own small electric motor mounted on the dash, with a metal rod protruding from the back so that the wipers could be operated manually if the motor failed. A massive spare tire was attached to the hood. The dash was a vertical metal panel with a layout that had changed little since the Second World War. I was delighted to learn that this old beauty had already led an adventurous life, crossing the Sahara and the lava fields of Iceland before ending up with a dozen or more of its brethren in the Wiltshire farmer's field.

"Where are you taking her?" asked the farmer.

"Greece."

He nodded, pleased with the answer. "Bear in mind, if you drive on the motorway, she won't go above forty-five miles an hour. Then again, she'll also do that towing a ton."

I told him I was looking for a trailer of some kind to carry our furniture, and he took me to another part of the field. An old rusted blue horsebox stood there—really no more than a cuboid of thin metal on six small wheels, the same length and width but taller than the Land Rover.

"You ever driven with anything on behind?" asked the farmer.

"No. Never."

"You might want to practise a bit before you set off for Greece. Especially reversing."

"I'll make a point of it."

"All right, then." The deal was done.

We moved out of my flat on the last day of January, ferrying my belongings to the family home—my mother's house now—in our articulated transport. The rear roll-down door of the horsebox opened of its own accord halfway along the Wandsworth Bridge Road, but I saw the tumbling furniture and tea chests in the side mirror and pulled over in time to salvage them, making a mental note to buy a stronger padlock.

For the next ten days, my mother's house was barely habitable as we packed and repacked the things we thought we might need to start our new life. The box spring and mattress of my double bed slid neatly into the trailer on its side, taking up exactly one quarter of the available space. Bent double, Wendy's grey carpet was wedged in above it. In the shed at the end of the back garden, we found a brand new kitchen sink—no one could remember why it was there—and we took that, too, if only to be able to say we had packed everything including it. Tea chests of books and bedclothes, tools and typewriter, LPs, record player and a collapsible basinet—like a box on wheels that could double as a cot and a pram—the desk and bookcases I had used as a schoolboy, our precious stamp collection, pots and pans, picnic basket, wooden spoons and liqueur glasses . . . for an inveterate list maker like Wendy, it was a time of glory. In the evenings, my brother and I spread out maps of Europe and attempted calculations of time and distance: London to Dover, then the ferry to Calais. Paris, Chamonix, the Mont Blanc tunnel and down to Milan, over to Rimini, then down the Adriatic to Ancona for the long ferry ride to Corfu.

Daniel would have to fly back to England as soon as we reached our goal, but I was delighted he had agreed to come with me, sharing the driving and keeping me company. He knew a great deal more about cars and their engines than I did, having rebuilt a BSA motorbike from scratch in his student days, and more recently restored a classic MGA 1600. Should anything go wrong with the Land Rover, I imagined he would have no trouble with its admirably accessible engine. We had allowed ourselves five days for the journey, aiming to reach Corfu the day before Wendy flew in from London. Six months pregnant, she would be much more comfortable in an airplane than a Land Rover.

The paperwork was my own responsibility. Two full days of interviews and explanations in various departments of Her Majesty's Customs and Excise had generated a heavy folder of documents, ferociously detailed inventories and bills of lading in pink, green and yellow triplicate. Assessing the value of the goods—all second-hand except for the kitchen sink—had been a matter of guesswork, and the clerks I dealt with seemed as confused by it all as I was, passing me from office to office.

The day came. My mother had made sandwiches and filled a bag with apples and chocolate bars. I kissed her goodbye, trying not to notice her anxiety, hugged Wendy, and then we were off.

The first leg, to Dover, took longer than expected, but the Channel was calm and we were in Calais by early afternoon. None of the customs men in England or France had been remotely interested in looking at my portfolio of papers, merely waving us on when we said we were making for Greece. Given our cruising speed, Daniel and I had agreed it would be just as quick to avoid the motorway from Calais, travelling by smaller roads in what looked on the map to be a straight line to Paris. The roads were almost deserted and we congratulated ourselves on the decision. Nevertheless, our progress was still slower than anticipated. By nightfall we were only at Abbéville, half as far into France as we had hoped to be. We were also running low on diesel, and the garages in the small towns and villages we passed were all closed for the night. We would have to take the motorway after all, if only to find fuel.

The rain grew heavier as we crawled along the slow lane in the darkness, peering ahead at the patch of road illuminated by our dim yellow headlights. The wipers created small, fan-shaped areas of clarity on the windshield, but their sweep was slow and the rain was gaining. We felt we were squinting through keyholes. Every few minutes, some huge juggernaut of a truck hurtled by us, lit up like a Christmas tree, its horn blaring, rocking the Land Rover and sending a wave of water across our bows. Somewhere near Beauvais, we ran out of gas. We had just enough momentum to glide onto the hard shoulder.

"At least it's quieter now," observed my brother. He reached out to touch the windshield wiper motor and swore. It was burning hot.

"What do you think we should do?" I asked.

I could feel him looking at me in the darkness. "I don't know. What do *you* think we should do?"

"We could sing?"

I started with the old Roy Rogers standard "A Four-Legged Friend." He did not join in.

We were rescued eventually by the largest truck I had ever seen, the size of an ocean liner, festooned with coloured lights. It pulled off the road ahead of us and started to reverse while we frantically flashed our high beams, hoping it knew we were there. At last it stopped, and I jumped out into the rain as the driver climbed down from his cab.

"You lot in trouble?" he asked. "I noticed the English number plate."

While we siphoned diesel from his massive spare tank into the Land Rover he explained that he drove from Edinburgh to Turin every week and made a point of helping out stranded drivers whenever he could. "You know your tail lights aren't working, do you, mate?" he asked. "Might want to fix that. There's a lot of big rigs on this road and you're well camouflaged."

My brother and I looked at each other in horror. Then we set to work, Daniel jury-rigging a cable directly from the battery to the trailer's tail lights, me holding an umbrella over his head.

We reached Paris in time for the early-morning rush hour on the notorious *périphérique*, the ring road, birthplace of all the most hair-raising legends of ruthlessly aggressive continental drivers. But the French sensed danger when they saw us and allowed the Land Rover unusual liberties where changing lanes was concerned. In Fontainebleau, on the other side of the city, we finally found a place for coffee and croissants and sat down to review our itinerary.

"Oddly enough," I pointed out, "we're exactly where we hoped to be at this time, except we've missed the good night's sleep in that hotel by the Seine you recommended. Do you think you could sleep while I drive?" Daniel stared at me through tiny crimson eyes and nodded. "Then we could take it in turns." He nodded again.

"Diesel," he croaked.

"Right. Absolutely. First we fill up."

So we crossed France, spelling each other at the wheel, sleeping as best we could above the roar of the engine and the spine-distorting vibration. We learned to top up the oil every time we bought gas and to do without the floor heater after it burned a brown patch on my trouser leg while I slept. We made good progress down the autoroute to Burgundy, then ran into snow as we entered the Alps. As we went down one steep hill, the trailer jackknifed behind us, slithering round until it was at right angles to the Land Rover, sticking out fifteen feet on the driver's side, its weight forcing us ever faster. My brother spun the steering wheel and we finally came to a halt facing back up the hill. Somehow, the frail ball-and-socket connection between vehicle and horsebox had held.

Daniel wanted to stop and find a hotel, but we were close to Chamonix and the Mont Blanc tunnel. Beyond that, I imagined, lay a different landscape—Italy, bathed in sunshine, welcoming, warm. I persuaded him to push on, climbing the laborious hairpins, mile after mile, until we came to the mouth of the tunnel. It was midnight. I bought our ticket, and a sleepy French douanier waved us through.

Into the narrow tube we drove, the mesmerizing orange

lights flickering past, mile after mile; above us an unimaginable weight of rock and ice. I had never experienced claustrophobia before, but I did so now. The wall of the tunnel seemed dangerously close. In the side mirror, the lights of a truck were getting closer, forbidding any thought of slowing down.

I still don't know how long it takes to drive the Mont Blanc tunnel—ten minutes? fifteen?—but it felt like an eternity until the signs to slow down began to appear, the baleful sodium glow changed character, and we glimpsed the welcoming darkness at the end of the tunnel. I pulled over into an empty parking lot, waiting for the thundering pursuer to roar past us, then switched off the engine and carried the portfolio of papers across to the Italian customs office. Half an hour later, Daniel appeared, wondering what the hell was going on. My precious documents were spread all over the desk.

"We have to go back to France and come back tomorrow morning when this gentleman's superior will be here."

The customs officer flicked at the papers disdainfully with his fingers. There was nothing for it. Back into the tunnel. The ordeal so soon repeated.

"What if the French customs won't let us back into France?" suggested my brother. "We could be trapped in the tunnel for ever."

But they did, and we descended the mountain through the falling snow, ever sensible to the trailer's propensity to start sliding away under downhill conditions. We pulled into a hotel car park, slipping between two enormous trucks, and turned off the engine. Snowflakes settled on the windscreen, slowly blocking our view. The silence was such a sweet benediction. "Just sleep here," muttered Daniel, and we would have if the cold had not set in so quickly. Within minutes we could see our breath. Crystal patterns of ice began to form like a skin on the inside of the windows. They would find us in the morning, frozen, wide-eyed, brittle and blue, and bury us at the foot of Mont Blanc.

The night clerk reluctantly let us into the hotel, insisting on cash in advance before handing us the key to a room.

Next morning, Daniel drove the tunnel. When we reached the Italian customs, he handed our passports to the military teenager in the booth, who promptly handed them back and waved us on.

"Don't you want to see our papers?" I asked, incredulous. But we were already moving and out of earshot.

Down the Aosta valley, out of the Alps, skirting Milan—snow a distant memory—across the buttock of Italy to a cheap but comfortable hotel in Rimini, checking in at a civilized hour. We ate dinner in the hotel, our first real meal of the journey, then walked up and down the promenade by the beach, enjoying the air of melancholy that descends on a seaside resort out of season. We found a gelateria and bought cones of lemon sorbet so cold they gave us crippling headaches deep between the eyebrows, but oh so delicious.

"I've never understood why you chose Greece over Italy," mused Daniel. "I suppose it's true that everything there is a quarter the price."

"You'll see why when we get there."

We slept late next morning, aware that Ancona was close, lingering over cappuccino, pastries and sharply refreshing blood orange juice. Reaching the port at eleven, we made our way to the booking office but found it closed. The next ferry to Corfu left the following May.

"Your best bet," said the mop-wielding janitor who seemed to have sole charge of the city's dockyards, "would be to go north to Venice, round by Trieste, then drop down through Yugoslavia, around Albania and into Greece that way."

We showed him our map of Italy, the dotted lines across the Adriatic allegedly connecting Ancona, Bari and distant Brindisi with Corfu by boat. He scoffed at Bari but finally admitted there were year-round ferries from Brindisi, down on the heel of Italy, steaming across to the island every evening. Three hundred more miles, as the crow flies. At forty-five miles per hour, 6.666 hours—an ill-omened number, but we could make it in time for the eight o'clock sailing. We ran back to the Land Rover.

Whoever designed the Adriatic autostrada had deadlines like ours in mind. It is a brilliant road, burrowing through hillsides and spanning deep valleys, and it swept us south into a country where there were leaves on the trees, olive groves and orange orchards, winter sunshine and pale blue sea. Uphill or down, the indomitable vehicle roared on, providing the changeless keynote while we sang the Roy Rogers song until our voices were hoarse.

Next morning at dawn, standing on the top deck of the ferry, we watched and waited for landfall. To our left, the barren mountains of Albania soared in silhouette against a sky that shimmered in faint pastel colours like opal or mother-of-pearl. To our right, Corfu glistened a fecund green. It looked to me the most beautiful island in the world. On one of the high ridges, if only I had known where to look, stood our house, roofless home to swallows and rats, lizards and scorpions, hornets and butterflies, with eleven olive trees on its acre of asphodel.

Chapter Four

Corfu airport in February was a very different place from the sweltering mosh pit of the summer months. Once a week, on Sunday, the Olympic Airways jet from London to Athens deigned to pause at the island, discharging a handful of passengers and most of their suitcases before lifting off again as quickly as possible. On those evenings, the lights in the deserted international lounge flickered on, and the black rubber luggage carousel wheezed into life. Whichever customs officer happened to be on duty stubbed out his cigarette, strapped on his holstered handgun and took up a pose of studied nonchalance, lolling against the glass doors that led to freedom. This time, Wendy surprised him. Carrying only hand luggage, she swept past the glum ensemble at the carousel with a radiant smile and was through the doors and in my arms before he had heaved himself upright.

The drive up to Loutses was the best possible illustration for the tales I told Wendy of the road trip. The heater scorched her shins but left the rest of her shivering with cold. The dim yellow beams of the headlights illuminated the rain, not the road, and the plunging cliffs on the right loomed large in our imaginations. The island was black, hunkered down for the winter. All the bars and restaurants, the shops, hotels and villas were shuttered, padlocked, boarded up, entire resort towns abandoned to the wind and rain.

But we were far too excited to pay much attention to the weather. Wendy had a thousand questions. She wanted to know how the house looked, if the garden was still a jungle, what I had felt when I saw it again. I tried to explain that first morning's confusion of emotions, to myself as much as to her. There had been a glow of proprietorial satisfaction as I walked along Zervou, barely glancing at the view, a glow that flared suddenly when I crossed the invisible line onto our own land. Every inch of it was ours. I had felt that way about my flat in South London, but here the sensation was a hundred times more intense. Almost as strong was the feeling that I was an interloper, a threat to the status quo. On the day the house was abandoned, thirty years earlier, a slow, gentle process of dissolution had begun, the organic shift back to a natural, elemental state. Wood turning to soil, stones slipping back to the earth to be reabsorbed into the mountain, metal rusting away to powder . . . We had sensed it eighteen months ago when we first saw the house, had admired and responded to it. One of the reasons why we loved the place was its ruined condition, the way it was already blurring into wilderness. Now we were going to arrest that devolution, wrenching it all back to wakeful servitude. And the thought of doing so was extraordinarily exhilarating. Everywhere I looked there was work to be done—an infinity of major and minor projects all clamouring for attention. Above all, I longed to get down onto the land, to discover and catalogue the wild plants, to set to work under the olive trees, which, incidentally, seemed laden, positively weighed down with olives, to make herb beds and terraces and stone benches and a folly at the end of the garden—as if the whole move to Greece, the reinvention of our lives, were not folly enough.

I looked across at Wendy. She was sitting uncomfortably, trying to minimize the vibration, the seat belt pressing against the bulge in her coat. If it weren't for the baby, we could take our sweet time with the renovations, stretch it all out for years and years. Instead, we had a frighteningly imminent deadline. The garden and the olives would have to wait.

It was late when we finally parked beside the chicken run, but Alexandra and Kostantes had waited up for us, sitting at the kitchen table. There was love in their greeting and tears in Alexandra's eyes as she laughed and murmured words of encouragement, putting her hand on Wendy's belly.

"Po-te?"

"Efta tou Maiou, the seventh of May," said Wendy, who had memorized the Greek date with just such questions in mind.

"Tris minas," said Kostantes, pursing his lips. Three months. "Poli thulia. Avrio—no efta, exi!" With so much to do on the house, we had better start work at six tomorrow morning instead of seven.

I had thought he was joking, but at ten to six he came knocking on the door, whispering an urgent "Dzimi!" until I mumbled an answer. I had been trapped in a dream, driving the Land Rover down an endless Mont Blanc tunnel that grew narrower and narrower until the weight of the mountain crushed the vehicle, pinning my arms to my sides. It might have had something to do with the burden of blankets, coats and clothes we had piled on top of the bed to keep out the cold and damp. I eased out from under it, dimly aware of Wendy rolling over into the warm hollow where I had been lying. I had slept in two T-shirts and two pairs of socks, but my feet were already cold as I pulled on a sweater, jeans and a pair of boots. The ice cold water from the bathroom tap finished the brutal journey into consciousness. At least water would not be an issue in wintertime. Kostantes's rain-catchment cistern would be brimming. Must remember to turn on the boiler so Wendy could have a hot shower when she woke up.

The kitchen, for once, was no warmer than the rest of the house, the wood stove unlit. Alexandra made me a coffee on the gas ring, then tied a scarf around her head and set off to walk halfway down the mountain to one of the olive groves the family owned. It was a day for gathering whatever olives had fallen into the nets during the previous week, and she would be gone until dusk.

Kostantes limped over to the dresser and fished out a half-empty bottle of cheap Botrys brandy. He poured us each a shot, then raised his glass with a grin.

"To spitisas!" Your house.

I had opted to walk up to the property that morning rather than ride on Kostantes's scooter. The sky was just beginning to brighten into dawn as I trudged through the puddles along the crest of Zervou. Over the water, the mountains of Albania were capped with snow, tier upon tier of peaks reaching farther inland than I had ever seen in the clear, crisp air. The tallest and most distant summits were already glowing the colour of coral as they caught the first rays of the sun, making the lower slopes and the sea look as deep a blue-grey as the western sky. The wind had gone and the slightest sounds carried miles—a dog barking down in Peritheia, a car on the coast road—then the sudden, deafening Bronx cheer of Kostantes's scooter rounding the bend, the cackle of his laughter as he passed me, accelerating down the last few hundred yards of the track.

He was already stumping about in the courtyard when I reached the house, peering up at the walls and windows, rubbing some warmth into his leather hands.

"Poli thulia, Dzimi! Poli thulia!" A lot of work.

I followed him round the corner and we stood and inspected the windowless southern wall of the building. This was the side that faced the mountains behind Loutses and that received more rain than wind. It was the only wall that had been finished with mortar and plaster, a protective measure, but when Kostantes picked up a stick, dug it into the surface and twisted it, a slab the size of a dinner plate fell away and split into crumbling pieces at our feet. He said something I didn't understand and went back around the house to push open the broken front door.

It was dark inside, the air cold and smelling strongly of damp. Kostantes barely glanced at the room before setting off up the stairs, climbing stiffly and talking to himself. At the top, he stood staring up at the missing ceiling and the holes in the roof. My own eyes were drawn to the window, and through it to the eastern view of olive-covered hills that fell steeply into a valley and then climbed to a distant ridge. Down to the left the sea looked flat and grey, but straight ahead the sun was rising, a huge tangerine-coloured orb, erupting over the black line of the ridge, dissolving it with its brightness. This was the sight that would one day greet us each and every morning.

"Ton 'elios," announced Kostantes unnecessarily—the sun—before turning his back and clumping downstairs.

In the few minutes we had been inside, the change in the light had brought the courtyard to life. A week of rain had cleansed every surface and there was colour in the stones—an infinity of greys and pinks. The leaves on the oak tree shone like gold, and the old, semi-cylindrical tiles on the little house opposite, grey a moment ago, were now a faded motley of every imaginable hue from beige to terracotta.

"Oreia!" I said, smiling, reaching up to touch a tile. Kostantes stared at me from beneath a cocked eyebrow, his expression, for once, disturbingly serious.

"Palio," he grunted—old—as if age was not implicitly desirable.

We pushed open the rickety twin doors of the little house and stepped inside. The ill-fitting floorboards were strong and trustworthy, though stained with water and animal droppings. We could peer down between them into the byre beneath. The ceiling boards were missing, but a couple of slender beams stretched across the width of the room. A large brown rat was sitting on one of them, trying to be inconspicuous. When it realized it had been seen, it trotted silently along the beam and slipped through a gap in the tiles, out onto the roof.

At some point in the distant past, the little house had been used as a kitchen. Over in the corner, flat stones had been set on the floorboards and though the wood stove that had once stood over them was long gone, the stones themselves were still blackened and cracked by heat. High on the wall above this spot was a hole for the stove's tubular metal chimney. It made sense to have a separate kitchen during the summer months, when the heat of a wood-burning stove would have made life intolerable in the big house. And during the winter this small single room would have been much easier to keep warm. Beds could have been moved across from the big house, and even the rising body heat of the animals in the byre might have made a difference.

The byre was our next destination. To reach it we clambered down from the courtyard into the steeply sloping garden and pushed our way through the waist-high jungle of yellow grasses, thistles and asphodel. At school, we were taught that the souls of the dead wandered through fields of asphodel in the ancient Greek underworld, but I had never been able to envisage the scene until now. Each plant was nothing more than a long, smooth stalk, as thick as my thumb and waist-high, sticking straight up out of the ground. Last August, those woody stalks had been glossy and brown and crowned with a plume of white flowers (if my pocket guide to the wildflowers of Greece could be trusted); now they were dead and dry and topped with a honeycomb of husks that might once have been seed pods. Wherever there was open land between the olive trees, the asphodel had taken hold. There must have been thousands of them.

Kostantes whacked at one with his stick. "Kakos!" Bad! He mimed a man digging out the bulbous roots of the plant and flinging it away. "Poli thulia!"

We had to duck to go inside the byre, stepping on rich brown soil. Kostantes turned a clod with his shoe.

"Kalo homa." Good earth. "Ollo exo. To kipo." Someone would have to scrape it all out and spread it onto the garden as fertilizer. Then he explained his intentions for the space. It took a while, using only a few key nouns and some very involved charades, but at last I understood. Wendy and I would have to abandon our plan to turn it into a charming underground library, reached from the upstairs room by a wrought-iron spiral staircase. This was to be our water-catchment tank, our sterna. He would seal up the byre's low doorway and the small square window through which the sun was now pouring. The walls and floor would be coated in cement six inches thick; a reinforced concrete ceiling could double as the floor of the room above. Gutters and pipes would gather the rain from the roof tiles of both houses and drain it into the sterna. A small pipe set high in the wall would take care of the overflow; another, set close to the ground, would lead outside to an electric pump that would send water gushing to our kitchen or bathroom whenever we turned on a tap.

"Good, Dzimi?"

"Oreia."

Running water would definitely be an asset when we moved in. But how were we going to make the cement to build the water tank without having water to begin with? With any luck, Kostantes had already thought of that. Of course, we would also need a kitchen and a bathroom and a considerable amount of plumbing before this grand vision could be brought to pass. And electricity to operate the pump . . .

"We'll make a list," said the ever practical Wendy when she arrived, just after nine. She had brought a Thermos of coffee, and somewhere within her bulky shoulderbag she found a pen and a scrap of paper. When Kostantes realized what we were doing, he sat down beside us on the ruined stone pigsty and began to recite.

"Prota, epano!" First of all, before anything else, the roof of the big house must be repaired. "Keramika!" That would require tiles. Did we want to do the job properly with the smart new flat red tiles that interlocked so beautifully, kept the water out and would last a thousand years? Of course not. We wanted the old, curved clay tiles that had to be held in place with a dab of mortar and that blew off in a high wind and shattered if you dropped one. Nobody made those tiles any more, but Kostantes knew where he could find some. He wouldn't say where; he just tapped his nose and put a conspiratorial finger to his lips.

"Amo aspro. Asvesti. Laspi!" Since we insisted on using old tiles we would first have to buy a load of fine white sand and some plastic sacks of creamy white lime to make the mortar. "Allo amo. Haliki. Tsimento." But not until we had bought some coarser sand, some gravel and sacks of cement to make a flat concrete area upon which we could mix the mortar. "Xylo!" And before anyone started doing anything like that, we would need to find some wood to replace the beams and slats that had rotted away in the roof and had made the original tiles fall off in the first place.

Each element of the master list required a similar prologue of other events and purchases. Eventually, Wendy learned to begin at the bottom of the page, working upwards to match Kostantes's preference for reverse causality. Meanwhile, the paper was quickly filled. The proposed inventory of materials was staggering, but of greater concern was the need for specialized personnel. While Kostantes answered to the title of *archimastoras,* or master builder, there were certain jobs he wished to delegate, and we would have to find an electrician, a plumber and a carpenter who were not only available at very short notice but prepared to work within our minuscule budget. There was also the question of a builder's mate. Since his accident, Kostantes had problems with ladders, and someone would have to be mixing the next batch of mortar or cement while he was applying the first if we were to stand a chance of making the house habitable in a mere three months.

Wendy put down her pen. Her eyes were very wide.

"All right," she said, without any trace of concern leaking into her voice. "Let's start with the electrician. Ton elektrologos . . ."

Kostantes nodded. There was an excellent electrician in the village, but he had died some years ago. Electrocuted while on the job. However, there was another man, even more skilled, who might take on the work.

"A plumber?" Yes, he was also a plumber.

"A carpenter?" Kostantes knew just the fellow. In fact, he intended to take us down to the coast the following evening to show us a beautiful ceiling made of Oregon pine that the man had just installed in one of the new tourist villas in Akharavi. As for his own assistant . . . We could not afford to hire a second builder full time, but there were any number of men in the village who had no work during the winter—

waiters, most of them, but certainly capable of stirring a batch of cement and shinning up a ladder. The great thing would be to find someone who also had a pick-up truck, someone who could bring building supplies up to Zervou from the coast.

"What about Babis?" suggested Wendy. Babis! The son of Stamati and Maria, who owned the village shop. He was a waiter, silver service trained. He had a truck. He spoke English. His English wife, Michelle, had just had a baby and they could probably do with some money. Kostantes approved, and Wendy put her second tick on the list with a satisfied flourish.

Now there were other things to discuss—minor details we wanted to add to the house, beginning with a bathroom. We went inside and stood beside Kostantes while he gave the matter thought.

"Etho," he said, pointing at the darkest corner of the room. He drew a line in the dirt with the toe of his boot. It would be easy to build a bathroom there with two brick walls, leaving enough space between the inner wall and the staircase for a kitchen. A shower, a toilet, a basin: who could ask for more? We could even give the bathroom its own window by knocking a hole through the three-foot-thick stone wall. With great concentration, he mimed someone flushing, then said "Whoosh!" and gestured dramatically towards the base of the wall.

"Where's it going to go?" I asked, suddenly realizing how little I knew of the ways of the world.

"Exo! Sto kipo!" Out into the garden.

"Oh . . ."

He switched into mime.

"A man digging," guessed Wendy at once. "Digging a hole. A cesspit! A man digging a cesspit and he's happy. It's easy work. He looks at his watch. It's quick, happy work. Dzimi . . . Even Dzimi could do it!"

"Machina?" I suggested. Could we not hire a machine, an excavator, to tear a hole in the limestone hillside big enough to serve? Kostantes frowned at the thought. Very expensive, very difficult, and fraught with problems involving licences.

"To kivernisis," he said, with a look of mock terror on his face. The government. In the months that followed, we came to appreciate that Kostantes had no wish to involve the authorities in our great project in any way. Let them get even a sniff of it and there would be so much red tape, so many permits, papers and taxes, such an expense, that we would never finish in time for the baby. Far better to keep things on a cash basis and go quietly about our business. He pointed at me. "No machina. Inglis. Sitheronia!" It was the same word he had used in our first conversation, eighteen months earlier, to describe the wartime British commandos. Englishmen. Men of iron.

BUT THE AUTHORITIES were already involved. The horsebox containing all our worldly goods was still down at the harbour in bond, under lock and key. My name and the number of my passport had been entered in the Black Book of the Douaniers, from which no name could be expunged. On Monday morning, therefore, looking shaved and reputable, I parked the Land Rover outside the customs sheds and presented myself to the officer in charge. Wendy was with me, wearing a jumpsuit and very obviously pregnant, hoping it might make the authorities a tad more sympathetic. The dawn ferry from Italy had come and gone long ago, there was no one else in the office except for a man in a black leather jacket, smoking and reading a newspaper, but five minutes passed before the uniform felt inclined to acknowledge my presence.

"Do you speak English?" I asked as he scanned the bundle of papers I had surrendered.

No answer.

"Stay cool, darling," murmured Wendy, squeezing my hand.

At last he looked up, tapping the papers with the back of his fingers.

"No good. This. No good."

"But they come from this office only three days ago . . ."

He jerked his chin upwards in a gesture of dismissal.

"Why?"

He embarked on a long explanation in Greek, then I saw his eyes slide away to the man in black leather, who was suddenly standing beside me. He took the papers and looked through them.

"You are a merchant?" he asked at last.

"No, I'm a writer."

"What do you write?"

"Fiction."

"Then why are you bringing merchandise into this country?"

"I'm not! It's just personal possessions."

"Electrical items? A typewriter, perhaps?"

"Yes, a typewriter."

"An electric typewriter?"

"No. A very old portable one."

"I think perhaps we should see this old portable typewriter."

"Okay."

We stepped outside into the cold sunshine and walked across to the customs shed. The doors were wide open. Our horsebox looked small and beaten up, sandwiched between a truck and a motorboat, like a suspect between two burly cops. The men watched me pull on the shaft, straining under the weight until it began to roll slowly forward. I found the key for the padlock and pushed up the flap at the back. From the look of disappointment on their faces, it was clear that they had been hoping for something more interesting. Leather Jacket pointed at a cardboard box and the customs officer opened it—nothing but old books.

"The typewriter's in one of these tea chests."

"Unload them, please."

Half an hour later Wendy and I had unpacked enough of the horsebox to satisfy the most bloody-minded curiosity. The customs officials had not offered to help, ignoring Wendy's condition, merely indicating which tea chest or box or suitcase they wished to inspect. They had barely glanced at the typewriter when I finally produced it. Then everything had to be put back.

In the office, I signed the Black Book and handed over nine hundred drachmas. The uniform found a cardboard box full of stamps and attached one to my papers. Then he opened my passport and began to write across the last page.

"It says you have been permitted to bring a typewriter into the country," explained Leather Jacket. "The next time you leave Greece, that typewriter must go with you. And you may keep the trailer here for three months. After that, it will no longer be legal."

"Why?"

"An unlicensed commercial vehicle. Serious business."

"How much is a licence?"

"It is not eligible for one. It wasn't purchased in Greece."

"So I have to take it to Italy and then bring it back?"

"It would not be allowed back in the country."

"So I'll have to sell it?"

"That would be illegal."

"Then what can I do?"

He shrugged. "You will have to leave it here with us. As a gift to the Greek people."

We had other errands to run in Corfu Town that morning—tools to buy from a list dictated by Kostantes, a withdrawal from the bank—but the thought of manoeuvring Land Rover and trailer through the narrow streets and Byzantine one-way system was not attractive. We set off on foot, returning laden with carrier bags full of food, a new shovel, pickaxe and mattock over one shoulder, trowels and nails, a small, two-bar electric heater for our bedroom, and a percentage of our precious funds stuffed into an envelope in my jacket.

It was comforting to feel the familiar deadweight of the horsebox behind me again as we drove back to Loutses. I unhitched it outside Kostantes's house, then we carried on up Zervou. Babis's patched yellow pick-up truck was parked on the steep slope where the road ended on our property. It was facing up the hill and there was a mound of sand on the ground behind it.

"Have they started?" said Wendy, half jubilant, half disbelieving.

Babis sauntered around the side of the house, a trowel in his hand.

"'Allo, mate!" he called.

The two men had been working quickly. They had decided not to bother making a flat cement pad on which to mix the mortar. They just spread a big piece of heavy plastic over a corner of the courtyard and used that. Babis had brought the wood and a hundred or so roof tiles in his truck that morning and was about to carry the last of them up to Kostantes.

We followed him upstairs. A long, very thin wooden ladder, so old it might have been used to construct the ark, was wedged under the window. Babis climbed up through the biggest of the holes in the roof and crawled out onto the tiles. I followed, sticking my head through the hole, blinking in the sunlight. Kostantes was sitting on the tiles, his bad leg stretched out straight, his good one curled around a sawn-off rectangular cheese tin with a piece of dowel nailed across the top to form a bucket. A cigarette was stuck to his lip.

"Whoa, Dzimi!" yelled Kostantes.

"You got a bloody nice view up here!" added Babis with a grin.

"How's it going! I can't believe you've done so much!"

I watched them work for a while.

"Babis? You can't put tiles on from inside, can you?"

"'Course not."

"Then, how are you going to finish the job?"

"What?"

"To finish it, you'll have to be out on the roof. But then you won't have any way to get down."

After a moment's thought, Babis started to talk to Kostantes in Greek. The old man shot me a piercing glance. A long pause. Then he said something. Babis laughed.

"No a problem," he explained. "We're goin' to build a door."

"A trap door?"

"Yeah."

"Right . . ."

I climbed down the ladder and went into the inner room, where Wendy had started sweeping.

"What is it?" she asked.

"Nothing. Improvisation."

We heard Babis descend the ladder and clump downstairs in search of something. "Hammer and nails," I said.

"What?"

"Just a wild guess. Part of the improv on high. They're building a trap door."

"I wondered how they'd get down."

Looking through the old window, we could see the yellow pick-up below us. Babis appeared, rummaged around in the cab for a while and drew out a hammer and a bag of nails. As he turned, he caught sight of the old stone pillar. He walked up to it, touched it, frowning.

"More Akropolis jokes," I sighed.

He pressed his hands against it, still holding the hammer and nails. I saw him push out his leg, looking for a purchase in the loose stones. Then he heaved. The pillar trembled, then tottered and fell, breaking into a hundred pieces as it hit the ground. Babis walked away, disappearing from view.

"It's the same impulse that makes a schoolboy burn ants with a magnifying glass," I sputtered furiously.

"It was already wobbly. Maybe he thought it would collapse onto our unborn infant one day. He did us a favour."

"He's a Philistine."

Wendy and I spent the afternoon scraping swallow guano off the roughly plastered downstairs walls. The birds built their cup-shaped nests of mud and spittle against the sides of the ceiling beams, each pair making a new one every year, raising their young and then departing for a balmy North African vacation when winter set in. Any pang about displacing them soon vanished as we started to chisel away at decades of petrified black droppings. They were hard to dislodge without gouging the plaster, and when they fell they left an indelible stain like a dark brown comma on the old whitewash that then had to be scratched away. I thought about my brand-new electric sander sitting in its box in the trailer, useless without electricity. Instead we rubbed at the wall with sandpaper until our arms ached, handkerchiefs tied like bandanas over our noses and mouths, clothes and hair soon powdered with fine white dust. Without ladders or scaffolding we could barely reach halfway up the walls, but by the end of the day a considerable expanse of thoroughly scoured plaster gleamed as white as a bank of newly fallen snow.

Kostantes and Babis, meanwhile, finished repairing the roof. With the tools Babis had brought him and the last long ceiling board from the other upstairs room, Kostantes built a square frame for a trap door, nailing it to the sturdy beams above us. Babis explained that we would commission a metal cover from one of the tinsmiths who worked in the old Jewish quarter of Corfu Town, close to Kostantes's urban pied-à-terre. Lawrence Durrell had described the metal workers of that particular area in *Prospero's Cell,* including a family called Iskariotes, reputedly descendants of the more famous Judas. The grimy old alleys of the neighbourhood still rang with the sound of hammers on metal. In the meantime, four wooden battens made a temporary hatch, with a square of heavy plastic nailed across it as tightly as the skin of a drum.

Kostantes was pleased with his day's work. He and Babis shared childish jokes as they came down the ladder for the last time. Wendy paid Babis a thousand drachmas (ten dollars) for the day and gave him the money for the supplies he had brought in his truck, then the men went home.

The noise of Kostantes's scooter finally faded over the hill. We stood under the oak tree looking down into the garden, listening to the breeze moving gently in the long grass, hissing through the dried seed pods of the tall asphodel. The sun was behind the house and there was a definite chill in the air. Shadows were gathering under the olive trees.

"I salvaged something from the horsebox this morning."

"What?" asked Wendy.

"I'll fetch it."

The pretty blue hurricane lamp from England. We had bought a half litre of paraffin, decanted into a wine bottle from a tank in the shadowy recesses of the tool shop in Corfu Town. I filled the lamp, trimmed the wick, lit it, and we carried it inside. Set on the windowsill, it did not cast much light, but it seemed definitely symbolic, a first personal incursion into the property, something of ours. After a while, I blew out the flame, pulled the broken door shut, and we drove back along Zervou and down into the village.

Dinner that evening was a hurried affair. Alexandra came home from the olive groves at dusk, looking as though she might collapse with exhaustion, arching her back and pressing one fist hard against the base of her spine.

"Oh, Dzimi, poli thulia . . ." So much work . . . Wendy and I offered to cook, but she would have none of it. Then Kostantes stepped jauntily into the room and her face was suddenly illuminated by a smile. He stoked the wood stove to a cheerful blaze while she put a pan of water to boil on the gas ring, and in no time at all we were tucking into day-old bread, slippery fried eggs and khaki-coloured spinach seethed in water and liberally dressed with cold olive oil. Alexandra had looked pleased when I showed her the food I had bought that morning, but she left it untouched in the refrigerator. It would have to earn the right to a place on the dinner table.

After dinner, Wendy, Kostantes and I piled into the Land Rover and set off down the mountain to view the potential carpenter's ceiling. The town of Akharavi lay west along the coast road, a fifteen-minute drive away but still within the traditional ken of the Loutsiotes. Here the mountains drew back from the sea, creating a plain that had been farmed for millennia, for the soil was rich and well watered, even in summer. Many of the families from the mountain villages owned land there, using it in years gone by to grow the fruits, vegetables and tobacco that could not be farmed in the hills. Chickpeas from these market gardens had been particularly prized, for they carried a subtle salt tang of the sea. Historically, however, few people had dared to actually live on the plain, partly because they would have been easy prey for Albanian pirates and partly because of the malarial mosquitoes that bred in the brackish coastal lake known as Antinioti, the Enemy of Youth.

The mosquitoes had been eradicated in the 1950s and no pirates now ventured to sea past the Communist gunboats of Albania. So the hamlet of Akharavi had spread along the coast road and down the lanes that led to the beach. Landowners had abandoned their chickpea gardens and melon patches and built studio apartments and villas on the precious soil. Wendy and I deplored such development as a matter of principle, though we had to admit it was handy having a hardware and plumber's supply store so close to Loutses.

Kostantes guided us through the dark lanes and finally told me to pull over beside a recently constructed villa. He retrieved a key from a hiding place under a brick and with a conspiratorial wink ushered us inside and turned on the lights. It was strange to see a *new* house, every wall sleek and plastered, every floor glistening with glossy ceramic tiles in a turquoise and tangerine motif. The ceiling was indeed very fine—slender boards, flawlessly interlocking, the pine stained a colour that lay close to the point where brown becomes orange, varnished until it shone like glass. Wendy glanced at me, her frozen smile eloquent: if we do hire this carpenter he must not be allowed to choose a finish for any wood. Kostantes was beaming, and we acknowledged the ceiling's beauty over and over again until he was satisfied. Then he pulled the ace from his sleeve. The carpenter himself was waiting for us at a nearby bar, and if luck was with us that night we could hire him to work on our house.

Luck was busy elsewhere. Dmitri the carpenter was a no-show. We waited an hour, Kostantes drinking brandy, Wendy aching for a shower and bed, then set off back along the coast road. Not far from Aghios Spiridon, a pick-up truck passed us. It was the carpenter. Kostantes almost grabbed the wheel in his excitement. I made a reckless U-turn and set off in hot pursuit, flashing my feeble headlights. Dmitri did not pull over. Instead he sped away into the night, his truck plunging through puddles and potholes, skimming the verge, swerving madly from one side of the road to the other. We caught him on the outskirts of Akharavi, riding his tail until he slowed and pulled over.

Kostantes clambered out of the back of the Land Rover and hobbled around to the driver's window. By the time I joined him he was speechless with laughter. So were the two young men in the passenger's seat. Even the dog at their feet seemed to find the situation funny. Dmitri the carpenter did not. In pretty good English he explained that they had been out shooting duck on the lake, not necessarily with a licence, and had thought we were the army, come to investigate the gunfire. And anyway, what were we doing chasing people in a military vehicle?

We waited for him to calm down before asking whether he might come up to the house next day to see about working for us. He promised he would be there. Then he got out of the cab and pulled back a tarpaulin in the truck bed. Two ducks lay dead, a small brown female and an extravagantly beautiful drake, its neck plumage matted with blood.

"I've been after these two for weeks," said Dmitri with ugly satisfaction. "The last pair on the lake."

WE WERE at the house early the following morning. The blue hurricane lamp was gone from the windowsill, stolen during the night. It was a small matter, but it left a disproportionately large sense of violation in our hearts. Wendy grimly added "padlock" to her list.

"When the carpenters come, the first thing we'll ask for is the new front door. Everything else can wait."

"And shutters for the windows."

But the carpenters did not come. It was our first inkling that the Greek word *avrio* did not mean "tomorrow" as the dictionaries promised but in fact referred to a far more abstract concept of the future. Compared with *avrio,* the Spanish *mañana* was a Swiss-precision descriptive. As for *methavrio,* "the day after tomorrow": that was a term so broad it stretched as far as "never in my lifetime, buddy."

Babis also failed to appear. Kostantes volunteered to root him out and came back an hour later with brandy on his breath and the news that Babis felt he could continue working for us only if we paid him double the agreed price—as much as we were giving Kostantes. Not possible. It was a general assumption in the village that we were millionaires—

all tourists were—and fair game for the occasional scam. There and then, I swore myself in as Kostantes's official apprentice, cement mixer and all-purpose construction slave, much to the old man's amusement. In the absence of Babis's vehicle, the Land Rover could be commissioned as a pick-up truck for sand and building supplies, and the trailer, assuming its wheels could stand it, might also be pressed into service. Its contents could be unpacked and stored in the corridor outside our bedroom in Kostantes's house.

He handed me a scrap of paper with words and numbers scrawled in a crabbed and painstaking hand. Seven hundred bricks and six sacks of cement.

"Akharavi," he instructed. "Presto!"

So my life as a construction worker began. As the days passed, I became aware that our relationship had subtly changed. Kostantes had no qualms about issuing orders or criticizing my work if it did not come up to his sometimes rigorous standards. He also began to teach me tricks of the trade. He distrusted spirit levels, determining whether a vertical line was truly vertical by squinting at it over his thumb. If a horizontal measurement was required, he achieved it by first hammering a nail into the wall. Then he filled a length of transparent plastic hose with water, spilled a little of it out and handed me one of the ends. He held up the other end and positioned it so that the water level was exactly flush with the nail. The water at my end would settle at exactly the same level, which I marked with a pencil. Hammer a second nail into the mark, stretch a string between them, and we had a perfect horizontal.

This struck me as a brilliantly ingenious alternative to the cold technology of a spirit level, especially as the system even worked around corners. In reality, and probably because of some fault with the string, none of the angles in the house were ever exactly true, which to my mind only added to its charm.

Dmitri the carpenter arrived unexpectedly one morning, three days late but cheerfully unaware that he had been missed. We went through the house together, listing our needs. Front doors. Beams and boards for a ceiling in the upstairs room. A cupboard to support the kitchen sink we had brought from London. Five windows with frames and shutters.

"What about this?" mused Dmitri, pushing against the wall that divided the upstairs rooms. To my horror, it moved slightly. "It's not safe—made in the old way—wood frame, then bamboo, then mortar, then plaster. Very, very heavy. Very hard on the floor." He repeated all this in Greek to Kostantes, who rubbed his bristly chin and then nodded in agreement.

"Knock it down," advised Dmitri. "I'll build a new wall in the same place with wood and board. You can keep the old doorway and door."

Out in the courtyard, he called for silence and began his calculations. We had braced ourselves for the worst, but his price was not exorbitant, especially after Kostantes bargained him down by 25 percent, explaining that, being English, we loved wood more than plastic and that many more commissions, for banisters, bookcases, cupboards and shelves, would surely follow.

"And how much would it cost to put in a wooden floor downstairs?" I asked innocently. Dmitri's ears pricked up. His long, hinged yellow ruler was opened out again and measurements taken. More mathematics.

"I could do it for four hundred thousand drachmas."

"No, really, how much?"

"Four hundred thousand. And I throw in the ceiling and wall for nothing."

"That's one third of what we paid for the whole property!"

"Floors are tricky. They have to be flat."

We decided against the floor. Dmitri didn't seem to mind. He promised to return in ten days with everything we wanted.

Amazingly, he was as good as his word. The twin front doors opened inwards—beautiful panelled doors of an elegance we had not dared to expect. The window frames were sturdy, and Kostantes had them set in place and the surrounding walls smoothed with cement and plaster in no time. Because the walls were so thick, each window had an inside sill two feet deep. The ceiling of the upstairs room was a small masterpiece of new beams and dovetailed boards, and the carpenters had even remembered to include a trap door so that we could climb into our loft and out onto the roof when the time came to add the guttering.

For days the sun had shone, taking the edge off the cold breeze that blew from Albania, but as March deepened the rains came, a week of unremitting water that brought outside work to a standstill. Wendy despaired of ever getting her daily loads of laundry dry. Still, we went up to the house every day and toiled away on the interior, sanding wood and smoothing the rough plaster walls. Out in the courtyard, the dune of sand I had laboriously ferried up from the coast for mixing cement turned to milk and ran down into the garden.

Wendy's special project was the inner chamber upstairs. Because it had a ceiling and a functioning window in the north wall, complete with the original, elegant shutters, she had developed a great fondness for the room. It was so much closer to being habitable than any other part of the property, cosy, self-contained, with a faint, warm aroma of wood, like a dusty cigar box. Dmitri the carpenter had admired the floor, telling us it was made of cypress wood, properly aged and seasoned, and only needed cleaning to be a highlight of the property. Forced indoors by the rain, Wendy spent an entire weekend on her hands and knees with a bucket of soapy water and a scrubbing brush—not the most comfortable chore for somebody seven months pregnant. On Sunday, Alexandra appeared and good-naturedly set to work beside her. By late afternoon, the plain, dust-grey floorboards gleamed a deep, rich gold.

Next morning the weather decided we had suffered enough. The sun shone from a cloudless sky and with enough heat that it seemed as if steam was rising from the olive-covered hills. Spring had arrived, and our irritability and anxiety over the delays evaporated with the puddles. We went down into the garden and found green shoots everywhere among the flattened yellow grasses. The almond and plum trees were on the brink of blossom, and a patch of what looked like giant irises already stood tall with tight, glossy buds.

As we climbed back to the house, we noticed a child peeping at us shyly from behind the oak tree in the courtyard. She was a strikingly beautiful little girl with black hair and green eyes, the daughter of the family who had the fine house with the mulberry tree on Zervou. She would say nothing as long as I was there, so I disappeared into the house. Wendy came in fifteen minutes later. They had had an interesting talk.

"Her name is Ranya. She's really sweet and gentle and she even speaks a little English, though she has forgotten the number for how old she is. She thinks it's nine. Her grandfather is in a wheelchair and he has taken it upon himself to educate her and her little sister, Letta, who is still only two. They have a subscription to *National Geographic* and they own an encyclopedia. Guess what her father does for a living?"

"Tell me."

"He's a carpenter. A good one."

"Then why aren't we using him? Why didn't Kostantes tell us?"

"Why, indeed."

"No wonder he seems a tad cool when I pass him on the road."

"Anyway, Ranya and I have decided we will be good friends. She'll teach me Greek and I'll teach her English. I asked her if she would like to earn some money babysitting for us in a couple of years."

"Brilliant!"

"She said no. She said she didn't think anyone would ever babysit for us because this house and the other ruins are well known to be haunted. By a ghost she called the Moro."

It was almost certainly a tale told by local parents to prevent their children from playing in the ruined houses where floors and walls were not safe. That night we went up to the kafeneion, and while I tried in vain to telephone England from the village phone, Wendy asked Philip what he thought of the Moro. We had expected a long stream of oaths and mockery from our pragmatic friend, but instead he just shrugged and gave a half smile.

"Old people and little childrens," he growled, low enough that the card players at the other end of the bar could not hear, "they, maybe, believe this shit."

"So you don't?"

"Me, man? You're crazy. Anyway, you'll be all right. The Moro only comes to people who are alone at night."

Next day, Philip showed up at the house to see how things were going. With him was his friend Maro, the woman we had once seen cutting a chicken's throat, and her father-in-law, Old Tomas, who picked his way over the rubble in the courtyard very nimbly for a man of ninety-two. We knew him by sight—the old man who had smiled at us so pleasantly in the taverna on our first night in Loutses—but we had never spoken to him beyond saying hello. Maro had brought a gift, a cutting from the white lilac tree that was one of the splendours of her garden. I watched her plant it in the small flower bed I had begun at the end of the courtyard.

Tomas was looking at the new windows we had put in, nodding and smiling.

"You know he used to live here, don't you?" said Philip.

"What!"

He said something to Tomas, and the old man nodded again. Then he started to speak and Philip translated. When Tomas was a boy, his family, the Vlahoses, had lived in all four of the ruined houses. They had donkeys and pigs, chickens and vegetable gardens, and baked their bread in the huge stone oven that stood apart from the houses. Our courtyard had been covered by a great vine trained across bamboo poles between the big house and the little house, and every summer the children had gorged on juicy pink grapes. It was a good place to live. When he was a young man, in 1921, he had gone to fight the Turks, though it scarcely felt like Corfu's war. He had no grudge against the Turks. Then he had come back and resumed his life, never leaving the island again. In the 1950s, the families had abandoned the houses and moved off Zervou into the village where the land was more fertile and the winters easier. He had seldom walked back up the hill to look at his old home.

Tomas wandered off and started to poke about in the heap of stones near the new lilac bed. I had not yet started to clear that particular patch of ground.

"Maro!" he croaked. She went to see what he had found and then called us all over. We moved the stones aside, scraping away layers of leaf litter and dead plants. It was the thick stump of an old vine, its boughs bent and crushed beneath the rubble. Maro broke off the end of a twig. The wood was green with life.

"Is this *the* vine?"

Tomas raised his arms and spread them like some Old Testament prophet, indicating where the vine had once spread its fruitful shade. The gesture seemed more like a blessing.

Philip started to chuckle. "I'll send my father down here," he said. "He'll look after it for you."

"And can you please ask him if there was ever a ghost up here?"

Tomas mumbled something in reply.
"He says only children and idiots believe in ghosts."

April 8, 1983
4 weeks and 4 days to go!

Dear Ros,
I am sitting propped up on our beautiful double bed upstairs! We moved it up here two days ago, a morning when the carpenters were supposed to bring the banisters for the staircase, but needless to say they didn't show. The jerks. The box spring would not fit up the stairs anyway and it looked for a while as if we would have to build a new one in the bedroom, but Kostantes sawed it in half, folded it over and tied it with rope, then he watched while James hauled it up the outside of the house to the bedroom window and dragged it in over the sill. The rope came undone halfway up and nearly pulled your son out the window, but K managed to tie it properly the second time and up it went. It's a little the worse for wear but at last we can get some idea of what this room will look like now that it's clean (relatively). Of course, we're still living down at Kostantes's house until we can get water and electricity up here.

James is working in the little house today, preparing the "pit" below that will be our water tank. He's hammering old mortar from the stone walls and not enjoying it as there are lots of spider webs and scorpions. They tore up the floorboards yesterday and K filled in the door and window with stones and cement in about an hour!! He is working in Nissaki for the next two days so Jim can get a lot done. Today the temperature is about 75 degrees Fahrenheit—I think I have a sunburn (reading outside). It will be glorious when you come in May.

My mom sent me some baby moccasins and a baby duvet which are wonderful. Jim said he told you about the baby "dropping"—it's magic, though I can't cross my legs very well. I went back to see Dr. Babalis, the gorgeous, very young obstetrician that Michelle recommended. He doesn't speak a word of English, which adds a surreal quality to the examinations, but he seems to think the baby will be early—the last week of April. Not good news, since we certainly won't have running water by then. We went to the post office in Corfu Town (the postal strike is still on where Loutses is concerned) and found your parcel! We are THRILLED about the brass door knobs. We admire them all the time and because they're so beautiful we've decided to stain the front doors and not paint them green after all. Thank you for them and all the other wonderful things you sent. Alexandra just cooed and gloated over the packets of seeds. Kostantes showed them to Maro (who has the best garden in the village) and she asked if she could have a few. "No," he said. He seemed to think this very witty. What a bugger he can be.

Big news: we now have a floor. Temporary, cement, but so much better than dirt. I was sweeping it out prior to K & Jim putting down the first layer (little stones, then iron rods) and when the dust settled I saw a small area still had some of the original flagstones—beautiful, unpolished pink marble, ten inches thick. Most of them were cracked and displaced but a few were in their original positions fitted side by side as snugly as the blocks of an Inca wall. Tried to imagine what it must have looked like. I called Jim in and he loved them as much as I did. So we went outside to ask K about having a new pink marble floor. He finally understood what we wanted. He seemed surprised. I think he'd assumed we'd prefer linoleum . . . He knew a man who could sell us the most beautiful pink-and-white-striped marble on the island. It comes from a quarry at the foot of our own mountain, which pleased Jim very much. So we drove down to see him—miles along a very bumpy dirt track through the olive groves. His house looked like a charcoal burner's shack and the quarry was just a small area in his back yard. The marble was stunning and turned out to be half the price the carpenters had wanted for a wooden floor. Go figure. So we have that to look forward to soon. K won't lay it himself. He says you need a special marble man with complicated equipment to do the job properly. Meanwhile we would have to put a cement floor under the marble anyway so they went ahead with that. Jim took a magic stone he had found in the forest in Canada and buried it under the cement just inside the front door. He had to mix about thirty loads of cement—his hands and back very stiff—and after lunch his boots just dissolved. They were so saturated with cement and water that they simply came apart. Thought K would die laughing.

We are very tired and very happy—just fall into bed at ten every night and Jim reads out loud to me until we fall asleep.

A swallow just flew in and out, looking for its nest. The garden is suddenly alive with birds every day. We think the ones who nested in our house have found a new place next door. Wood pigeons coo in the morning and evening. Bees everywhere, lizards too, dozens of stray cats who come in and out of the house as they please. And a scorpion. Jim was working on the ruined pigsty after K went home last week (he's turned it into a stone bench for sitting out under the oak tree) and he picked up a small rock and there was a scorpion on the underside. It clung to his hand and stung him between the fingers. He waited for the agony to begin but there was no pain or anything. He says it's because he's a Scorpio.

I had a million other things to say, but I've forgotten them all of course. Thanks for EVERYTHING. I know you think we're crazy to be doing all this. We think so too sometimes. We miss you so much, Ros, and can't wait until May—for a great many reasons.

Lots of love,

Wendy

Chapter Five

The pleasures of mixing cement are not always apparent to the uninitiated, but pleasures there are. Beyond the obvious satisfaction of physical exercise lies the childish delight in playing with mud and water, bucket and spade, and in stirring things together. Mixing a good batch of mortar is part building a sandcastle and part making a cake, the whole activity dignified by manly practicality.

One begins by seizing a shovel and moving a quantity of sand from the main heap to the newly swept and pristine mixing pad. The obsessive workman will seek to create a conical mound with the perfect profile of Mount Fuji, judging this part of the operation complete when the summit is about knee-high. Now he exchanges the shovel for a mattock, scrunching its blade down into the soft peak and pulling gently, moving to left and right, pulling some more, pushing a little, until the mountain has a deep crater. His eye falls upon the heavy brown paper sack of cement emblazoned with the manufacturer's name—usually Titan but sometimes Erakles, either way, a worthy foe. A swift, sudden, arcing blow and the mattock blade pierces the top of the sack, sending up a small cloud of fine grey dust. Through this wound, the cement can be shovelled into the crater of sand, the perfect amount judged by eye and instinct. Mix dry ingredients together thoroughly until a new, slightly larger Fujiyama looms on the mixing pad.

The next crater is larger and broader than the first. Indeed, the mountain is all but pulled down, spread into a ring of smooth hills around a peaceful valley. If making mortar for stone, the lime is now added—half a bag should be about right—pure white and with the soft texture of toothpaste, an alien lump in the centre of the valley. Pour on half a bucket of water, pick up the mattock and start blending the lime into the sand-cement mixture, pulling the encircling hills into the mud, adding more water as needed. One must work quickly now, in case the water finds a way through the shrinking hills. In a minute or two, the danger is past, the dry and liquid ingredients are thoroughly mixed and the mortar exists, a quivering mudlike form, solid enough to hold its shape, wet enough to make a cheerful splat when dropped from a shovel into the carrying bucket. A single batch will serve one old Greek builder for twenty minutes if he's working hard and if you've remembered to take him enough lumps of stone. The recipe can be repeated twenty-seven thousand times for larger projects, or until back breaks.

THE BEST REFRESHMENT from the long hours of mixing cement was to glance up from time to time and absorb the view from the courtyard. To the north lay the sea and the mountains of Albania, endlessly fascinating on these clear spring days when there was always a chance of seeing a ship in the straits. To the south, looking inland, the horizon was dominated by the yellow hills that towered over the village. In a Celtic country, each blunt peak would have a name and a personality, perhaps even a concomitant legend or two. The Loutsiotes, for all their superstitions, felt no need to identify them in this way. And yet there was an other-worldliness to the high plateau behind the hilltops, when the wind sighed over the outcrops and stirred the dried yellow grasses, something more than solitude—especially around the great crater.

Wendy and I had discovered the crater during our first summer, while following the traces of an old sheep track that meandered across the plateau. It was shaped like an amphitheatre, but many times broader, deeper and steeper than that of Delphi or Epidauros. Tens of thousands of seats could be set into its vertiginous sides if anyone wished to clear the jagged scree and the impenetrable, snake-infested undergrowth. Where the stage might be, there was a soaring cliff face of pitted stone, hundreds of feet high, streaked orange and grey, black and white, where crows and pigeons roosted, their calls echoed and amplified by the vast bowl.

We stood and marvelled at its size for a while, then Wendy noticed something at the foot of the cliff, far below. From this distance it looked like a long black slash, a grimacing, down-turned mouth, half hidden by rocks and stunted trees: the entrance of a cave. The sheep track continued over the lip of the crater, not really a path so much as a suggested obstacle course between the boulders and thorn bushes. Tapping a stick against the ground to scare away any snakes, we clambered down and after twenty minutes reached the mysterious opening. It was much larger than we had guessed, hundreds of yards wide. We stepped in out of the hot sun and entered a different climate, cold moist air tingling on our bare, sunburned backs. But it was the size of the cave that made us gasp. We were actually close to its ceiling, just under a massive domed roof split by crevices and knobbed with stalactites. At our feet, a steep slope of red clay and fallen boulders fell away, plunging down onto terraces and ledges until it reached the bottom, a flat area of mud and puddles the size of a football field, kept constantly wet by water dripping from the roof. I picked up a rock and hurled it as far as I could. It hit the ground at the foot of the slope, never even reaching the flat.

Everyone in the village knew the cave. For centuries, small boys had gone to the crater to look for fledgling crows that had fallen from their nests, and shepherds occasionally spent the night in the cavern itself, penning their flock with a barricade of thorn bushes. During the Second World War, when the Italian air force bombed Corfu before invading the island, the Loutsiotes had hidden up there for days. And inevitably there was a legend of a monster. One morning, at the kafeneion, Philip had told us about a German archaeologist who had been looking for evidence of Neanderthal occupants and had found a strange footprint in the mud—like a lizard or reptile, but much, much bigger . . . He took a cast of the footprint back to Germany with him and later wrote to Philip saying it could not be matched with any creature living.

"A dinosaur, man," said Philip, nodding wisely. "And you know there are many smaller caves and cave systems coming off the big one. Who knows what you might find in thems?"

The crater could double for Conan Doyle's Lost World, or for the extinct volcano that led Jules Verne to the centre of the earth. But it was not a volcano. Our mountain was made of limestone. Where the rock was exposed to wind and weather it was a dull battleship grey, eroded into sharp formations, painful to clamber over. A loose stone made it rattle and ring like crockery. Freshly exposed, however, the limestone was far more beautiful. There were places where the coast road had been widened where one could study a cross-section of hillside—white marble veined with chocolate brown earth, the tough roots of olive trees twisting and writhing downwards, seeking out meagre pockets of soil. Up in the mountains, beside the track to Ano Peritheia, the landscape's infrastructure was even more apparent—whole slopes of flat, layered slabs of stone, as smooth as a tabletop.

Nothing, however, gave me a more intimate impression of the local geology than the week I spent hewing a cesspit, a *borthro,* out of our steeply sloping garden.

I viewed the project with mixed feelings. Kostantes had determined the dimensions of the hole we would require—nine feet by nine feet by nine feet. He continued to make light of the project, but I found the thought of manual excavation on that scale a tad daunting. On the other hand, it would be a heavenly break from mixing cement. And I would have help. Before we left England, I had issued a general invitation to all my friends: Enjoy a Greek island holiday, free food, wine and accommodation in a charming

150-year-old villa (some assembly required). There had been only one taker. Eddy was an old friend from university, a guitar-playing Buddhist with a ruthless talent for poker. He was also a devoted amateur rugby player who liked to keep fit in the off season. Wendy and I were delighted when we received a telegram announcing his arrival in mid-April, though we were uncertain how he would react to the chain-gang conditions of life *chez* Kostantes. And how would we feed him? That problem, at least, was solved the day before he appeared. As if at some given signal, all the artichoke plants in Loutses suddenly came into season, and generous Maro came by every morning with a bulging bag of them. Put a cauldron of water to boil on the Primus stove in the putative kitchen, mix a jugful of vinaigrette, buy a loaf of bread, and lunch was taken care of.

Kostantes took to my friend immediately, and he to him. Eddy's first morning up at the house began with the initiation rite of mixing a load of cement. He passed the test, making up in enthusiasm what he lacked in finesse. Then we jumped down into the garden and made our way to the spot Kostantes had selected for the borthro. In no time at all we had cut down the undergrowth and raked it away, scratching off the meagre six inches of topsoil with a mattock and hoe. After that, however, we hit living rock and set to work with our picks. *The living rock.* An odd phrase, but it pleased Eddy and me and we used it so much in our conversation that it began to annoy Wendy, whose ear for cliché is unforgiving. The first blows of the pick failed to make much impression on the sloping sheet of marble that lay beneath the grass. The stone was as white and pristine as nougat, except where some seam bore the delicate black traceries of primeval plants. We smashed the points of our picks down as accurately as possible wherever we spotted a flaw, prying and levering any hairline fissure until the stone suddenly gave way, yielding a chunk or a plate-sized slab or a shower of sharp marble chips. These we dumped behind us down the slope. By lunchtime we had broken both our pick handles and blistered our hands, and we stood looking foolishly at the dent in the ground, secretly proud of the strength in our shoulders and backs. In an hour, I was back from Akharavi with half a dozen new pick handles, big and sturdy as baseball bats, and a four-foot crowbar.

Every day, Wendy took a photograph of the borthro boys' progress, and I have them still—a sequence in which Eddy and I appear to be sinking into the ground as the pile of rubble behind us grows larger. In the early shots we are in shorts, but these changed to jeans as our legs were lacerated by flying chips of rock.

And here are snapshots of Kostantes at work, standing behind a gap in the wall, a cigarette stuck to his lower lip, feeling the heft of a stone in his brown hand, scrutinizing it. With a couple of quick taps from his hammer, he shapes it and fits it in place in the wall, pressing it gently into the wet mortar, smearing the grey paste around its edges . . . The wall grows.

This one is of Eddy and me at the end of the day that saw us put the concrete cap on the finished borthro. Our clothes are stiff with dried cement, our fingers curled like claws, hands numb and tingling from pick work, shoulders aching. Every night, in my dreams, I was hammering stone, breaking through walls, this time *building* the Mont Blanc tunnel.

And here is Wendy, out in the courtyard, very pregnant, bending over the door of the bathroom, which has been taken off its hinges and laid flat for sanding. The cypress wood gleams like whisky-coloured glass under her hands.

The last photograph in the group seems at first glance to be an aerial shot. Eddy and I took a Sunday afternoon off to walk up into the mountains, following the road through the village until it diminished into a track, slowly zigzagging into the hills across the valley from the track up to Ano Peritheia. It was a warm day, and we saw many snakes and lizards basking among the rocks on the path. There were signs of sheep, though the ruined pens of weathered stone had been empty for decades. Green plants thrust up beneath the tall yellow grasses and spiky undergrowth wherever there was soil between the ridges and outcrops of pitted grey limestone. Where a fold in the land offered a modicum of shelter, some stunted tree had taken root—laurel or arbutus or ilex, not much bigger than a bush. We reached the plateau, but there was not enough time to get to the crater or the cave, so we sat on the hilltop we had seen every day from the garden, feeling the breeze in our faces, watching a flight of crows winging their way across the valley below us. I pointed out landmarks: the tiny pink church, the rooftops of outlying farms no more than specks of brown and wisps of smoke among the olives. Zervou was one ridge among many, our house a toy, though even at such a distance a toy with remarkably fine lines. The breeze died away to a whisper. The sun sank from yellow to orange, darkening the sea, throwing the distant islands of Othoni and Erikoussa into brown silhouette. The light was thickening, the air an opaque coral colour as we made our way back to the track, pausing to cut a bough of glossy green bay leaves for the kitchen.

For *our* kitchen. Slightly larger than an alcove, squeezed between the bathroom wall and the stairs, it was almost ready to use. Earlier in the month, Wendy and I had bought a small fridge in Corfu Town and carried it down through the rubble in the courtyard (a stupid thing to do in her condition) and installed it under the staircase where the space was tallest. Beside it, also under the stairs, we had built shelves for pots and pans. The sink we had brought from England was against the back wall, supported by a wooden cupboard that contained the gas cylinder for the dollhouse-sized stove. Beside that was a second tiny cupboard topped with a square of dark green marble. There was room for one person to cook, and to my eyes it was as neat and cosy as could be. All it needed to be perfect was running water and electricity.

Therein lay the problem. One of our first tasks in February had been to apply for a licence from the national electricity company in Corfu Town—a morning of standing in line, filling out papers, queuing again, and again as each sighing official moved aside coffee cups and ashtrays to find his particular rubber stamp. It had taken ten weeks for the actual licence to be approved, a flimsy scrap of pink paper upon which all depended.

Tasso was to be our electrician and plumber. He was Philip's cousin, spoke good English and was universally considered to be one of the best and smartest engineers on the island. He had given me a list of the materials I had to buy from the electricity company warehouse—everything from cables and wall sockets to a massive fuse box—very little of which had actually been in stock. "This has to come from Athens," explained the gentleman in charge with considerable glee. "It's such a big fuse box! Are you opening a restaurant?" There was no point in explaining that we hoped one day to be able to heat water and turn on a light without blowing every fuse in the house: he would only have thought us eccentric.

When the materials finally arrived, Tasso and his young apprentice, who gazed at Wendy with a fourteen-year-old's intense longing whenever she passed by, had worked like fiends for three days, cutting trenches in our walls, upstairs and down, installing more power points and switches than they thought we could possibly need, and mounting the fuse box in a place of honour beside the front door. A channel was dug across the courtyard so that the little house could have light. It only remained for the power to be connected to the cable that ran up the mountain on tall poles to our neighbour's house.

When might that happen?

"Listen, James," said Tasso in his gentle way. "It's something the company must decide. Ask them again next time you're in town." But the company was strangely reticent. They were so busy, there was so much building going on in the resorts, a question of priorities . . . When at last I was able to wring an answer from one of the clerks, the news was not good. With luck they would have a truck in our area sometime during the summer.

I had an appointment with our lawyer later that morning and he listened politely to my tirade of complaint.

"Of course, there's another way," he explained with a shrug. "Something everyone does. But it costs five thousand drachmas."

"Anything!"

He made a short phone call. Two days later, on Saturday, I drove into Corfu Town and picked up an employee of the electricity company, setting his tool box in the back of the Land Rover. It took him an hour to connect us. I handed him an envelope of money, then drove him back to town. That night, Wendy and Eddy and I stayed late at the house, switching lights on and off for the hell of it, merry as schoolchildren. The next morning, two weeks before the baby was due, we finally moved in.

Kostantes and Alexandra were as happy to see us go as we were to leave. We had tried to be model guests and to remember at all times their great generosity in letting us live with them rent free. But tensions had started to build. It was far worse for Wendy than for me. Our laundry was endless and her back was sore, her hands red from washing cement-covered jeans, socks and T-shirts in a plastic bowl in the bathroom. The work was even harder when there was no hot water. Alexandra was too shy and Kostantes too proud to ask us to help with the electricity bill. Instead they would tiptoe down the corridor outside our room and switch off the water heater at random times, usually just when Wendy was looking forward to a shower. Or else the monthly bill would be left prominently on the kitchen table, but when we offered to pay it they would look hurt and angry and refuse to take any money until we literally begged for the privilege of taking the cash into Corfu Town and settling the account. It was the same with the water. In spite of the rains of February, our showers and laundry had all but drained their sterna by the beginning of April. Alexandra told Wendy, who offered to buy a truckload to refill it, but she would not hear of such a thing. Neither would Kostantes, though he led me through the chicken run to the big concrete tank set into the hillside and showed me how little was left. It took all evening to persuade them that we were happy to pay, had expected and indeed longed for the moment when we would at last be able to pay Kostantes's cousin, Diomedes the water man, to drive his tanker up the mountain from Peritheia and replenish the supply.

"Not Diomedes," said Kostantes darkly. "Tatsi Rizzi."

"Whoever," we said eagerly. The next day, Kostantes and I drove down to find Tatsi Rizzi. He lived halfway to Corfu Town and was using his truck for building materials these days. The empty tank and great hoses had been removed until the summer—no one ever needed to buy water in April! For a price, however, he would bring us water the following day. Inevitably, Diomedes happened to be driving through Loutses next morning, just as I was standing beside the reconstructed water truck handing a telltale white envelope to Tatsi Rizzi.

"Why don't you buy water from Diomedes, man?" exclaimed Philip that night at the kafeneion. "It's better water and costs maybe three times less."

I did not have an answer for him. We relied on Kostantes's goodwill and connections, which meant we were at the mercy of his private, incomprehensible world of feuds and favours. To have taken the advice of others—even Philip himself—

would have alienated our friend, and I doubted we would be any better off. We would simply have swapped one coterie for another.

For both Wendy and me, the biggest problem with life at the Villa Parginos was the lack of privacy. Soon after we had arrived, Alexandra had got over her unwillingness to let us share any kitchen duties. For weeks now, I had done all the food shopping and cooked the evening meal for the family, leading them gently into unfamiliar gastronomic waters, introducing them to curries and Lancashire hotpot, ratatouille and Spanish omelettes. We ate every meal with them except for the two or three occasions when we broke our budget and drove into Kassiopi for a pizza. Life revolved around the kitchen, and one or both of them were always there. Our freezing, spartan bedroom was the only place we could go to be alone or have an uninterrupted conversation. After Wendy had done the dishes we would say goodnight and retreat there, climbing into bed to get warm and reading for hours until we fell asleep.

Eddy's arrival changed the routine. Alexandra was in town, so Kostantes spent hours drinking at Stamati's shop before coming home for dinner. After the first couple of evenings, his backslapping bluster lost the charm of novelty, as did his long rants about the parlous political state of the world. It was a great day for Eddy, too, when he pitched his sleeping bag in the spare upstairs room of our own house and fell asleep without Kostantes's distant snoring to trouble his dreams.

I AWOKE on the first morning to the sound of hoofs in the courtyard. For a moment I was back in my mother's house in Chelsea. When I was very young, one of the vivid figures on the edge of my awareness was a man called Jimmy who sold fruit and vegetables from the back of a horse-drawn cart. He came from south of the river, clip-clopping over the Albert Bridge in the early evening. If I was still up I was allowed to go outside and hold out a sugar lump on my flattened palm for the horse's warm, wet muzzle. If he was late, I was already in bed, long before nightfall on summer evenings, but I would hear the horse in the street outside.

The hoofs in the courtyard slowed. Whoever was riding or leading the animal was now scaling the mountain of rubble outside the bathroom window. I heard a voice, indistinguishable words, soothing the beast without. It was Spiro Vlahos, one of our neighbours on Zervou, and his donkey, passing by to offer the implicit reminder that our courtyard was still a legal right-of-way for any member of the local Vlahos clan, as agreed when we bought the house. At least he had not woken Wendy. So pregnant and so exhausted, she slept deeply these days. The sounds faded. I lay there, grinning like a fool, basking in the idea that we had finally moved in. A thin bar of hot yellow sunlight lay across our bed. The room smelled of wood and clean linen. There was still so much to do, so many things to buy, but whatever happened in the future, this was surely a victory.

I slipped out of bed and dressed silently, eased open the handle of the door and closed it behind me. Eddy's sleeping bag was empty. So was the downstairs room and the soon-to-be-bathroom. He couldn't be making cement at this hour. I stepped outside into the bright sunshine and heard the sound of a guitar from down in the garden among the olive trees. Eddy was writing a song for us as a housewarming gift, a ballad of the borthro. I could see him now, a distant figure sitting on the flat white stone beside the plum orchard.

The garden had changed again a few days earlier, though we had been so busy we barely noticed. The tall white and purple irises were fading under the almond trees—the air was no longer heavy with their extraordinary incense—but now the whole hillside was covered in bright red poppies, thousands of them, so many they seemed to emit a scarlet glow in the early-morning sunshine. There were patches of pink mallow too, and exquisite miniature Persian cyclamen nodding small mauve heads among the old rock piles, but everything else looked dowdy beside the poppies. Here and there, two or three at a time, the poppies would tremble and bow, though there wasn't a breath of wind. Tortoises were busy in the garden, males seeking the larger females, moving surprisingly quickly. When one of the little studs found a mate he would heave himself clumsily up onto her back without further ado and the sound of shell clacking against shell would break the silence of the olive grove.

I had such plans for the garden. Pathways and terraces and stone benches to take advantage of the view, beds for those herbs that did not grow wild, beds for vegetables . . . I had made a start on a vegetable patch one evening after the cement mixing was over for the day. Alex, a gentle, soft-spoken boy of eighteen whose family owned a house farther back along Zervou, had come by to see what we were up to and stood watching me dig. Progress had been slow. There was so little soil once I started to pry out the rocks and rubble and clustered bulbs of the ubiquitous asphodel that I quickly lost heart. One huge spherical bulb with damp, brown papery skin was particularly hard to dislodge. It was about the size of a melon and reeked of onion where my spade had cut into it.

"That's a wild onion," said Alex. "Very useful."

"You can eat it?"

"Oh no. But you should take it out carefully and put it on your windowsill, outside the house."

"Why?"

"It's the best way of keeping vampires away when the baby is born."

Alex was at agricultural college on the mainland, so he ought to know.

"And what about the soil, Alex? How do I grow vegetables without soil?"

He suggested I follow the old ways since I was so determined to be traditional about everything. When the first families settled Zervou, they had encountered the same problem. They were patient people. They built a stone wall around the area they wished to cultivate and filled it with the small oval leaves that fell from the olive trees in autumn. In a year or two, the leaves decayed to loam, enriched, of course, with the precious manure of the family donkey.

It seemed an admirable method, especially as I loved building stone walls much more than I enjoyed digging.

"Of course, you'll still have to water your crops," he pointed out. "Every day, from May to October."

Water again. It all came back to water. Ironic that *loutses* meant "puddles"—or, more accurately, "holes in the ground where water collects." I looked down over the courtyard wall at the new pump, an expensive little item, like a red basketball on a green box set onto a small concrete pad. Tasso had already wired it to the fuse box and plumbed it into the house. In three more days, by Kostantes's reckoning, the bathroom would be finished and by then the cement walls of the sterna would be dry enough to hold water. We had ordered a tankerload to be delivered—by Diomedes, not Tatsi Rizzi (it seemed Kostantes's argument with his relative was over). Meanwhile, we were still filling our plastic demijohns at the town pump every morning, flushing the toilet with dishwater and boiling a kettle whenever we needed to wash.

Eddy came slowly up from the garden, carrying his guitar and smiling delightedly.

"You've got some very randy tortoises there, Jim," he observed.

"Randiest on the island. That's why we bought the place."

It was Eddy's last day with us. The following morning he was flying back to England. Without his help, we could never have finished the house in time, but he had grown tired of us telling him so.

"Let's make a start on this rubble before Kostantes gets here," he suggested. The remains of the upstairs dividing wall, torn down at Dmitri the carpenter's suggestion and dropped out of the window, had lain in the courtyard for weeks, a mountain of broken plaster, bamboo, wooden slats and rock. We pulled on our tattered gardening gloves and started to shovel and heave the stuff over the low wall to the right of the little house, taking care not to hit the thick black plastic pipe that emerged a couple of feet below us and then plunged vertically down for another ten feet before disappearing underground. It was our sewer pipe, the conduit to the borthro in the garden below. My plan was to bury it beneath a solid slope of rubble, which I would then turn into a broad and majestic flight of stairs leading down to the concrete cap of the borthro. A stone wall around the cap, at the right height for sitting, a fringe of flower beds, and we would have the first of many handsome terraces in the garden.

We had almost cleared the entire rubble pile when we heard Kostantes arrive on his scooter. He, too, would soon be taking a break from the project. The building season was already under way down on the coast and his presence was required. Foreigners who had bought land the summer before and had gone home for the winter imagining that a dream home was under construction in their absence would return in May. The contractors had a hundred watertight excuses to explain why nothing at all had been done, but even they felt obliged to make some token display of activity now that the weather was warm enough for comfort.

"Today," said Kostantes, slapping Eddy on the back and giving my shoulders a hug, "No tsimento!" He waited for the cheering to die down. "No tsimento. Sofa!"

Plaster. For the inner walls of the bathroom. Groans. Mixing batches of plaster was less arduous but far more painstaking than mixing cement. It called for the finest white sand and the creamiest lime, which then had to be tossed up and down in a cradle of small-meshed chicken wire until the smooth, heavy plaster dribbled out into a spotlessly clean trough, leaving a gritty residue in the cradle. Hard on the arms, but there was a huge sense of satisfaction in having progressed from basic construction to cosmetic work.

Today was also a fine day for painting the inside walls of the house, added Kostantes. He waited for me to start complaining.

"We have no paint! Why didn't you tell me we had to buy paint the last time I was in Corfu Town? Now I have to make a separate trip!"

The old man was grinning. We did not need to buy paint, he explained as I finally ran out of pidgin Greek. We would make our own using lime and water, and add a little olive oil so that if you happened to brush up against a wall you wouldn't get a white smudge on your clothes. Another use for olive oil! And Wendy could do the painting while we stripped to our shorts in the warm sun, taking it in turns to mix paint or plaster.

Some time later, the first of the day's visitors showed up, an elderly man called Thanos who had spent much of his life in Athens and returned to Zervou each summer. We had given up counting the villagers who happened to wander by as the house neared completion, some intensely curious, some more discreet, all of them desperate to find out how much we had paid for everything. The men felt obliged to comment on whatever chore was under way. "You'll need a bigger borthro than that!" "Plenty of rock down there!" "What's with the fuse box—are you opening a hotel?" The women would speak only to Wendy, sharing advice about pregnancy and invariably remarking that she was dangerously slim. One weathered old grandmother, a total stranger, suddenly reached out and gripped Wendy's breast, cackling some long invocation in Greek. Luckily, Michelle and her baby were also visiting. Michelle giggled as she translated. "If the milk won't come, eat black-eyed beans and rub half a lemon over your nipples! Well, it might be worth a try."

Many of the women brought their daughters along for the outing (it had been years since a male child had been born to a Loutses family) and some also arrived with gifts—usually eggs, or a jar of honey, or a plate of fruit—which were always very welcome. When I saw that Thanos had a bulging plastic bag in his hand I assumed that he too had a housewarming present, but he clutched it to him as he poked around the courtyard, looking for something to criticize. He stayed only as long as manners required, then strolled off down the path beside the ruined houses. Just as he reached the edge of our land, he dropped the bag over the wall.

This time it was my turn to be curious. I jumped down into the garden and looked in the bag. It was full of chicken feathers, blood and the few internal parts of the chicken that not even Thanos would eat. I could see him watching me from among the blackberry bushes farther down the path.

"Oh, Thanos, did you forget this?" I asked when I caught up with him.

"That? Oh no, that's skoupithia. Garbage."

I handed it back to him. "Not in my garden, please."

He shrugged and took back the bag.

An hour later, I was outside the house mixing more white-wash when I saw him drop the bag into our garden again. I began to wonder if there might be some sort of voodoo going on. Thanos's wife was well known as a wisewoman whose herbal remedies were much in demand among the older generation.

"Please," I repeated, handing him the bag again. "Not here."

"Why not?" he protested. I lacked the Greek to argue a point of principle and realized that it would be unneighbourly to push him over the wall. He made a face as if to say that the eccentricities of foreigners were unfathomable and shuffled off.

Garbage disposal had long been a problem in Loutses. Organic waste was tossed to the pigs and chickens; non-perishable items were usually thrown into the nearest ravine or taken secretly and by night two miles along the coast to the Kassiopi town dump. This salubrious site lay in a fold in the hills just out of sight of the coast road. A fire smouldered there perpetually, and when the wind was in a certain direction a cloud of foul-smelling smoke hung over that stretch of the shore. Soon after we arrived, I had made the mistake of approaching the gentleman who tended the eternal flame to ask when would be the best time to bring him our garbage. He said it was forbidden to dump in the dump and if he saw my Land Rover again there would be trouble. So we had fallen into the habit of burning our garbage in an old oil drum, halfway down the garden, starting the fire by sousing everything with diesel fuel from the Land Rover's emergency can. The resulting inferno would have incinerated asbestos.

We kept up a Thanos watch for the rest of the morning, but it was hard not to concentrate on the effect the whitewash was having on the interior of the house. We had become used to the stains of time and the blemishes of construction, the patches of new plaster and cement above the windows, until we scarcely noticed them any more. Now, as they all but vanished beneath the first coat of paint, we were aware of a transformation: the building site was becoming a room. The whitewash soaked into the old plaster as though it were blotting paper, drying in minutes.

"It's so white!" marvelled Wendy, brush in hand. The paint seemed to draw in light through the windows and door; the scrubbed-down cypress wood of the staircase took on a new lustre. Even the ceiling, so high we had to stand on the top of a ladder even to touch it with our fingertips, looked more dignified. The most satisfactory change was to the bathroom in the corner. The brick had been plastered over, but the messy seams of grey mortar where the new walls met the old were a constant reminder of the way we had commandeered the space. Now the seams disappeared and the fresh plaster merged with the old as we gleefully slapped on the whitewash. The whole room was taking on a most satisfactory coherence. Even so, the ambience was still spartan, largely due to the floor of battleship grey cement, patterned with the dark stains of bootprints, and the absence of any real furniture. Aside from the kitchen, the only creature comforts were the three cushions on top of the stone ledge that ran along the back wall, and two bookcases I had brought from my flat in London and carefully reassembled. The books themselves were still upstairs in cardboard boxes and in the six tea chests we used as a table. I longed for the day when I could unpack them.

Choosing which books to bring and which to leave behind in my mother's house had been a traumatic process once the obvious dictionaries, atlases, star charts, do-it-yourself and gardening manuals, demotic Greek primers and childcare texts had been given priority. Poetry seemed like a good idea—words in concentrated form, taking up less space in the trailer. But should it be poetry I already knew and admired and liked to have about me for emergencies—Byron and Rochester, Pope, Marvell, Yeats, Dylan Thomas—or should it be the stuff I had always meant to read but had never been able to face—the precious Romantics, the ponderous Victorians? Affection beat duty easily. And what about fiction? My last enthusiasm before leaving England had been for the short stories of Buchan, Kipling and Somerset Maugham, but I had an uneasy feeling they would not bear repeated rereading. In went Márquez and Calvino, Borges and James Stephens—windows of wonder and escape. A couple of dozen ancient Greek authors in the black Penguin Classics translation provided necessary intellectual bottom. While studying classics at school I had bought one a week at my teacher's insistence, but most had remained unopened. It seemed proper to embark upon them now in the land of their creation. Wendy's books were in Canada, but she had amassed a small new collection over the last six months—Willa Cather and Gabrielle Roy, Mary Shelley, Virginia Woolf and Ruth Prawer Jhabvala's short stories. Dostoyevsky's *Crime and Punishment* stood alone on the male side of her literary fulcrum. Outnumbering any other genre was the section of our miniature library devoted to travel writing, partly because I felt that our own adventure might draw inspiration from the wanderings of others and partly because these were the books that Wendy and I loved to read together. In my innocence, I imagined that we would continue to do so. Long afternoons in shady hammocks as soon as the house was finished, long evenings of leisure while our calm, thoughtful baby amused itself silently for hours on end . . .

The books could wait another day in their dark confinement, but there was one thing we could do to enhance the look of the room. The only possession we had that could truly be called a treasure was a framed fifteenth-century map of Corfu Town in the days of Venetian rule, a beautiful map that showed every rock and reef, every house and defensive emplacement around the old harbour. My best friend had given it to us as a wedding present before we left England. Now I hung it, with a small, silent fanfare, over the fuse box beside the front door. Wendy called Kostantes to come and see. He peered at it with gratifying intensity, pursing his lips and nodding at the detail, pointing out buildings that still existed, awed by its age and accuracy.

"But why hang it there, Dzimi?" he said with a look of concern. "Now you can't see your beautiful fuse box."

OUR LAST NIGHT with Eddy began with a candlelit feast in his honour. Planks were laid across the tea chests and dressed with a blanket and my grandmother's embroidered tablecloth, unpacked for the occasion. Jars filled with scarlet explosions of poppies from the garden adorned the bookshelves. We began with hunks of soft, crusty white bread and saucers of new, green olive oil for dipping. Then fresh baby sardines, tossed in flour, pan-fried in olive oil and dressed with pepper and lemon juice. The best way to eat them was to pick them up by the tail and pop them into your mouth, biting off the tail and crunching down. A preliminary decapitation with knife and fork was a permissible option. Our main course was a shoulder of lamb baked in the Greek way—long and slowly until the tender, juicy meat almost parted company with the bone and the skin was crisp beneath its marinade of garlic, salt and oregano. Artichokes, haricot beans and tomatoes had shared its roasting pan, while in another dish sweet white onions braised in white wine, pepper and bay leaves. It was the first real meal I had cooked in the little gas stove, and it turned out well. Dessert was less elaborate—apples and bars of chocolate—and then we cleared the table, leaving the dishes for tomorrow, and played poker for hours, until Wendy went up to bed.

Voices would have kept her awake, so Eddy and I went outside into the warm night and sat on the old stone wall. There was no moon, but the stars were bright. Down in the blackness beneath the olive trees, fireflies danced. A tiny scops owl was using the oak tree above us as a watchtower, and its single, high-pitched peep marked the time at regular intervals, answered by other owls below us in the valley.

"It's all about to begin for you two, isn't it," observed Eddy quietly. "Not a bad place to raise a family."

May 3, 1983

Dear Ros,
There ought to be a very good reason why I haven't written in a week, like having a baby, but nothing yet. There have been plenty of times in the last three months when I have longed to postpone the event. Now we're here and I want it to happen SOON. I've been getting lots of abdominal cramps in recent days, and thought it might be labour. Spent all day timing the cramps and cleaning the house in case we had to suddenly LEAVE, but no dice. My stomach is as hard as rock and the baby is constantly on the move. After months of assuming it was a girl, I now feel convinced it's a boy. I went to the doctor's again and this time he says I'll be right on time—May 10th!! On the way back we stopped at the Nissaki Beach Hotel, which has just reopened for the season. It's a beautiful modern hotel halfway along the coast between Kassiopi and Corfu Town. We went to the bar and your son ordered a cocktail (don't worry—I just had orange juice) and we sat looking out at the beach and the sea. Then we both just started to laugh. I suppose it's the first time we've actually relaxed since we arrived here. We felt like two ragged explorers returning to civilization after a gruelling expedition. All the tension lines seemed to fade from Jim's face, then he caught sight of himself in a mirror and laughed again. There's a hairdresser's in the hotel and he went and had a haircut—quite a good one and very cheap. This will be a good place to take bored guests (the bar, not the salon). I do miss my friends so much and am anxious for them to visit this summer.

And in a week, my mom will be here. I spoke to her on the phone and she's so excited, praying I don't have the baby until she arrives.

Jim went back into town to hand the horsebox over to the customs. It still seems unbelievable that they are entitled to it, and so unfair. Even so, I think we were both a little bit glad to see the last of it. The suspension had never recovered from using it to bring the marble window lintels from Corfu Town and we had stopped using it for sand and cement because it always got at least one puncture. What with rust and the residue of building materials, it was pretty much scrap, though useful as a tool shed. But now when we look out the ground-floor window we see Albania instead of a blue metal trailer. He came back with four chairs inside the Land Rover and a dining table tied to the roof—all modern and made of highly varnished pine, not particularly attractive but the best the island had to offer—at least that we could afford—so we don't have to eat off tea chests any more. We think we may strip off the varnish one day when we have five minutes.

While he was gone, Kostantes finished tiling the shower. He had had a long "lunch" at Stamati's shop and when I went in to see how he was doing, the tiles were a total mess. He had started halfway up the wall, for some reason, and the line of tiles he had stuck on just drooped as they got farther away from where he was standing. He muttered something then blurted out, "You should have SAID you wanted them straight!" I made him start again. Later Tasso came by and finally finished the plumbing—everything except the bathroom basin. Although we thought it was the end of the world when he gave us his estimate all those weeks ago, I have to say he has earned every penny. The hot weather these last few days has dried out the sterna at last and yesterday Diomedes (who looks like a forty-year-old movie star—all the women in the village think he's dreamy) drove up in his huge tanker. He had to park on the track (a great deal of shouting and instructions from every man on the hill as he did a three-hundred-point turn), then he ran a huge hose down into the sterna and we all watched it fill. It took about twenty minutes. K said it should last us a week, the way we use water. We asked K when he was going to put a concrete cap on the sterna and he said October! Aaaarrrgghh!!! Meanwhile he will put a sheet of plastic across the top to stop rats and lizards and centipedes falling in and then we will replace the old floorboards. He's going to leave a hole in them so we can lower a bucket for water whenever the pump fails, and Jim has made a heavy wooden trap door for it. One day the room will be a beautiful spare room for you to stay in. Meanwhile, Jim is going to use it as a study. He has put plastic over the window until we can afford to have a proper window made and is working on a scheme to stop the rats and snakes coming in through the old tiles above his head.

So we have running water at last. We aren't drinking it yet—it still tastes cementy and Jim still has to fetch drinking water every morning from the village—but we have had hot showers and feel pretty much as if we're in heaven. But . . . Major news! He saw a shop in Corfu Town that sells washing machines!! The way he described it, it's just a cylinder with a sort of paddle inside that swooshes the clothes around and you have to pour the hot water in through the top. It has gone to the top of the list of priorities, though we can't afford to buy it quite yet. We're saving everything to pay the clinic when the baby comes, because of course no one will tell us how much that's going to cost. My bag is packed and by the front door for when the big moment arrives. After that, who knows!

I've just realized that you will already be a grandmother long before this letter reaches you, and Jim will have called you and the baby and I will be home again in our cosy little house. Oh well. I'll send it anyway, with all our love,

Wendy

Chapter Six

The prayers that Audy uttered proved extraordinarily powerful. Wendy and I were still childless when I met her at the airport and drove her home to Loutses. This was her first trip to Europe, and we would have loved to have shown her the island, but long excursions seemed unwise. Instead, she entered into the spirit of our adventure, helping me shift rubble and painting the window frames.

The days passed with no sign of the baby. A week went by. All of us, especially Wendy, were getting tired of staying at home. We decided to risk a trip to the beach—not to Kalamaki, but farther along the coast where Wendy could reach the sand without clambering down through the olive groves. The water was cool, but Audy, used to Muskoka lakes, didn't think so. Then we went down to Kassiopi and bought a rug for the baby's room, just in case it ever showed up. With only four days left before Audy had to leave, we decided to have dinner at Akharavi, at a restaurant right on the beach, and ate grilled shrimp and devilled chicken livers while the sun set self-consciously into the sea.

I believe the chicken livers did the trick. That night, just after two o'clock, I felt Wendy shaking my arm.

"You're sure it's not indigestion?" I mumbled.

"They're fifteen minutes apart. But maybe we'd better wait and see."

At three-thirty, the contractions were coming more rapidly. We closed up the house and climbed into the Land Rover. Not the most comfortable vehicle for a woman in labour. No fun for Audy, either, perched on the hard metal bench behind Wendy.

"The trick is to find a speed that will get us there in time without giving you too much of a bumpy, bone-shattering ride," I explained helpfully, while Wendy gritted her teeth and clutched her mother's hand. The sky was beginning to pale as we reached the outskirts of Corfu Town and pulled up in front of the clinic. The building was dark and the big glass front doors were locked. It seemed an age before a sleepy nurse answered our knocking. She led us to the reception desk and opened the heavy appointments book, looking for our names.

"Can we do the paperwork later!" gasped Wendy.

The room was comfortable, with its own bathroom and a spare cot beside Wendy's bed. While Audy helped her undress, I opened the windows and stepped out onto the tiny balcony. Cement stretched away to the horizon, fringed with blue and white lights—the clinic lay at the end of the runway of Corfu airport. I was about to share the news when the peaceful morning erupted into an apocalyptic roar and the underbelly of a plane appeared about fifty feet above my head. I watched it land, then went back into the room, still grinning at the exhilaration of the spectacle. Wendy was in the throes of another contraction, understandably seething at my sense of priorities. A nurse appeared at the door. She promised us that she had telephoned Dr. Babalis and that he would reach the clinic in time. Then she took a quick look under Wendy's nightgown.

She smiled. "Mia ora." One hour.

Sixty minutes and five aircraft later there was still no sign of the wretched doctor. The nurse had been in two or three times and repeated her cursory examination. This time she saw something that galvanized her into action—the baby's head. She helped Wendy to stand and led her away down the corridor to the birthing room. Babalis was already there, scrubbed and gowned. They seemed surprised I might want to be present but told me I could wait at the other side of the room while Wendy climbed up into the birthing chair. Almost immediately, I heard Babalis tell Wendy to "poosh." Minutes passed. "Poosh! Poosh!" Then suddenly, "No poosh!"

The cord was wrapped around the baby's neck. "No poosh!" The nurse fled in search of an anaesthetist while Babalis prepared to perform an episiotomy. Wendy was groaning deeply. The nurse came back, alone, and pulled a curtain around the chair. I heard Wendy yell out in pain, heard Babalis urging her again to push. "It's a boy," called the nurse as the anaesthetist entered the room and vanished behind the curtain. A moment later our son gave his first cry for attention. Whatever the anaesthetist had done appeared to have worked, for Wendy was unconscious in seconds while Babalis worked away with needle and sutures, stitching the incision he had made. Now the nurse appeared, holding the baby. Wrapped in a towel, his fists clenched, his face fading from blue to a dappled red and yellow, he was carried across to where I stood and laid in the weigh scales, looking like an angry little gnome. Then his eyes slowly opened—huge silvery blue eyes that stared up into mine with a gaze of calm wisdom and reassurance.

Back in our private room, the baby slept, untroubled by the periodic roar of the planes passing fifty feet overhead. Wendy slept, too, thanks to the heavy-handed anaesthetist, who had shot her full of enough narcotics to tranquilize a gorilla. Hours passed before she finally began to moan and stir towards consciousness. She was in great pain from the stitches but it didn't seem to matter once I had lifted up the baby and laid him in her arms. With Audy beside us, we settled down to admire him, pointing out various aspects of perfection in careful whispers.

We had found Audy a room in a hotel close by; I took the spare cot beside Wendy. At three in the morning, the baby's crying woke us. Peering groggily into the crib by the glow of the night light, I wondered what on earth to do.

"Maybe we should change his diaper," whispered Wendy. But how was that done? Working very slowly and carefully, I unfastened the pin and peeled the cloth away.

"Oh my God . . ." It was a scene from *The Exorcist,* a black, tarlike substance everywhere. Wendy turned on the light and frantically thumbed through her copy of Penelope Leach. I pulled on my jeans and went to find help. The night nurse must have seen the terror in my face, for she flew along the corridor behind me, only to chuckle when she reached the crib and understood our alarm. It was all perfectly normal, she cooed, a good thing. She handed me a box of wet wipes and returned a few moments later with a baby bottle of tepid camomile tea. I had never heard that newborn babies drank tea, but ours sucked away thirstily for a while, then went back to sleep.

Next morning, Kostantes and Alexandra arrived with a box of biscuits and a bottle of orange squash as gifts. She leaned over the crib, laughing quietly, not quite daring to touch anything. He kept giving me bristly hugs and telling me the baby was a boy.

"And he has a house to go to, eh, Dzimi?"

"Thanks to you, Kostantes."

"And he's a boy!"

An airplane passed overhead and we both hurried out onto the balcony to watch.

Wendy, Audy and I took Joe the baby home two days later. We agreed that the noise and vibration of the Land Rover would be traumatic for the young master and profoundly uncomfortable for her. A taxi was also ruled out, since the cab drivers all drove the coast road like demons with one hand on the horn. Audy figured out a solution. I would take the Land Rover to Kassiopi, rent a small, smooth, quiet modern car and drive everyone to the house. It seemed simple enough.

Land Rover owners never worry about skidding, even at the end of the olive season when five months of ripe olives have been crushed into the tarmac and a light rain lifts the oil back out onto the surface without washing it away. Land Rover drivers take corners for granted, but the drivers of small, unfamiliar Japanese rental cars should not. On a curve of the corniche just outside Kassiopi, I felt the Suzuki start to hydroplane, sliding gracefully off the road. Luckily, the car went right, not left—into the cliff, not over it—but the flank of the vehicle was crumpled like shiny yellow paper. Naturally, I had waived the insurance option in the rental office, hoping to save a few hundred drachmas. Now they would squeeze me for millions, finding all sorts of double-secret codicils in the fine print. But was there any need to tell the swarthy, chain-smoking pirate who leased me the car about the accident, or in worrying Wendy with the tale, come to that?

The Suzuki was still roadworthy, and a careful hour later I was in one of the seedy auto body shops behind the clinic, explaining the situation to three frowning mechanics. The ringleader spoke a little English, but, more to the point, his wife had recently had a baby. In no time, they had the miserable car up on a hoist and were pounding away with rubber hammers, spraying with cans of yellow paint, playing a hair dryer over a final coat of varnish. Obviously, they had done this sort of thing before. They took a sizable but not exorbitant portion of the cash in my wallet. To this day, neither Wendy nor Christos the car guy is any the wiser.

So we drove, *en famille,* back to Loutses, Wendy sitting in relative comfort on an inflatable rubber ring painted with pictures of Smurfs that I had found in a tourist shop, Joe wearing a knitted woollen cap and scarcely crying at all in the arms of his doting grandmother. I settled them into the house and left to swap vehicles. Everyone was asleep when I came back.

It was a time for reflection, and I stood outside under the oak tree with a cigarette, gazing at the incomparable view, mulling over the fact that we were now three. The afternoon was simply perfect, cloudless but not too hot, and I waited for insights and revelations to well up like answers in a witch ball. None were forthcoming. The old stones and the olive trees basking in the sun looked exactly as they had done three days before.

Audy left the next morning. Carrying the suitcases out to the car, I didn't see her say goodbye to Wendy and Joe but she was tearful and pale on the drive to the airport.

"You know I'd stay if I could," she exclaimed. "But I have to get the flight."

A long time later, Wendy told me how she had held her mother and sobbed, asking her not to go, crying that she didn't know what to do. Audy didn't mention the scene and by the time I got back to the house, Wendy had decided to trust to luck and tough it out. She was up and dressed and determined to take Joe into the village to show him to Michelle. I couldn't persuade her out of the plan.

News of the expedition travelled fast. If we were out and about, we were obviously up to receiving well-wishers. Six o'clock was the hour for formal social calls in the village, after people had risen from their siesta and the heat of the day had relaxed. Today, however, was a special case, and the visits began around four. First to arrive was Ranya, the carpenter's daughter, peering shyly around the corner of the house until I saw her and beckoned her closer. She carried a bowl of cherries protected from the elements by a paper napkin, and a small bunch of camomile daisies. I carried the gifts into the kitchen and she watched me put the flowers in a jam jar of water.

"My mother says I must wait to hear the baby before I can look," said Ranya. "In case Wendy is sleeping."

She followed me up the creaking staircase and into our bedroom. Wendy was sitting up in bed, Joe beside her in the bassinet box. Ranya looked at him, smiling but saying nothing. Then she reached out and touched Joe's tiny fist with a finger.

"My mother says can we have the bowl back when you've eaten the cherries."

Maro was the next visitor, bringing a two-litre bottle of new yellow oil from her trees and a cutting from one of her famous gardenia bushes. I remembered my manners and asked if she'd like a coffee, but she smiled and said she couldn't stay. Petros and Eleni, the parents of our old friend Ilias, also brought oil and they did accept my offer, perching on the edge of the cushioned stone bench while I filled the long-handled briki with coffee, sugar and water and stirred it over the gas jet. I had not yet mastered the art of making Greek coffee, and they winced as they sipped it. When Eleni went upstairs, Petros stepped outside with me.

"Those olives need work," he muttered, glancing down the garden. He crossed the courtyard to the resurrected vine and fingered the papery bark with gentle fingers, tutting with disapproval. Small pale green shoots grew out of every knuckle of the wood—signs of life of which I was inordinately proud—but he began to rub each one off with his thumb, leaving only three or four near the ends of the two sinuous branches. He laughed when he saw my dismay and patted me on the back. "You do want fruit, don't you? Not just leaves? Well, then . . ."

In the black middle of the night I awoke to feel Joe sleeping peacefully between us—a curious discovery, since Wendy had changed his diaper and tucked him into the bassinet box at the end of the bed hours earlier. What if Wendy or I rolled over in our sleep and smothered him! I sat up and tried to lift him but his faintly shimmering, silvery shape glided up into the darkness without my assistance and floated back to the bassinet. My hands were under Wendy's body.

"What are you doing?" she moaned.

I felt for the flashlight, shone it into the box. Joe was still tucked in, breathing quietly.

For the next five nights I woke up before dawn to find our son's astral self sharing our bed. Then the sweet visitations stopped. Perhaps his rapidly developing ego disengaged his spiritual ability to project; perhaps I simply grew accustomed to it and no longer felt any anxiety at his presence. Whatever. He and Wendy and I had plenty of other nocturnal activities to keep us busy, involving diapers and bottles of milk.

WHEN JOE was one week old, my mother came to stay for a fortnight, bringing good advice, suitcases full of food, presents and baby clothes and a brilliant all-terrain British pushchair that could handle the rubble slope we called a driveway. She persuaded us that Joe would survive an outing to Peritheia and might even enjoy it, but her real target was Wendy, who had not left the house since her visit to Michelle. It was time she re-entered the world. So we drove down the mountain in the comfortable car my mother had rented and had lunch at the small taverna opposite Spiro's shop. The tables were set outside, and many passing Peritheian ladies took the opportunity to peer down at Joe and to tell us that he was clearly too cold or his blanket should be tucked in much more tightly or that he would certainly catch a sore throat from being out in the open air. I could see Wendy bridling at each new admonishment. Even women we had come to know fairly well insisted on adding their two cents' worth. They would ask if he was a boy or a girl, but none of them asked his name. When we volunteered the information they continued to call him *to moro* or *to mitzo,* the baby, the little one. It was a matter of superstition, we later discovered from Michelle. No one used a baby's name before he or she was christened, an event that usually happened when the child was one year old. Given the historically high rate of infant mortality in Greece's poor rural areas, perhaps there was no point in the community affording a baby the full status of a name until its survival was assured.

Audy and my mother were the first of many visitors that summer, so many that our tiny house soon began to feel alarmingly like an inn. We later figured out that we had only eight days to ourselves between May and September. Of course, all our friends missed us and were dying to meet the baby, and if that meant having to spend two rent-free weeks on a Greek island, they were prepared to make the sacrifice. Some arrived by taxi or bus, others took the initiative and rented a car of their own in Corfu Town; most had to be met at the airport before being wined, dined and entertained for a fortnight. We enjoyed their company, catching up on gossip and news of the outside world. We took pride in showing them the house and the land and explaining the minutiae of our long-term plans for this wall or that pile of rubble or the next potential herb bed until their eyes glazed over. But sooner or later during their stay, Wendy and I would find ourselves looking forward to the day of their departure and a couple of moments of solitude in which to catch our breath before the next party arrived.

We were the first in our circle to have a baby, and none of our guests seemed to grasp what that involved. Coming downstairs in the middle of the morning, hungry and blinking from sleep, they were surprised to find Wendy bent over a tub in the courtyard washing baby clothes and me lugging plastic demijohns of pure water from the pump in the village that could be boiled and cooled to make formula.

"Is that for tea?" they would yawn when they saw the kettle. "Good-oh!" And they'd wander out to the patio to look at the view.

Sometimes people we had never met appeared at the front door, usually while Wendy and Joe were asleep and I was in the shower. They were friends of friends who happened to be on the island and thought they'd pop by with greetings from London or Canada. Eager, confident faces, trusting in our hospitality . . .

The more sensitive guests eventually understood that though they were on holiday, we were not. They volunteered for service as dishwashers, grocery shoppers or plant waterers; some even helped in the endless task of repairing the low stone semicircles that helped keep a little soil around the base of the olive trees in our vertiginous garden. Real keeners had to be kept in check. One morning, Wendy and I awoke to find the baby coughing and thick clouds of dust billowing like smoke in the bedroom. Our current visitor, a kind, funny and companionable man called Stephen, had crept downstairs at dawn intending to surprise us by spring cleaning the house. He had taken a stiff broom to the cement floor, but the more he swept, the more cement dust he created—we could barely see the bookshelves through the whirling grey sandstorm. Everything we owned was coated with a fine soft powder. It took all three of us the rest of the day to clean up.

In the end, Wendy and I developed a system for surviving our guests. While one of us looked after Joe, the other looked after the visitors. One morning, I might drive them into Corfu Town for shopping and sightseeing; the next day, Wendy would drag them off to the beach. On Friday night, she took them to Georgie's taverna for dinner, and after to Philip's bar, leaving me to put the baby to bed and steal a couple of hours for writing. On Saturday, I would organize a trip to the casino south of Corfu Town so Wendy could read or write letters—or just revel in the luxury of solitude.

The casino, easily the most charming in Europe, was always a hit. In those days, it operated inside the Akhillion, the palace built in 1892 by the tragic Elizabeth of Austria as a distant retreat from the spite of the Hapsburg court. Lawrence Durrell once called it "a monstrous building," and ever since then, guidebooks have tittered nervously when describing its pillared portico and terraced grounds. In fact it had a distinctive, melancholy beauty. A sense of resignation and romantic failure permeated the cracked facades and empty rooms, while the chocolate-box fresco of the death of Hector on the grand staircase and the statue of the death of Achilles in the garden only added to the poignancy. I liked to arrive at dusk, showing our passports to the prim concierge (locals were not permitted to gamble lest Corfu become an island of bankrupts), then climbing the stairs to the gaming rooms. Because it was built into the crown of a steep mountain, the top floor opened onto gardens and the French roulette tables were set outside on warm summer nights, beneath massive cypress trees surrounded by rose beds and ornamental pools.

Like all sentimental gamblers, I had my own private rituals, strictly enforced on anyone who was with me. A preliminary Campari and soda was to be sipped on the other side of the terrace while we watched the burnt orange light of sunset fade from the crumbling balustrades and the shadows deepen around the statues in the garden. Inside the old throne room, chandeliers sparkled and we could hear the murmur from the blackjack and American roulette tables. The urge to join in was most compelling but had to be overcome, partly because my paltry stake could be gone in half an hour of even the most parsimonious betting, and partly because I loved to see the croupiers open up the French roulette tables out of doors. The posse would uncover the green baize and sort the columns of coloured chips in their various denominations, counting out loud for the benefit of the house cashier and his assistant. There was a liveliness and a meticulous energy to their calculations that seemed quite different from their cool, withdrawn behaviour when play began. Dextrous fingers cut and splayed the coloured piles, pencils scribbled feverishly. The wheel and the cloth were forgotten, the impatient punters ignored. For those few minutes, one could glimpse the real soul and purpose of a casino—the manipulation of money.

At last play began. I bought my colour and placed the same bets for the first spin of the wheel—a carré of five and nine, a carré on each of the corners of seventeen. What happened next lay in the hands of the Fates, but more often than not my hunches were close enough to sustain my little stack of chips. After an hour or so, or before I had used up my small allowance, I'd take a break, heading inside where the action was livelier. Around the American roulette wheels Athenian men bantered with the croupiers, the latter in dinner jackets, the former in shirts split to the navel, rivers of gold looping down through their hairy chests. Their mistresses sat within earshot, nibbling nuts and sipping thick liqueurs. There were the usual student types, betting in tiny amounts and marking wins and losses on a notepad with tight-lipped anxiety. At the blackjack tables a scattering of single ladies in Athenian silk and their own gagging microclimates of Chanel No. 5 tossed their hair and flirted with the dealers. The pit bosses on their high tennis umpires' chairs scanned the play with catlike nonchalance, while one of the managers of the place—a melancholy Greek who looked just like King George V—sat at the bar, waiting as always for an incident that never happened. Whatever it was—the gentle night breeze wandering like a ghost between the tables or the tranquil elegance of the old palace—the Akhillion brought out the best behaviour in those who gambled there.

But while the casino was a delightful expedition, the real *coup des vacances* was always Ano Peritheia. For once, Wendy and I would both escort our friends, with Joe in his bassinet, driving deliberately slowly into the mountains. We enjoyed watching our guests discover the old, abandoned town, falling under the inevitable seduction of its spell. And now there was an added attraction. Kosta, who lived in the last house in Loutses, had opened one of the tavernas in Ano Peritheia's piazza. Like Philip, he had been a steward on a merchant ship and he cooked the most delicious food we had ever had on the island. We placed our order when we reached the taverna and then set off on our exploration, for everything was made from scratch and we wanted to give Kosta the time he needed. He had three great specialties. The first was sofrito, steak pounded thin and braised in an opulently heavy sauce of brandy, vinegar and garlic with a pinch of fresh mint to cut the richness. The second was calf's liver, which he cut into slivers, sautéed quickly and served piping hot, still juicy beneath the salty, crusted surface, with a slow-cooked sauce of onions, tomatoes, fresh herbs and red wine. Sometimes tiny morsels of the liver were included on the plate of mezethes that came automatically when one ordered beer or retsina. The third delight was the keftedakia, tiny, soft balls of finely ground veal mixed with chopped olives, onion, oregano and a whisper of cumin. He fried them for a moment to fix their shape and give them a golden crust, but they finished their cooking in the oven with a fresh-tasting tomato sauce. We never knew which of these dishes he might have on the menu, but it didn't matter. Each one was a masterpiece.

Kosta's wife, Lydia, waited table, a strikingly beautiful Chilean woman with flashing eyes and long, very straight black hair who spoke English well. He had met her some years ago when his ship put into Santiago and had wooed her with tales of the bright lights and high life of Athens. She followed him to Greece but found herself living in the last house in

Loutses and spending every working moment in Ano Peritheia, lonely as Rapunzel in the tower, with only her husband, her young daughter and the sporadic, usually accidental clientele of the taverna Kapricorn for conversation.

"What about the old woman who lives up here?" Wendy asked. We sometimes saw her, bent double by age, dressed in layers of black, shuffling through her front door into the darkness of a ground-floor room near the square. She kept herself to herself, Lydia told us, living on little more than bread and water. Though she had family down on the coast, they were infrequent visitors. Either they did not want her with them or she preferred to remain in the mountains—no one was exactly sure.

"We'll all end up like that, Wendimou," said Lydia with a grim laugh and a toss of her head. "If we live so long."

One night, as we sat over our sofrito under the spreading poplar tree in the square, the old woman appeared beside Joe's bassinet.

"Aigori i goritzi?" she whispered. Boy or girl?

"Aigori," I stammered.

She made a small noise of satisfaction and bent over the bassinet to look more closely. She began to mutter indiscernible words, and her arthritic fingers made curious gestures over the baby, sometimes gently stroking the thin woollen blanket that covered him. Then she smiled at Wendy and at me and congratulated us.

"Oh my God! Was it a blessing or a curse?" murmured Stephen when she had gone.

"It was a blessing." I had never been so sure of anything in my life.

SUCH MEMORIES were rare that first summer. Weeks passed too swiftly to leave much impression, built around the intricate, unrelenting, rapturous routine of parenthood. To avoid any suggestion that one of us might be exploiting the other, Wendy and I divided our baby time to the minute and made elaborately balanced lists of the chores that had to be done in the garden and the house. Partly in the spirit of modern egalitarian notions of childcare and partly so that each of us had hours alone to write, we were most meticulous timekeepers. At night, when Joe went to sleep, we sat slumped at the table, playing poker or Scrabble. We no longer played for sexual favours. Now, the loser had to clean the bathroom or make the next batch of formula.

"What we need is a little spontaneity," sighed Wendy one evening, a week or two after the last of the summer's house-guests had gone home.

"Add it to the list."

"I mean it!" So we put on our smartest clothes, loaded Joe into a blanket-filled box on the floor of the Land Rover and drove down past Corfu Town to the casino. We gambled in thirty-minute shifts, one of us staying in the vehicle with the baby, the other dashing in for a half-hour of black-jack or roulette.

"If ever we're both ahead at the same time, we should just go home," suggested Wendy during one fleeting rendezvous.

"Or not?"

"Or not," she agreed. Joe didn't seem to mind. Born on a runway, he found any commotion relaxing. Luck was with us that night—our last visit of the year. A week later the casino closed for the winter.

The season was changing and the whole island seemed aware of it. At night, we lay in bed listening to the house rustle and creak and tick as a breeze picked up, cooling the roof tiles and the old stone walls. Creatures who had lived in the building before we moved in and had spent the summer down among the plum trees and rubble piles in the garden crept back inside. There were scrabblings and scurryings on the other side of the wooden ceiling above our heads, and once a dry and ominous slithering. When the rain finally came, the first drops hit the tin trap door in the roof with a startling metallic resonance, like ball bearings falling into the kitchen sink.

The shutters on the bedroom window were our weathervane. They were the original set, lighter and more finely made than the ones we had ordered from our carpenter, and they led a life of their own, as if determined to pay no attention to the return of humans to the house. I had made the mistake of oiling their hinges, and now they swung freely, overdoing it, showing off with articulated grace at the merest hint of a breeze, suddenly clattering and banging in the middle of the night like shutters possessed.

As the weather cooled, the village began to stir itself. Our long afternoon walks with the baby were no longer solitary. Men were busy in their apothikis or down in their sternas cleaning the great tanks for the second coming of the rain. The first big rainstorm was not collected—it rinsed the dust off the rooftops and out of the eaves. Before the second, however, pipes and tubes that had been stored away all summer were brought out, patched and reconnected.

Every day now the women were off at dawn to work in the olive groves, scything the undergrowth and raking it into long piles for burning. When the land was clear, the big black plastic olive nets were dragged down among the trees and unrolled like carpets, overlapping one another, weighted with stones or sewn loosely together with twigs poked through the mesh. Philip could remember the invention of the nets and the way they revolutionized the olive industry on Corfu. Before that, farming olives had been a back-breaking business, for the Corfiots have never picked the olives from their trees, the way they do in Kalamata and other parts of the country. They let them ripen until they fall, which maximizes the amount of oil in each olive (as much as 60 percent by weight). In the old days, an army of itinerant workers and gypsies would arrive on the island in the winter to pick up the olives before they began to rot, staying until the last of the harvest was over, which might be as late as June. When the nets first appeared, in the early 1960s, the work of ten could suddenly be done by one person walking slowly across the black carpet, lifting it and twitching it with a hooked stick until the fallen olives all rolled down the netted slope to be easily gathered at the bottom. It was the first evolution in a farming system that had remained unchanged for two thousand years.

"What about your trees, man?" Philip asked me one night at the kafeneion when I had been urging him to teach me the way of the olive farmer.

"We're going to harvest them."

Philip made a small noise of satisfaction. "That's good, because some peoples have been wondering if you were going to ignore them again like last year. You have a responsibility. It's bad to waste olives."

So Wendy and I set to work, spreading a rug on the hillside in the cool morning sunshine and setting Joe upon it in his bouncing chair. I had no idea how to use a scythe, so I snipped away at the undergrowth with the gardening shears we had brought from London, while Wendy raked everything into a massive hill of dead vegetation. Backs and hands were soon aching, but it was fantastically exhilarating to be busy with the land again. This was why we were living here, I explained earnestly to Wendy, for the hands-on intensity of these kinds of experiences, the elation of physical work. I showed her the soil under the trees and we were both amazed to see tiny white seashells in it. Had the mountains once been beneath the surface of a primordial ocean?

"No, man," said Philip when we proposed our theory to him that evening. "In the old days, peoples would use drying-up seaweed as some kind of fertilizer, digging it in around the trees. It's good and organic and it's free." I made a mental note to revive the tradition next year.

It took us a week to clear our land, though Alexandra could probably have done it in a single day. We bought nets in Corfu Town and laid them out, weighting the edges with rocks, and invested in a giant plastic barrel in which we could soak our olives in water until we had enough to fill a sack that could be taken down to the olive press. That might take a while, for olive trees produce a good crop only every second year, and the wasted harvest of the winter before had been spectacular.

In the end, we collected four and a half sacks of olives from our eleven trees, driving them to the olive press that stood by the roadside halfway between Loutses and Peritheia. There had once been twelve olive presses in Loutses, each one powered by a horse that walked in circles around the stone crushing trough, turning the massive granite millstones. The slough of crushed olives, like shiny, black, pungent porridge, was shovelled into bags of knotted rope, which were set beneath the weighted blocks of the press. A wooden mechanism like a capstan was turned, the farmer heaving on poles, until the oil drained out into storage jars.

The current press was not horse-driven, and the rope bags had long since become obsolete. A centrifugal crusher did the work ten times more efficiently, delivering golden extra-virgin oil of great beauty and purity. The peaty residue of the press was sold to a baker in Kassiopi who used it as fuel for his ovens.

Making our own olive oil was enormously satisfying. Friends from abroad were always given a bottle to take home with them, which left us more than enough for our own use. We stored the red plastic five-gallon flagons in the little house across the courtyard, refilling our kitchen bottle whenever we needed to. I could look across at them as I sat at my desk in an overcoat, scarf and fingerless mittens, trying to get on with my novel, listening to the rain on the tiles and the sound of the water splashing into the tank beneath the floorboards. Our water no longer tasted of cement.

The winter was a particularly cold one, according to the village savants. Loutses itself was sheltered by the surrounding hills, but the northeast wind blew straight across the snow-capped mountains of Albania and over the sea to our front door. On some January mornings, the puddles in the courtyard shone with a brittle layer of ice. Our small electric radiator kept Joe warm in his cot but made little headway against the damp in the rest of the house, and Wendy was uncomfortable having to sleep in layers of sweaters and a winter overcoat. So we drove into Corfu Town one day and bought a small wood stove from a tinsmith. Basically a brown, rectangular metal box on legs, it stood demurely in the corner of the downstairs room. Standing on the step-ladder, I burrowed a tunnel through the wall and ran the metal chimney pipe outside, sealing the hole with cement. Then we fired it up.

All her life, Wendy had been addicted to cosiness, and she was delighted with the little stove. Its heat spread through the house like a sigh, warming the rooms above in no time. Now each day began with me running downstairs, teeth chattering, to rake the soft grey ashes from the stove and lay and light a new fire before running back up to bed. During the morning we slow-cooked a casserole on the single hot plate on top of the stove; in the evening, we bathed Joe in front of it in his blue plastic baby bath or draped the wet laundry around it to dry on a clothes horse.

Inevitably, the stove created its own chores. Wood had been scarce on Corfu since the Romans deforested the island for their shipyards nineteen hundred years earlier, for though we were surrounded by tens of thousands of olive trees they never needed pruning and rarely shed so much as a single bough. So we scavenged for driftwood on remote, rainswept beaches and scoured the rubble pile in the garden for any splinters of timber. The problem was eventually solved when we discovered that one of our ancient almond trees had given up the ghost. Babis arrived with his chainsaw, and for months we luxuriated in warmth and the sweet, delicate aroma of almond wood.

THE WINTER wore on with days of monotonous rain and nights of bright starlight and clear, silent cold. We baked our own bread and tried not to eat the entire loaf while it was still hot from the oven. We turned the sweet oranges that grew in the valleys around Peritheia into marmalade and spongecakes that Wendy would give to her new friends, Michelle, Koula and Renna, returning with eggs, a bag of potatoes or some other edible barter. The women were all young mothers, and the evenings they spent together gave Wendy a social life of her own. It amused her to discover that in the privacy of their homes, with their husbands up at the kafeneion playing poker, the women behaved quite differently than we would have guessed, smoking and tucking into the local brandy, sharing the most scandalous gossip about their neighbours. Wendy's Greek vocabulary was vastly enriched.

Other than Michelle, Wendy's closest friend was Philip. Two or three nights a week she would make her way to the kafeneion towards the end of the evening and sit with him until the poker game ended and the men went home, then join him and his father in the kitchen of their house and talk late into the night.

"You know, man," he said to her one night, "everyone thinks I'm fucking you."

"Oh my God!" spluttered Wendy. "I hope you tell them you're not!"

Philip shrugged and laughed. "Come on, man. Of course I don't say that! They wouldn't be believing me anyway."

It was his company she enjoyed, his irreverent sense of humour and the endless fund of stories left over from his days in the merchant navy—wild tales of fights and whores and jumping ship in shark-infested waters. His nickname was the Grove because he was as silent and discreet as an olive grove where the sharing of gossip was concerned, though he was privy to most of the village's secrets.

Often Philip knew more news about us than we knew ourselves. It was he, for example, who told us that we would receive a visit on the following day from Christos the stonemason. The marble floor we had ordered a year earlier was finally ready.

We had grown used to the dusty grey cement beneath our feet. It was handily absorbent if we slopped water onto it when we were bathing Joe, and any cracks or gouges could be quickly repaired with a small batch of fresh cement and a flick of the trowel. If it had not been for the shocked double takes and polite silence of visitors when they first saw the floor—a reaction that always forced us to explain the glorious future planned for it—we might have forgotten all about the marble. But now it was about to become reality, and our excitement was intense. The stone itself was beautiful. The quarryman had cut it into long planks five or six feet in length, eight inches across and one inch thick. Just off-centre down each plank, the strawberry-milkshake pink faded to white, then back again to pink, with a meandering seam of snowy quartz close to the edge.

Christos might have been cast for the part of a master mason. He was short and powerfully built, with long hair, a bushy beard and hands that looked as though he could break rocks without any need for a hammer. His own house, halfway down the mountain, was an illustration out of the Brothers Grimm, its walls completely faced with randomly shaped paving stones of pink limestone.

"It will take a week," he said when he had finished unloading the marble and taken the measure of our house. "And you must move everything out of the kitchen and living room. Everything. Even the wood stove and the cooker. There will be a great deal of dust."

We assured him we were used to dust.

"I'll be here tomorrow at seven a.m."

To our amazement, he arrived precisely on time, with his wife and their new baby beside him in the van. While she sat and talked to Wendy, Christos immediately set to work, mixing a great batch of stiff cement with extraordinary speed and spreading a thin line of it every few feet across the width of the room, using a wooden rod and a spirit level to make sure the height was exactly uniform. While the cement dried, he set up a trestle for his circular stone-cutting saw and began to trim the ends of each length of marble to a more perfect right angle while his wife dribbled water onto the blade. The man was an artist, smiling to himself at the pleasure of feeling his strong hands working. I stood and watched for hours, marvelling at his skill.

By lunchtime, Christos was already laying the lengths of marble across the cement beds, tapping them carefully into place, his spirit levels in constant use. By teatime, we had ourselves a floor complete with a thin pink marble baseboard. The next day, he unloaded an empty vat from the truck and made a slurry of white cement, as smooth and liquid as single cream, into which he stirred a pot of red paint until it precisely matched the dominant colour of the marble. He poured it all over the new floor, spreading it into every corner of the room and into every hairline crack between the lengths of stone. Hours passed before he was satisfied.

At noon, we sat outside in the courtyard and ate bread and cheese and olives. Christos kept glancing at our doorstep, a great, flat-topped hassock of a rock that made a perfect step from the courtyard to the front door two feet above it. The stone wobbled a little when anyone stood on it, but Wendy and I were used to the effect. I had, from time to time, tried stabilizing it with small stones or wooden wedges, but they soon slipped out of position. Clearly, the arrangement offended Christos. He suddenly stood up and strode off into the garden, returning with three hefty rocks from the rubble pile by the pump. I helped him mix a batch of cement (light on the sand, heavy on the lime), and in twenty minutes and ten glancing blows of the hammer we had an immaculate, rustic stone doorstep that immediately made everything Kostantes and I had wrought in the preceding year look crude and malformed.

The last treatment for our marble floor was the hardest—two days of polishing with a machine so heavy that all four of us were needed to lift it up into the house. As noisy as the

Land Rover, it had three spinning discs on the base, covered by abrasive pads that ground away at the surface of the floor. The promised clouds of fine pink dust filled the room, and Christos had to wear swimming goggles to protect his eyes and a bandana over his nose and mouth. Every few hours, he put more finely graded pads onto the discs—the last set were as smooth as chamois leather—and then he was finished. It took a weekend to clean the house and move everything back, but the evening eventually came when we sat on our staircase and looked down at the most beautiful strawberry-and-vanilla-striped marble floor in the world, polished so perfectly it shone like a pool of water.

Joe was particularly pleased with the improvement, stroking the cold stone and pressing his palms against it. Best of all was the way in which a tiny toy car now travelled the length of the house, from wood stove to kitchen, with only the smallest push.

Almost a year old, with big blue eyes, skin tanned gold and hair so blond it was almost white, Joe was the sun around whom the rest of our lives revolved. Wendy had made it her life's mission to keep him constantly amused and mentally stimulated, and her efforts had paid off, for he was precociously intelligent. To the village he was still *to mitzo,* the baby, though now May was upon us, that was about to change.

The preparations for Joe's christening had begun months earlier with a trip to the Metropolitan in Corfu Town, headquarters of the island's Orthodox clergy. Armed with a letter from our village priest, I sat in a dry and sombre anteroom, listening to a clock ticking for the best part of an hour before I was called into the presence of a stern, grey-bearded, black-robed potentate and his much younger assistant. He read the letter carefully, frowning and pursing his lips or glancing up at me with raised eyebrows as if something in the document had surprised him. At last he spoke, a question smoothly translated into English by the secretary.

"Your own faith is Protestant, not Roman?"

"Church of England." I wondered whether it would further our cause or damage it to add how long ago and how thoroughly I had lapsed.

"And the mother?"

"Also Protestant."

"But you wish the child to be raised in the Orthodox Church?"

"Yes, please."

"And the godparent?"

This was the important point, according to the best advice of Michelle. A Greek godparent who would keep Joe on the straight and narrow was an absolute prerequisite, and Wendy and I had chosen Philip. He had been both surprised and moved when we asked him, then he had burst out laughing, reminding us of his letter campaign against the religious establishment. This was a small island, and it was possible someone at the Metropolitan had read Philip's correspondence and might recognize the name.

"He's Greek," I answered.

And that was the end of the conversation. A letter for our priest was typed and stamped, a small administrative fee paid, and I was released into the cold sunshine, feeling exuberant and slightly guilty, like a schoolboy who has survived an interview with the headmaster through the timely use of a lie.

Towards the end of April, the tempo of preparations began to quicken. A necessary step was a visit to the christening shop in Corfu Town, one of several emporiums dedicated to the outfitting of weddings and christenings. Based upon a conversation with Michelle, I knew what I had to buy: gifts for the guests (in this case, small white china ashtrays filled with coloured sugared almonds and tied up in muslin with blue and white ribbons) and a white beeswax candle, four feet long and garlanded like a maypole. I could take the candle now but the sweets would not be ready for a month.

Wendy had also been making plans. There would be a party, of course, after the service, and the traditional form of such celebrations was a sit-down lunch or dinner at Georgie's taverna, which my mother had generously insisted on paying for. With Michelle acting as interpreter, and her own daughter's recent christening as an example, Wendy sat down with Georgie's wife and made the arrangements, drawing up a menu and ordering copious amounts of wine, beer, ouzo and brandy. Philip knew a band of musicians down on the coast that we could hire for the dancing.

The highlight of the feast would be two lambs purchased from the small flock that Michelle's mother-in-law, Maria, tended on their land at the top of the village. She was happy to sell them, but we would have to find someone else to slaughter them, since she hadn't the heart for such work. Neither had I, but our neighbour Spiro volunteered for the deed. He was also prepared to dry and cure the fleecy hides, which Joe could then keep, as was the custom, to use as rugs beside his cot.

All things considered, the organization was surprisingly easy. Then again, Joe was not the first baby to be christened in Loutses and an established pattern for such occasions already existed, made simpler by the fact that the village had only one church and one taverna. During the winter, there had been some speculation among the local gossips about whether we would have a christening at all, and if we did, whether it might be as strange and chaotic and penny-pinching as most of the other things we attempted. Once they realized we had opted for a decent, traditional affair, they were able to anticipate our plans even before we had made them.

The one great unknown was who could expect to be invited. From our point of view, the list virtually wrote itself: everyone we knew at any level of intimacy beyond a polite nod was included. Kostantes and Alexandra, of course, and their extended family, all our neighbours, all the people who had worked on the house, its original owners, Old Tomas and Maro, Michelle and her in-laws, our lawyer, Kosta and Lydia from Ano Peritheia . . . In no time, we were up to fifty people and the numbers continued to climb. Since Philip was to be Joe's godfather, he was now our *koumparos,* related to our entire family, and we were koumparos and koumpara to his. So his elderly, dignified aunt, also our new koumpara, was added to the list. But I was still nervous that we were forgetting someone significant, someone who might be mortally offended and would turn up like the wicked Maleficent in the fairy story to heap curses and doom on our heads.

"Don't worry, man," said Philip. "If they think they should be there, they're coming anyhow."

Wendy's childhood friend Chris was flying over from Toronto to represent Canada at the great event; two of my oldest friends were coming from London, joining my brother, my mother and half a dozen of her famous, more or less eccentric friends. Some would be staying in hotels on the coast, but others would be billeted in the village, wherever anyone had a spare room. We had put together a fairly exhaustive itinerary for their entertainment. It was important to me that they should understand why we had made the decision to move here. I wanted them to fall in love with the island, too.

The month of May seemed determined to back me up in this ambition, for Loutses had never looked lovelier. The long days were idyllically warm, the nights full of starlight and fireflies in the blackness under the olive trees. It rained just enough to please the gardenias and jasmine we had planted in the boxes and beds around the courtyard and to bring out the last of the wildflowers in the garden. The swallows were back, nesting in the ruined houses next to ours, and so was the owl, peep-peeping all night long in the oak tree outside our bedroom window. It had been absent during the winter, not actually migrating, just visiting some more sheltered spot in the folded hills.

Joe's first birthday came and went, marked by a small tea party with Michelle and her daughter, Louisa, but by then the christening was less than two weeks away and everything else was doomed to play second fiddle. We had taken to going to church on Sunday mornings, partly to get Joe used to the place and partly so that we wouldn't feel like complete hypocrites on the day of the baptism. The priest approved of our zeal. Come the day, it was explained to me, he would like his fee in cash and in advance and would also need to be fetched from his home near Karousades, half an hour's drive away.

And there were other details to be considered. As godfather, Philip would provide the olive oil, pressed from his own trees, that would be used for the baptism. Koula had a galvanized metal baby bath that could be borrowed for Joe's inundation, but it was up to us to bring the warm water to fill it. A special loaf of holy bread had to be ordered from the baker in Kassiopi and picked up on the morning of the christening.

One by one, as the days went by, crucial details were ticked off Wendy's master list. The wood stove had been dismantled and stored away for the summer when the marble floor was laid, and I finally got around to blocking the chimney hole with plastic bags full of rags and hiding the round scar behind a picture. Ranya and her little sister were out in the courtyard as I worked, and I scared them cruelly by making ghost noises through the hole in the wall. The cupboards and fridge were groaning with food so that we could offer appropriate hospitality to who knew how many guests. When I drove into Corfu Town to pick up the *bonbonieri* of sugared almonds, Wendy suggested I might also want to buy a pregnancy test from the pharmacy.

"You . . ."

"Quite possibly."

"Oh . . ."

"I know."

I bought the test and we watched it turn blue. In less than eight months, Joe would no longer be an only child.

The days before the christening were a blur of meetings and ferryings, reunions and rendezvous. One Land Rover and various rented cars buzzed up and down the main street of Loutses like foraging bees. Old Tomas, sitting on his wooden chair in a patch of shade against the wall of his house, blue suspenders most debonair against his grey shirt, watched all our comings and goings and smiled at the parade.

Down at the taverna a long shallow pit was dug and filled with brushwood. The roasting spit with its twin *souvla*—long metal spears as thick as a London street railing—was erected over it with the sacks of olive-wood charcoal close by. The carcasses of the lambs were in Georgie's big fridge together with several rolo—yard-long roulades of pork stuffed with feta and herbs—and two spits loaded with kokoretsi—plump, tubular bundles of the lambs' coarsely chopped offal, everything except the kidneys, which the Loutsiotes found unpalatable.

The morning itself arrived, and I set off to fetch the priest and the christening bread, a round trip that took the best part of an hour. By the time I returned, the guests were standing about in the courtyard in their best summer-holiday clothes. At noon, we all set off along the path up Zervou and down the other side into the village, walking in a straggling line that grew ever longer as friends and neighbours joined us. Some of the local men peeled off as we reached the main street and the taverna, ostensibly to check the charcoal pit where the lambs had already been cooking for hours, but another contingent was waiting under the cypress trees up by the church. In the end, sixty or seventy people must have crowded into the little church to welcome Joseph Thomas Chatto fully into the spiritual and temporal community.

Inside, it was hot and smoky with incense and votive candles. The double doors on either side of the building stood open, admitting a ray of sunshine and the song of birds and cicadas. Usually the women stood at the back during a service, but my mother and the other foreign ladies of the party were urged forward into vantage points close to the iconostasis. Wendy and I stood front and centre holding Joe, who had begun to fret as he eyed the curious metal bath of warm water and the bowl of oil. When the priest held out his arms for him, Joe began to cry in earnest.

"Who names this child?" asked the priest. Philip muttered something and stepped forward, looking, I thought, a tad sheepish.

"What is his name?" asked the priest.

Philip cleared his throat. "Philippos." Somewhere a camera flashed.

The photograph has come down to us—Wendy standing open-mouthed staring at me; me standing equally shocked, staring at her; Philip looking grave; the priest repeating "Philippos." Joe was wailing as hands unwrapped him and he was lowered into the water, the priest's beard wagging over his face, an oil-dipped finger marking the sign of the cross on his forehead.

Soon we were out in the sun again, strolling in another happy procession down the steep path from the church to the taverna. The Greek women were making a huge fuss over Joe, pinching his cheeks and chucking his chin and calling him Philippos and Philippakis.

"It's a good name," said Philip with a shrug when we finally cornered him. "It means 'the man who loves horses,' and that's a good thing to do. And it's true! Whenever I'm meeting the horses they really are fucking loving me." Then the musicians started to play—a guitar, a bass guitar, a bouzouki and a violin—and no further conversation was possible.

That christening lunch rates pretty high in my all-time list of parties, certainly in the top two, though my memories of the afternoon are an impressionistic blur of music and dancing, sunshine and heat, the dappled shadows of the trees on the long table. There were salads and plates of feta cheese, taramasalata and tzatziki, bowls of olives, platters of french fries and rice pilaf (the two starches a traditional sign of prosperity and largesse). I remember the lamb arriving, carved into juicy, crisp-skinned hunks, heady with the aroma of oregano and the meat's own sweet, decadent fragrance. The rolo and the kokoretsi were grilled to perfection, salty, rich and gamy, cut into round slices. The lambs' heads were split in two and presented to the guests of honour—Philip, Wendy, my mother and me. We ate a little, as custom demanded, then passed them to the middle of the table where everyone could take what they wished, washing it down with red or white wine, beer, ouzo, brandy or all of the above. There were no speeches or toasts—nothing so formal—though a great many people called my name or Wendy's from up and down the table, met our eye, raised a glass and drank. Some of them we had never seen before. Other strangers passed by, pausing to find out what was happening, and those with friends at the table smilingly accepted a glass of wine and wished the baby luck.

In spite of the dozen or so English and Canadian guests, it was an entirely Greek occasion, a very local party, and, in retrospect, it changed everything. After that day, we were no longer the foreigners who had bought property on Zervou. We were now Loutsiotes, with a son born and baptized into the village. Philippos . . . It seemed appropriate that he should have a special Greek name of his own.

Chapter Seven

Corfu. For rent: private home in remote mountain village, ten minute drive from coast.

"It's good," said Wendy. "Clear, succinct, accurate."

"Then my mum's phone number."

"Right."

"And once initial contact is made, we inundate them with information and glowing descriptions until they simply have to come."

The idea that we should go into business as a rental agency had come from Kostantes. One morning, some months before Joe's christening, he had come limping across the courtyard with a plastic bottle of oil as a gift from Alexandra, and settled down for a chat. His manner was unusually diffident and fidgety, as it always was when he wanted to talk about money, but at last he came to the point. He and Alexandra wanted to rent out their house again during the summer and it occurred to him that Wendy and I should act as agents.

But didn't he already have an agent, we asked—the man we had paid when we first stayed in Loutses?

Kostantes threw his hands in the air and brought them down heavily onto his legs. That one took so much commission it was almost a criminal act. "Sixty percent, Dzimi! Maybe even seventy! Don't you remember?"

"So we could do the same job but for a much smaller commission?"

"Exactly!" He beamed, proud of us for grasping the matter so quickly. "And there are other people in the village who would like to rent their houses, too. Nikolakis. Sotiris down in Peritheia. Maro. My brother. You, Dzimi, will be a millionaire."

To have an income . . . Math was never our strongest suit, but that night Wendy and I worked out what we could make from five houses in a four-month summer, taking only a very humanitarian 20 percent of the rent, enough to cover the creeping expenses of life with a toddler and a new baby on the way. There would be overheads—postage, telephone calls from Philip's bar, the cost of an advertisement in the *Sunday Times*—but all things considered, it could be a tidy little earner. And, of course, we would be helping out our friends in the village.

The ad had gone into the paper in February, three tiny lines lost in a sea of holiday villas, apartments, farmhouses and mansions. But the price we quoted was in our favour—half what the established agencies were charging. Then again, our properties weren't quite on a par. Kostantes's house we knew well, and Petros's was its equal in every way. Maro's modern bungalow opposite the taverna was the most finished of the group, and the only one with a bona fide garden—perfect if you didn't mind Georgie's jukebox playing late into the night. Nikolakis owned a substantial house on the flank of the steep hill beside the church. He and his wife,

Vassiliki, a jolly, round-faced woman who took great pride in their flock of chickens, lived on the ground floor with their daughter and various elders. The upstairs rooms had their own entrance, kitchen, living room and bathroom and fabulous views down across the olive groves to the sea. Furniture was rudimentary, but anyone would be lucky to stay there—the jewel in our portfolio. We weren't so sure about Sotiris, down in Peritheia. His was the taverna where we had taken Joe on his first day out, and the rental accommodation amounted to four bedrooms above the bar.

"Of course they'll be plastered, painted and furnished by the time the tourists come," he assured us as he showed us around. We asked where the bathroom was. He indicated a closet-sized space with a partially bricked-up window. "It will be here. In fact, if you can give me their rent in advance, I can start working on the plumbing immediately." We decided to leave Sotiris off the list until the interior design was a little more advanced.

The day after the advertisement appeared I called my mother from the kafeneion to see how many responses we had received. Dozens! This was excellent. True, almost all of them wanted the same two weeks in July, but there was an air of excitement in the homestead that night as we folded a hand-drawn map and a copy of a six-page letter into each of twenty-two envelopes. The letter had taken days to compose. It was descriptive, sometimes lyrically so, but also honest, hinting at the ungentrified realities of village life and making no false promises about the accommodation we could provide. Such phrases as "the true Greece," "authentic rural experience" and "you'll feel like one of the family" were surely accurate, while the total absence of any entertainment or nightlife beyond Philip's kafeneion and Georgie's taverna was turned into an asset—"so quiet at night you can hear the owls." I made much of the fact that we lived in Loutses ourselves and would be on hand if help or advice were needed.

The replies and deposits reached us in April. Now it was June, and the first tourists were due to arrive on the four o'clock bus—a family from London who would be spending a fortnight at Nikolakis's house. I waited for them in the shade of the fig tree outside the silent taverna. Loutses was deep in its afternoon siesta and there wasn't a soul to be seen, and not a sound but the hiss of the cicadas. Then I heard the distant horn of the bus coming up the mountain, and a few minutes later the great blue machine was gliding around the corner, wheezing to a halt outside Kostantes's house.

The family that disembarked were touchingly English, burdened with luggage and overdressed but very polite and determined to make the absolute best of whatever they found. The two silent, preteen daughters shook my hand while their mother smiled and said, "Gosh, it *is* hot!" I picked up two of their suitcases and we started to stroll along the deserted street, climbing the track past Philip's kafeneion to the cypress grove outside the church, where we stood in the shade, enjoying the faint breeze. They admired the view of the olive groves and the colour of the distant sea and we chatted about the possibility of their renting a car.

"It's funny," said the father at one point. "We assumed from the letter that you were much older."

"Frank had a friend who retired to Majorca," explained his wife.

"But this is first class," said Frank.

"It *is* beautiful!"

"I can see how a chap could end up here and go native."

We walked on, past the place where Nikolakis made charcoal, past his beehives and his old Toyota truck to the house. Had I gone native? I still felt as English as Pimm's, though I suppose I looked foreign to their eyes—bearded and brown in old tennis shorts and a faded blue shirt.

Nikolakis and Vassiliki were asleep, of course, but their teenaged daughter, Maria, had stayed awake to greet the new tenants. It had long been the custom in the more old-fashioned Greek high schools that boys should learn the rudiments of English while girls were taught French, considered a more feminine and decorous language. Maria gave the family her best *bonjour* and led them through the farmyard, pointing out *"notre chat"* and *"nos poulets."* Then we all filed up the steep stone staircase and into the sparsely furnished apartment. The family appeared to like it.

"Please come and find me if there are any problems or questions," I suggested. "Maria will show you the way."

"Righto," said the father. I thought he wanted to shake my hand but, to my surprise, he pressed a tightly folded hundred-drachma bill into my palm. "Right, then," he added while his wife smiled and nodded.

In the summers that followed, our small business flourished. Every year brought a dozen or so families to Loutses, and most of them loved the experience. We would introduce ourselves (after the first time I made sure to shave and dress up in a clean shirt and freshly pressed white trousers, while Wendy was her usual elegant self) and invite them up to our house for drinks early in their stay, regaling them with local anecdotes and telling them about the best beaches and walks, shops and excursions. It was interesting to watch them relax into the rhythms of the village as the days went by and to listen to them describe the discoveries they made for themselves—the charm and mystery of Ano Peritheia, how excellent Georgie's souvlakia were, what a colourful life the man who ran the bar had led. Both Georgie and Philip were delighted with the sudden surge in business the strangers provided, and Kostantes and the other householders revelled in their new income.

Only two of the tourist families were ever disappointed enough to demand their money back. "There's no pool!" one woman exclaimed. "I just assumed there'd be a pool!" And off she went to Kassiopi, where she found an apartment, hemmed in by discos, that shared a swimming pool with two other properties. The other couple had come all the way from Hong Kong for their annual summer fortnight and had also hoped for something more glamorous than Petros's house. But it was the bird life that distressed them most. In my letter I had referred to the swallows swooping about at dusk. The couple were avid birdwatchers and were barely able to conceal their anger and disgust as they informed me my "swallow" was in fact the common European house martin and not at all what they had travelled halfway round the world to see. I could only plead ignorance, hand them back their deposit and drive them down to the coast to look for better accommodation and more interesting wildlife. We felt those failures were balanced when two other women, each of whom had made a point of returning every year, eventually bought and renovated their own houses in Loutses.

There was only one real calamity, and it happened during the first summer. A very pleasant family of four from the north of England were coming back up from the beach one afternoon and had reached a particularly steep and sharp bend in the road. Kostantes was freewheeling down to Peritheia on his scooter, cutting corners as usual. They collided.

The first we heard of it was when Michelle's teenaged cousin from England, who had been in the car with the family, came running down Zervou to our house. Kostantes had been taken to hospital in Corfu Town, injured who knew how badly. The man and his family were also in Corfu Town, in police custody. Michelle was with them, acting as interpreter. As rental agent, I knew I should go to the police station and try to get the man out of a jam—my duty was clear—but I was more concerned for my old friend. I went to the hospital, where I found him heavily sedated, with Alexandra sitting beside the bed, murmuring to him with tears in her eyes. Kostantes was bruised and scraped and his good leg was broken—a nasty fracture just above the knee.

"Oh, Dzimi," he whispered. "This isn't too good." Then he mustered a tiny smile. "Still, you have to look at the bright side. Now my legs match."

Weeks passed before Kostantes was allowed home, and he was on crutches for the rest of the summer. As for the Englishman, the police kept him in the station for hours, then sent him back to Loutses. No charges were laid. He felt, quite understandably, that I had let him down badly.

THE LIGHT and heat of another Greek summer . . . I was addicted to it, working up a sweat every silent afternoon, dragging stone from the rock piles at the bottom of the garden to extend our patio past the vine to the edge of the property, filling it in with the last of the rubble. We used the money we made from the tourist business to build an apothiki on the garden side of the little house across the courtyard, a long narrow room like a tunnel with a green metal door. It gave us somewhere to store our tools and our olive oil and the useful things I found on the land and kept in case they might one day be needed—small pieces of wire or wood, bottles and jars, iron nails, a couple of rusted horseshoes. Everything could be recycled, and I took pleasure in my thrift, gloating over the collection.

Because of the dramatic slope of the land, the apothiki's flat roof was level with the courtyard, and we connected them with a balcony along the side of the little house. With Kostantes still laid up, Koula's husband, Haridimos, built a waist-high brick wall around it, then plastered it and painted it white. We called it the new patio and delighted in the slightly different view it gave across the top of the olive trees and down to the sea. We might have been standing on the bridge of a ship or behind the battlements of a castle, gazing down at the garden fifteen feet below. And there were enough bricks left over to build a permanent open-air barbecue at the far end of the patio—a blessing since cooking in the kitchen added uncomfortably to the heat.

For Wendy, five months pregnant and weary, the endless days of record temperatures were a profoundly uncomfortable ordeal. In town for a check-up with Dr. Babalis, she was working her way through a list of the usual peripheral errands—shopping, paying the electricity bill, buying a new pick handle for me—and ended up standing for half an hour in a queue at the bank. The place was so hot and so full of cigarette smoke she fainted. People helped her outside with her bags, and she burst into tears of embarrassment. She took a taxi back to the village.

One day in August, when the heat was at its most intense, Michelle brought Louisa up to the house to play with Joe. They had been there an hour before she mentioned that Louisa might have caught German measles from another child in Kassiopi. Inevitably, Joe soon began to complain of a sore throat and cover his eyes when he was out in the sunshine. Wendy nursed him for days before she, too, woke up with spots on her body and a throat like fire. She had never had measles as a child and had never been vaccinated against it. The doctor told us that the disease was a serious matter, given Wendy's pregnancy, and the upstairs rooms became a dark and shuttered isolation ward, with Wendy confined to bed and Joe imprisoned in his cot and crusted in calamine lotion to relieve the itching, if not the boredom. Our guests during those weeks were left to their own devices.

By September, the heat had become more tolerable and the two invalids finally began to enjoy what was left of the summer. Many mornings were spent at Kalamaki beach. We would drive down at nine when the air was still cool and the sun not too ferocious and lay out our towels at the edge of the bamboo thicket. At such times, the beach was deserted, as smooth and perfect as it had been when Kostantes first showed it to me, with an archipelago of newly formed sandbars in the motionless water. Tiny fish darted about the shallows, to Joe's delight, and even smaller hermit crabs in borrowed periwinkle shells like red-and-white-striped turbans made their slow progress from one rock to another.

But Kalamaki was changing. Entrepreneurs from Kassiopi had begun to bring boat tours there in the early afternoon, spewing out tourists who stayed for an hour or two before embarking again to disturb the tranquility of the next bay on their itinerary. They left litter behind and we hated them.

Yanni the fisherman, whose vegetable garden and orchard Wendy and I used to raid during our first summer, had built a small hut among his lemon trees. With his wife, Chrisoula, manning a Primus stove, he had set out three or four rickety tables in the shade and now offered lunch to anyone who wished it, charging next to nothing. Chrisoula was a fabulous cook. The vegetables came from the garden, of course—ripe, juicy tomatoes chopped up with delicious cucumbers and sweet, crunchy onion, salads of grilled zucchini and more onion tossed with a fistful of chopped parsley. Wine, feta and eggs came from their farm in Loutses. Sometimes Yanni fired up his barbecue and grilled chicken; on days when he went fishing, Chrisoula would make a sort of bouillabaisse out of the little rockfish he caught, stewing them with onions, garlic, oregano and lemon juice. It was magnificent, but so were all the lunches she prepared, seasoned by our own voracious appetites.

"It's all thanks to you," Yanni said to me cheerfully. "The tourists you bring to Loutses are my customers! And things will get even better next summer when the guys from Kassiopi build their jetty. Then they can bring the caiques in—hundreds of people. And when the man who bought Spiro's land up above the road builds his hotel—"

"What!"

"You haven't heard? They start work this winter. It's going to be a beauty."

After that, our mornings at Kalamaki seemed more precious than ever.

Loutses, too, was edging slowly into the modern age. The most obvious evolution was the arrival of street lights on the main street and on the last stretch of road into the village. Joe and I were out for a walk one morning when we came across the electricians from Corfu Town bolting the heavy metal shades to the tops of the poles that carried the power lines up from the coast. A group of men had gathered to watch and comment on the operation and were enjoying a joke.

"This is the spot where your father was chased by the cypress tree, isn't it, Stavro?" chuckled one of them. Stavro scowled, but the others insisted on telling the story again. In the old days, Stavro's father would often come back up the mountain from Peritheia after dark, riding his horse—the animal could be relied on to find the way. One night, at this very bend in the road, a cypress tree had lain in wait for him and chased him into the village. The same thing happened on the following three nights, until Stavro's father took some advice. He wrapped an oily rag around a stick and when he drew close to the bend in the road he set the rag on fire and passed safely on.

"The tree never bothered him again," spluttered the raconteur, barely able to finish the story he was laughing so hard.

"It's all rubbish," said Stavro crossly. "But one thing's for sure: horses always shy when they pass by this place."

"And now you'll have light from dusk to dawn," added the foreman. "No more encounters with ghostly trees." I thought it a poor exchange, but I was clearly in the minority.

The street lights were installed by the end of the week, casting their hideous white glare into the soft darkness of the Mediterranean night. They were mounted high enough to be visible above the tops of the olive trees on the mountainside, and we found to our horror that we could see one of them from our courtyard. It seemed a violation, the worst possible kind of pollution. I sulked about it for days. Then, one night, the light was gone. A youth with a slingshot was said to have smashed the bulb, though he denied it. Years went by before it was replaced.

September also brought a more tangible threat to our peace of mind. We were sitting at the table one day, having lunch, when a group of six middle-aged men and women came strolling through the courtyard, dressed in their Sunday best. They paused at our open doors and peered in, not saying a word, then moved on again around the corner of the house.

I went to see what they wanted, but they hadn't been looking for us. They were all members of the extended Vlahos family, aunts and uncles visiting from the coast, and had come to look at the ruined building next door. "Our nephew in Athens gets out of the army in ten months' time," they explained, "and he's going to be fixing this place and living here. There's a lot of work to be done, obviously, but he's young and he's got money."

The aunts and uncles clearly didn't approve of my look of horror. They turned away and began discussing the project. Wendy and I stood out of sight inside our doorway and listened, understanding almost everything they said. The old brick beehive oven would have to go, they agreed. An extension could be added that would fill the little patio in front of the ruin and it would look marvellous with an impressive balcony built out over the pathway. From there one could have the view right down the length of our courtyard and across to Albania. "If only the oak tree next door was gone . . ."

Wendy and I went back to our lunch in despair. It seemed so unfair after we had put all our hopes into our own place. We had been naive to suppose that the other houses would never be restored. "And doubly naive," added Wendy, "to imagine that if we did have neighbours they might be courteous and considerate and respectful of our privacy. If only it wasn't going to start so soon." We talked about her great friend Chris, a successful businessman who had been out to stay several times since Joe's christening and had mentioned buying the house next door and doing it up as a holiday home of his own. He had been serious about the idea. What if the four brothers who shared ownership of the property could be persuaded to sell?

A week later, the father of the young soldier appeared to make his own assessment of the property. He was rude and dismissive, but I kept my temper. I asked if the family would consider selling and mentioned that I might know a buyer.

"No," he grunted. Then he stamped into the building, sending an angry squadron of house martins flying from the upstairs windows.

More misery—but Wendy seemed strangely confident that things would work out.

"Four brothers own it," she explained. "This one wants it for his son, but don't you think that at least one of the other three—maybe all of them—will start thinking that a fistful of dollars wouldn't be such a bad thing to have? We just have to sow the seed."

That night she went up to see Philip and casually asked him if he thought the other brothers wouldn't rather make some easy money than spend a fortune restoring the house. Philip agreed it was a reasonable premise. She left it at that, knowing that the idea would spread through the neighbourhood in no time.

"It may never happen" had become one of our mottoes and a standard response to a threat. A year earlier, rumours that two Albanians were thinking of opening a discotheque on Zervou had proved unfounded. Likewise the scheme to develop Ano Peritheia into a huge Italian-owned resort with five hundred time-share condominiums, or the plan, endorsed and perhaps even created by Philip, to turn the crater outside the great cave on the mountaintop into a vast amphitheatre where classical Greek drama could be performed to the wonder of the world. Such schemes helped pass the long winter, providing subjects for endless debate and conjecture up at the bar.

Our own future was more certain—at least in one respect. The new baby was due in mid-December, and the more we thought about it, the more we realized it would be better if we were in London when it was born. After the trials of her labour with Joe, Wendy had set her heart on an epidural, something not then offered by the heavy-handed anaesthetist at the Corfu clinic.

"And you know how damp and cold the house is in December," Wendy insisted. "I don't want to bring a new baby home to that." So it was decided—the child would be born in London, at the Westminster Hospital, and we would stay with my mother until March brought the first intimations of spring to the island.

There was also another reason for going back to England. Our beloved Land Rover had outstayed its welcome on Corfu. George the lawyer had fought several valiant battles on its behalf, wringing extensions out of the customs officers, but nothing more could be done. We were not allowed to put it up for sale. The vehicle had to be out of the country by the end of the year or it, like the poor old horsebox, would become a compulsory gift to the Greek people. The plan, therefore, was for Wendy and Joe to fly to England at the beginning of November while I took the ferry to Brindisi and drove to England. An old friend of mine who lived in France agreed to come down to Corfu and help me get the Land Rover as far as his apartment in Paris.

That autumn was particularly lovely, October bringing an endless succession of perfect warm, cloudless days. There were no more tourists to worry about, and the island breathed a long sigh of relief as life settled quietly back into its proper rhythm. The necessary chores of autumn were many, but they were familiar and brought no stress, no problem that had not been solved two thousand years ago.

When the sun was high, I would make my slow way down into the garden, following one of the delta of meandering summer pathways I had tramped through the waist-high vegetation, spending long afternoons learning to use my new sickle—don't hack; slice slowly and smoothly—then raking the yellow hay into heaps. A day for burning. Another for hauling the black plastic olive nets out of the apothiki and laying them under the trees. Alexandra was too busy with her own crop this year, but Wendy's friend Koula from Zervou had agreed to gather and press our olives while we were away, in return for half the oil. Two mornings were spent on the guttering that would fill our tank with rainwater in the coming months. Just as important, the overflow pipe had to be checked so that any excess would drain into the garden when the sterna could hold no more. Our small store of driftwood, laboriously collected over the summer, could be moved into the apothiki to keep it dry for our return.

Wendy had her own chores, packing for such an extended absence and gradually closing up the house, but she still found time to take Joe into the village three or four times a week, going through the olive groves to save herself the climb up and down Zervou. Such expeditions had their own occasional dramas. About halfway between our house and the village, the rough pathway curved around the side of a hill. A slope fell away to the left, carpeted in black olive netting; to the right, the hillside rose equally steeply, protected from erosion by an ancient wall of stacked stones. Funnel-web spiders had colonized the deep holes between the stones, and one could lure them out by tickling the mouths of their webs with the end of a blade of grass. Safely in my arms or Wendy's, Joe enjoyed watching—half fascinated, half terrified, entirely intent on the experiment.

One day, he and Wendy had paused to coax out a monster when they were suddenly attacked. A huge turkey cock, followed by a harem of ragged females, appeared out of nowhere, thrumming and furious, flapping and gobbling as it charged down the slope towards them. Joe was wearing a navy blue windbreaker with a red-lined hood over his head, and the bird had identified him as a rival male turkey. Both of them wailing, Wendy and Joe raced off down the pathway, pursued almost to the village by the myopic fowl. They came home along Zervou and did not venture into the olive groves again until the owner of the flock had corralled all the creatures back into his yard and mended the hole in his wire fence.

Mad turkeys aside, those were days of rare calm. We knew our lives were about to change again with the arrival of a second child but were equally sure we could take that in our stride. Going back to London for the winter was the greater unknown. After so long away, our interests and conversation had acquired a very narrow focus—babies, olive trees, drystone walls. Though we talked with glee of the theatres and movies, restaurants and reunions that lay ahead, we still came outside at the end of each day to sit on the old stone bench under the oak tree and gaze at the view. While Joe crouched to study the ant lines or played with his cars, we watched the light of the setting sun fade from the distant mountains of Albania, until the dusk thickened and drained the colour from things and the cool evening air sent us reluctantly indoors.

November 10, 1984

Dear Mom,

Well, THAT was an ordeal. While Jim and his friend are driving back to London, Joe and I had to fly back through Athens and we were interrogated by the airport police! Picture me, enormously pregnant and already tired as hell from the flight from Corfu and the taxi ride to the other Athens airport terminal, pushing Joe (the angel) in his pushchair all bedecked with baby bags, toys, beakers of juice, coats for London, etc., when I'm stopped at passport control. It never even occurred to me that Joe NEEDED a passport. He was written into Jim's when he was born and registered as a Brit, but of course we never thought about that. Are we out of the loop or what? Anyway, we were taken into this smoky interrogation room by two undercover malakas in big leather coats where I was asked for proof that Joe was my baby. Did I have a paper from his baptism? Something signed by the mayor of Loutses, or by a priest perhaps? No . . . But they wouldn't give up. Eventually I blurted out, "You can TELL he's my baby! He looks just like me!" They just shook their heads! One of them said to Joe, in Greek, "Where's your papa?" They thought I was some holiday wife who had married a Greek and was now trying to abscond with his precious son. If Joe had been a girl, I bet they wouldn't have given a damn! Then they poked at my pregnant belly to make sure I was really with child and not trying to smuggle a television set out of the country. I could see that the only way out of the mess was to cry . . . It worked, thank God.

And now here we are in London. Jim called last night from Urbino and sounded as if he and his friend were having a fine old time. He should be back in two or three days. Flying in from the airport, I could TASTE the filthy air. After being in Loutses so long I feel I'm in the middle of a pinball game. Still, it's wonderful to be able to have a hot bath instead of a trickling shower, and eat pork pies and watch television and take Joe to a proper playground. He loves the one in Kassiopi but it's all rusted iron and gravel. I'm pretty exhausted looking after Joe and being so hugely pregnant (I've gained 50 pounds!) and my spirits have been quite low for the last few weeks. Very low, in fact. I don't know why. There doesn't seem any reason for it. And now I'm happy to be in London and looking forward to culture and civilization for a while, but I have this entrenched bleak feeling. I hope it passes.

James has nearly finished his novel. It's all about gambling and numbers, synchronicity and magic, and between you and me it's all a bit contrived—like the magic realism books he loves and I don't. The characters talk a lot but don't ever come to life. I think he has a better book in him—but, hey, what do I know?

I think about the island all the time, despite being happy to be back in the world. Everything here feels so closed in—

I'm used to open windows, wet rain on my face, the smell of the garden, the earth under my feet instead of sidewalks. I longed for London the last few weeks on the island; now I want to be back there ASAP.

Better go—Joe will be waking up in a minute.

I miss you, Mom, and I love you.

Love,

Wendy

Chapter Eight

Our second son was born in Westminster Hospital, a week and a half before Christmas. It was not the easy delivery we had hoped for. English obstetrics was going through a groovy phase—beanbags and laughing gas instead of epidurals. Combined with the blithely indifferent attitude of the nurses, Wendy had an agonizing time delivering a burly boy who weighed more than ten pounds. He hurtled out, eager for the world, three hours after the first contraction, full of energy and crowned with a mohawk of fine red hair. It had flattened out by the time he was christened in the church at the end of my mother's street in Chelsea—just as well, given the vicar's nervous disposition. He was already disconcerted by the decision to call our son Ford Lightfoot Martin, giving him Wendy's last name, not mine. Within weeks of his birth, however, we were calling him Nibby, and that was the name that stuck.

We lived in my mother's house, taking advantage of her boundless generosity and feeling as if we were on holiday in London. I had been away only three years, and my old territory was comfortably familiar. My friends still gathered for dinner parties and all-night poker games and we quickly resumed the familiar banter, reviving ancient jokes and picking up the threads of conversations that had started in university days. Some had already found their way into the foothills of serious careers—commerce, politics, the law—and others had chosen less certain paths as actors and writers, but we all shared the robust self-confidence of youth. Success would surely be ours: it was only a matter of time. Even when the publisher who had verbally agreed to buy my novel thought better of the idea (much as he liked it himself, he explained, his colleagues found it "impenetrable, obscure and unreadable"), the setback seemed no more than a tiny delay on the sure journey to stardom.

With very little pressure I could have slipped back into my former existence, if it had not been for Corfu. The dim, damp, shivering English winter was so much less vivid and intense than the heat and light of Greece. These months were just a sabbatical from what had become real life for Wendy and me, an existence we felt we had built for ourselves and our children. The long-ago decision to leave England could not be undone so easily.

Almost from the moment of Nibby's birth, Wendy's dark depression of the previous months evaporated, and now she threw herself into finding tourists for our friends' houses in Loutses and began making plans (and lists) for our return. We had sold the Land Rover back to the farmer who originally sold it to us, and again my mother came to our aid, lending us her Vauxhall Cavalier for as long as we needed it. Her business was doing well and she had decided to let her office buy her a Mercedes.

Wendy's mother arrived in March to take a first peek at her new grandson. She would have a week in London and then fly down to Corfu with Wendy and the boys. Meanwhile, I would set off by car four days earlier and be there to meet them at the airport. We had more good news to tell her. Though my literary agent had been unable to find anyone to publish the novel, she had put together a deal with a most reputable publishing house, Weidenfeld and Nicolson, for a different kind of book altogether. Its working title was "A Kitchen in Corfu," and it was to be both a cookbook and a chronicle of the traditions of daily life in our remote little village. Wendy and I were going to write it together.

We had thrown a party when we thought the novel was going to see the light of day—an embarrassingly premature gesture. This time, we waited until the contract was signed and the small but significant advance safely banked before telling our friends.

"It'll be interesting to be back there with an actual purpose," mused Wendy. "Something other than mere survival."

THE SOLITARY DRIVE down through Europe was a delight. The Vauxhall was an automatic, swift and silent, that sucked in the rainswept French autoroute and then the sunlit Italian autostrada the way cartoon characters suck in spaghetti. I made no detours, blocking my ears to the siren songs of immortal cultural landmarks that lay so temptingly close to the highway, promising myself that Wendy and I and the boys would take this road together in a couple of years and dawdle, if need be, for months. Now I craved only speed, eating at the gas station cafeterias that straddled the motorways, sleeping in motels, aching to see our house again.

I reached Brindisi earlier than planned, caught the evening ferry and stayed awake all night, watching the island come into focus on the horizon as the early-morning light gathered power behind the mountains of Albania. Passing Corfu's northeastern promontories, I could see our house like a tiny grey square on the high, distant ridge of Zervou.

The customs officer had his usual fun with my passport, filling a page with a detailed description of the Vauxhall, then rendering it all but illegible with the smudged black imprint of his official stamp. I smiled serenely. The car was packed to the gunwales with suitcases, supplies and stuff for the new baby, but he showed no interest in any of it, dismissing me with a jerk of his stubbled chin.

The island seemed more beautiful than ever as I headed north along the coast, swooping around each familiar bend until I reached the turn-off for Peritheia. A surprise—someone had planted tall flowering bushes on each side of the straight half-mile that led into the village. A charming idea! The second surprise was so significant I had to stop the car and climb out to see for myself. The winding road up the mountain to Loutses had been paved. Not only that, it had been widened at the worst of the hairpins—space blasted out of the hillside with dynamite, the rubble bulldozed over the precipice. The old rutted track was now a ribbon of glossy new tarmac, as smooth as an airport runway. This, certainly, was progress! And to have achieved it so quickly! How uncharacteristically efficient.

And yet, I felt a certain relief as I turned left onto the steep track that led up to Zervou and felt the tires slip a little on the good old dust and gravel. At the top of the ridge, beside Dee's rock, I got out of the car again to remind myself of the view. The clarity, the great distances, the silence under the sky, the shape of the mountains, the blue mirror of the Ionian far below—it was like drinking light, absorbing some potion that dissolved care and stress and recalibrated the soul. I climbed back in the car and drove the last hundred yards home.

We had been gone four months, but the courtyard looked pretty much the same as it had on the day we left. The geranium bushes were full and healthy, the vine was already in bud, and the air was sharp with the scent of new growth. Down in the garden, the black nets spread beneath the olive trees showed Koula's meticulous hand. The irises had returned—not yet open but thrusting up like sleek green rods. The only casualties of our absence were the two gardenia bushes, which had been lifted carefully from their pots and spirited away.

I checked the ruin next door for any sign that the Vlahos brethren might have started work and was relieved to see nothing. Then I unlocked the front doors of our own house and stepped inside.

A damp, musty smell, a thickness in the air, grew more apparent as I slowly crossed to the window, waiting for my eyes to grow accustomed to the gloom. The window frames were stiffer than I remembered, but the shutters swung open with their usual clatter, spilling light into the room. I turned—and gaped. In the kitchen and bathroom, up the stairs and in patches around the front door, our beautiful whitewashed walls had turned emerald green, sheened with a film of living mould. It was a science fiction moment. An alien life form had colonized our vessel, growing in the darkness until the unsuspecting crew member, all on his own thanks to an unlikely twist in the plot, stumbled into its embrace. The scale of the infestation was impressive. I climbed the stairs and touched it where the green was deepest. It was soft and spongy, and my fingertips were wet when I pulled them away. Here and there, tiny black snails were cruising across the vertical Sargasso.

I remembered knocking two of the ground-floor windows through those massive, yard-thick walls, discovering that they had been constructed like a sandwich of stone filled with a rubble of rocks and old mortar. That filling had sucked up the winter rains like blotting paper, and Kostantes's marvellous olive-oil-based whitewash had proved the ideal organic surface for this bloom of algae.

Upstairs, things were a little better. The inner room was completely unaffected, but the south-facing wall of our bedroom was floor-to-ceiling viridian. And then I noticed Wendy's treasured grey carpet—grey no longer but mottled and swollen with reeking black and khaki mould. It felt damp as I rolled it up and carried it downstairs and out into the courtyard. I doubted it could be saved.

There were other mysteries. On a downstairs shelf, the corners of certain books looked as though they had been rubbed with a coarse file. The paper labels on some tin cans stored under the stairs had been scratched away. One of my shirts lay under the sofa, though it was barely recognizable, more a rag of chewed and shredded cotton.

No time to be lost. Wendy and Audy and the boys would be here tomorrow. Throw open all the windows. Light the wood stove and move the electric radiator up against the wall. Lay newspapers over the floor. Fetch the ladder, scrubbing brush and scrapers from the apothiki and get to work.

The green was easier to remove than the guano of ages had been two years before. In some places whole strips of it came away like damp moss. The wind soon blew away the smell and began to dry the plaster. Tomorrow would finish the job. I slept in the boys' room that night and I slept deeply—until a crash from the kitchen sent me hurrying downstairs. A pot had fallen from the shelf but there was nothing else to be seen. The door and windows were secure. Clearly, I was not alone. A stray cat, perhaps, hiding somewhere in the house? I went back to bed, straining to catch any further noises, but soon fell asleep again.

Next morning, at first light, I made a quick search of everywhere on the ground floor an animal could hide, but found no sign of anything. With the doors and all the windows open, I hoped it might leave on its own while I was upstairs working on the walls. Either way, there was no time to spare. I was meeting the weekly Olympic plane from London in a matter of hours.

Driving back from the airport, I was able to reassure everyone about the algae. The little house across the courtyard where Audy was going to sleep had survived our absence in immaculate condition, and the boys' room was dry and cosy. Our bedroom would be fine for one night until the last of the green could be dealt with. There seemed no point in mentioning the intruder until it was absolutely necessary.

That night, it struck again. Scuffling in the kitchen. The clink of crockery under the stairs.

"Is that my mom?" whispered Wendy. "She'll wake Nibby."

"Don't think so," I said.

I tiptoed downstairs and thought I heard a metallic clunk from the little gas stove, but I saw nothing.

Next morning, while the boys were playing with Audy in the little house, Wendy and I stood halfway up the stairs, leaning over the banisters and gazing down at the stove.

"Do you think it's in there?" she asked.

"It's the only place I didn't think to check."

"It looks perfectly normal. Have you used it at all since you arrived?"

"No."

"Right, then."

"Right."

We went downstairs and stood in front of the stove. The oven door squeaked when I opened it, but it was empty. I remembered, from an accident during last year's plum jam-making, that the top of the stove could be raised for cleaning, leaving the four protruding gas rings in place. Gingerly, I lifted and we peered in.

"Oh fuck," I murmured.

"Fuck," whispered Wendy.

The entire space was stuffed tight with shredded paper and tiny flecks of fabric. Our stove had been turned into a nest. And there, lying on its side, motionless with alarm, its flank twitching and yellow teeth bared, was a monstrous rat.

I lowered the heavy top again and we both stood back.

"Okay, we stay cool."

Together we slowly dragged the stove out of its niche until I could reach behind and disconnect the rubber gas pipe. Then we carefully carried it out into the courtyard, expecting at any moment to feel movement from within. The rat must have got in and out of its borrowed lair through one of the ventilation holes at the back. It might do so again while we were carrying it. We set the stove down in the hot sunshine and stared at it for a while. Wendy thought to close the front doors behind us. I lifted the hinged top again. The rat was still there, hoping, perhaps, that it hadn't been noticed. Then it suddenly seemed to sense that the game was up. In a blur, it scrambled out and down the side of the stove, streaked across the courtyard and fled into the garden.

Scouring the stove took the best part of a day, and it had rarely been so clean by the time we had finished. Nevertheless, neither Wendy nor I felt we ever wanted to eat anything cooked in that oven again. We carried it down to the apothiki and bought a new one next day in Corfu Town. Babis drove it up to Loutses for us in the back of his yellow truck. For there would be cooking to do—recipes to be tried and tested for the new book, authentic local dishes, not the hybrid casseroles and soups that were our staple for most of the year.

For the first few days following our return, the late afternoon brought a steady line of visitors, all eager to see the baby and to pinch Joe's cheek. We told each one about the cookbook and asked if we could drop by their house sometime to talk about recipes that had been handed down, traditions, secrets, anything to do with cooking in this part of the island. Nothing, they assured us, could be simpler or more pleasant than to welcome us into their homes and have us standing at their elbow while they prepared the evening meal. Did they use cookbooks of their own? Nobody in Loutses owned a cookbook. Did they measure ingredients by volume or by weight? No, they measured by eye or instinct or long experience.

"That's exactly what we're looking for," Wendy explained.

Philip, above all, threw himself behind the project, especially when we told him we wanted the book to be as much a social history of the village as a collection of recipes.

"Well, it's pretty interesting, you know, man," he pointed out, a note of challenge in his voice. We were up at the kafeneion in the early evening when the only customers were the children from the schoolhouse next door coming in to buy chocolate bars.

"I was hoping you would teach us things. How olive farming has changed since you were a boy. How to catch octopus. How you go hunting and fishing and all about the things you grow. We want to know everything."

Philip laughed, and his father, Leonidas, who had been admiring Nibby in his carriage, asked what was so funny. The explanation made him smile, and he patted Wendy's back and went behind the bar to retrieve a folded sheet of newspaper. Inside it were some long, pencil-thin, dark green spears of wild asparagus. Leoni had gathered them himself early that morning in the hills above the village.

"This one is a very big favourite of my father," said Philip. "Usually when we are looking for horta—wild plants—we don't know what we'll find. With this one, it's more like hunting."

"Is he going hunting for it again?"

"Come on, man. Every day, while it lasts. For two or maybe three weeks. In most of Greece, they're forgetting this plant, except here on Corfu and maybe also Crete."

"Can I go with your father next time?" asked Wendy.

"Well, why don't you just ask hims yourself?"

Leonidas liked the idea of an accomplice on his asparagus hunt, and the next morning at seven, with the sun still a fat tangerine balancing on the ridge to the east, Wendy walked down to the village armed with an old plastic bag and a kitchen knife. It was a perfect spring morning, cloudless but cool. A faint hint of a breeze stirred the long, soft grasses along Zervou.

Leonidas was waiting in the road outside the bar, and the two of them set off immediately with Philip's old yellow dog quartering the path ahead of them, tail wagging and nose to the ground. They passed the paddock at the top of the village where Stamati's wife, Maria, was sitting on a stool, milking one of her ewes. Wendy made a mental note that we would have to include feta-making in the book. They strolled by Kosta, chef-patron of the Kapricorn in Ano Peritheia, a pre-breakfast cigarette stuck to his lower lip, busy beneath the hood of his truck. Then they were past the last house, climbing by a barely discernible track off the road and into the hills.

The breeze was stronger out of the valley. Philip's dog loped along at their heels.

"Does he think we're hunting?" asked Wendy in Greek.

Leonidas shook his head. "He can see we don't have a gun. He probably thinks you have some souvlakia for him."

The pace slowed as they mounted a ridge above a narrow fold of the land. Wendy had never been to this hillside before.

The view northward was spectacular, a broad slice of the glittering Ionian with Albania's mountains climbing sharp and clear on the horizon. All around, last year's yellow grasses and wild plants were thigh-high, a thick and spiky obstacle course that left her jeans covered with burrs. The dog picked his way behind them, treading in their footsteps, disliking the going. Here and there were patches of wild wheat, brown and dry as wire. Leonidas explained that during the end of the war, when the Germans had control of the island and the people were starving, some farmers had tried to sow wheat in high secret places like this. Nothing had come of it, but you could still find ears of wheat growing wild among the other grasses.

"What was it like here during the war?"

Leonidas shrugged but said nothing. Then an unexpected memory made him smile.

"Up there, in the mountains, we saw something drop from a British plane flying very low. We went to see. It was a sack full of pairs of shoes. Very good shoes."

He bent down, parting the stiff yellow grass with his hands. Close to the ground, the new plants of spring had started their struggle. They were too small to pick, but Leonidas recognized most of them—*lappato, sinapi, pikralithia, rathiki.* Wendy wrote down the names in her notebook and looked them up when she came home: burdock, wild mustard, a kind of chicory, dandelions. "They're for another day," he explained. A little farther on he found the first asparagus plants, just two or three stalks, each about four inches high, sticking straight up, proud amidst the tangle of undergrowth. A nick of his knife and they were in the bag.

"I could have stayed out there all day long," said Wendy when she came home in the middle of the morning, "but he had to get back to work on the vines with Philip." In spite of her protestations, Leonidas had given her the expedition's entire booty—enough wild asparagus for a small lunch, a couple of tiny grape hyacinths with blue flowers that could be boiled up with the asparagus, and some early mint that Philip had folded into a sheet of newspaper for keeping in the fridge.

Joe wasn't keen on the asparagus, but Wendy and I found it delicious, cooked that day according to one of Philip's proffered recipes—trimmed, boiled for fifteen minutes in a large pot of water, then dressed with olive oil, salt and lemon juice. Amazingly, the stalks were still a little tough, but their robust, slightly bitter taste seemed the very flavour of the colour green.

Leonidas took Wendy horta hunting again in April, and by the end of the season we felt confident enough about recognizing edible plants to go foraging on our own, though without the reassuring presence of Philip's dog we were obliged to thump the ground with a stick in the wilder, deeper garigue. The year's burgeoning heat made snakes bolder.

Slowly the book began to gather momentum. Philip's knowledge proved deep indeed. A couple of times he came to dinner at our house, arriving close to midnight after the kafeneion closed and his chores were done. He disliked talking into the tape recorder, feeling it cramped his anecdotal style, and his habit of emphasizing a point by thumping a fist on the tabletop invariably woke the baby. As the summer season kicked in and the nightspots of the coast opened up, there was also a sense that he would rather be relaxing in some bouzouki joint or favoured club. But he was patient with our endless questions.

He truly came into his own when we started to ask him about the sea. As a boy, he remembered playing truant, using a shortcut to run straight down the mountainside to the coast in fifteen minutes, swimming and diving for sea urchins, then running back up to the village, appearing at the kitchen door almost before he was missed. We asked him to show us how to dig for clams on the sandbars at Kalamaki and how to fish for octopus from the rocks during the springtime, with a cruel hook on the end of a long bamboo pole, a fluttering rag as bait. He said we had better ask Leonidas. "These are things, I can say, for old men to do," he cautioned. "Me, I prefer to dive for thems."

"Can you show us?"

"Maybe. It's depending on the wind. This wind, from the north, is no good. The blastards leave their holes and hide deeper, in the weed, when the wind is pushing the sea hard down through the straits. The best wind is the one who comes from the southeast. Maybe next week."

Next week it was, and Philip and I drove down the mountain one morning in his old orange Volkswagen van and parked by a cove called Siki, about halfway between Kassiopi and Peritheia. Down at the water's edge, under the silent gaze of a family of tourists, we prepared ourselves. Philip wore trunks, a faded purple muscle shirt, a mask and snorkel, a lethal-looking knife in a sheath that strapped to his leg and a pair of black flippers. He tucked a plastic carrier bag and a lemon into a canvas-backed net bag that fastened around his waist and finished the ensemble by tying his sandals to it with a piece of wire. I had nothing but trunks, flippers, snorkel and mask. "And keep your T-shirt on, man. It gets cold in the water." He picked up his spear gun, and I flapped after him into the sea.

I saw what he meant about the cold. There were no tepid shallows at Siki. Twenty feet from the beach, I was out of my depth. We pulled down our masks and began to paddle slowly along the rocky shoreline, gazing down into the green depths.

In the van, Philip had told me how much better it was to go snorkelling at night, when the sea seemed much more active and the narrow beam of his underwater torch took all sorts of creatures by surprise, from slender, green-boned garfish to the quick rust-coloured crabs that were the octopus's principal prey. There were few if any large fish left in the waters around Corfu. Even the winter shoals of sardines that had once choked the bay of Apraos (Kalamaki's real name), bringing the men of Loutses down to stand waist-deep in the bone-chilling surf, hauling in the heavily laden nets, had long since disappeared.

This morning, all I saw were black sea urchins and occasional glints of silver—the little wrasses and blennies that scooted away as our dark shapes passed above them. We looked into every cove, coming right into shore until our heads almost bumped the rocks. Then I would look up, the perspective would change, and I would find myself in the familiar, sunlit world, floating in a few feet of water. Duck back down and the green depths reopened to receive me. I quickly lost all sense of time. We might have been out there five minutes or an hour when Philip started to move his arms to attract my attention, pointing down at the sand and rock below us. Fragments of orange and white crab shell lay outside a dark crevice. He dived down—the water was much deeper than I had imagined—and gently prodded the barbed tip of his spear gun into the hole. He squeezed the trigger and the heavy elastic shot the trident about six inches farther. Then he dropped the gun and kicked for the surface.

"We wait, man," he panted, once the snorkel was free of his mouth. "You can't try and pull the blastard out. Wait for him to come." Grinning, he jammed in his mouthpiece and dipped his head back underwater.

I could hear the roar of my breathing in the plastic snorkel as we floated there. Then the tip of a tentacle emerged from the hole. Then another, and before I could react the octopus billowed out, heading for the depths. But the harpoon was in it and Philip was already down there, lifting the creature to the surface and into the air, pulling up his mask. The tentacles wrapped themselves around his arm, but he pulled them away with a sound like Velcro and quickly reached under the octopus's head, turning its body inside out with one deft gesture and plucking off the ink sac and entrails. Treading water, he slipped the catch into his pouch.

Blinking in the sun, we looked at each other. Philip was laughing. My own sense of triumph was tempered by pity for the gallant octopus.

"Come on, man," said Philip. "Think how happy thems crabs will be."

We paddled along the shore to a place where a flat black rock sloped conveniently into the water, and I hauled myself out. Philip was busy with his bag. Then he dived again. I pulled off my T-shirt and let the sun dry me, feeling the heat turn the salt to crystals on my grateful skin.

Philip emerged, holding the plastic bag. There were holes in it and the water drained out onto the hot, dry rock, staining its grey surface black until the sun corrected the colour. I watched him retrieve the octopus from his pouch and throw it a couple of dozen times against the rock—necessary tenderization, he explained. Then he rinsed it in the sea and began to rub it vigorously on the flat slab as if it were a slippery rag. At last, he sat down beside me.

The octopus looked white in the sun, except for a hint of pale pink along its suckers. Philip took his knife and cut off one of its tentacles, then cut me a thin slice. The meat was sweet and delicate and decidedly tender. "He's a pretty okay size. You take him home and cook him in wine."

He tipped a couple of purple sea urchins out of the plastic bag and set to work with his knife, knocking off the spines and enlarging the small mouth at the base of each one. Using the bag as a mitt, he picked one up, stuck the knife in and stirred. Then he cut a wedge off the lemon, squeezed some juice into the opening and handed it across to me. I ate it with my fingers, dipping them in as if they were toast and the urchin a soft-boiled egg, and, indeed, it tasted a little like egg yolk but infused with some quintessence of the sea, like the scent of rock pools on some pristine coastline. After a while, we swam slowly back to Siki beach—all of ten minutes away. We had been out two hours.

THAT SUMMER, both Wendy and I felt our lives had significantly improved. The house was working well. We were healthy and strong and used to the baby game, comfortable in our routines, far more relaxed the second time around. The old down-to-the-minute time-sharing regimen was no longer so strictly enforced. We spent the long mornings together doing family things, going down to the beach, shopping, cooking, keeping Joe and Nibby amused. After lunch, Wendy and I took turns seizing a couple of hours off to try to get some writing done. She was working on a short story, and the little she had let me read was excellent. There seemed more time to do whatever had to be done and more time for each other. We took greater pleasure than ever in the year's crop of houseguests, and they probably found us better company, less anxious as hosts.

Chris flew over from Canada and whirled Wendy and Joe to Vienna for a week's vacation on his generous dime. Nibby and I took advantage of the days alone to perfect the art of crawling across the bedroom unaided. At dusk, we would stand quietly outside in the courtyard and wait for the little scops owl in the oak tree to start calling—a single peep every twenty or thirty seconds. Later, in his cot, his favourite teddy bear held tight to his chest, Nibby would listen for the sound and imitate it with a whispered coo before finally falling asleep.

Eddy also returned, with his wife, and marvelled at the changes in the property. He was pleased to see his initials still graced the cement top of the borthro. For old times' sake, I soon put him to work, lugging rocks from the garden up to the steep rubble slope of the driveway, slowly transforming it into a smooth and elegant ramp. We worked hard, partly for the sheer pleasure of physical exertion but also because time was suddenly of the essence. Our neighbour Yorgos the carpenter had grown tired of the beating his van took on Zervou's uneven track and had organized for the road along the ridge to be cemented over. If we could prepare our drive-way, we could partake of the plan.

We were still dragging rock on the ordained day, using Joe's old blue plastic bath as a barrow, still stomping and raking gravel onto the surface as the road-making party came into view over the ridge. Twenty men from the village, the cement mixer from Peritheia, the old routine of borrowed hoses and water . . . Load by load, the tide of cement crept down towards us like cold grey lava, pushed and raked and patted by the men.

"It doesn't seem right, using a machine to mix cement," observed Eddy.

"The march of progress."

By nightfall we had a road leading onto our property. When the rains came in the autumn it proved a mixed blessing. The car could get up and down it with relative ease instead of spinning its wheels in mud. But the smooth cement acted as a chute, catching the water that fell on Zervou and channelling it neatly down onto our courtyard, together with whatever sticks and stones and other detritus the stream had gathered. Two precious flower beds were washed away before I figured out how to divert the flood down into the garden.

The new-and-improved road surface now allowed Dimitri the greengrocer to include Zervou on his route through the mountain villages. Two or three times a week, in the late afternoon, he appeared in his van, honking his horn to attract attention and parking just below Yorgos's house.

Dimitri was an exceptionally gregarious man, spreading news and gossip from one village to another, and even women who didn't want to buy his carrots or peaches, watermelons, potatoes, fresh herbs or whatever else was in season down on the coast sauntered out of their houses to see what he had to say. I told him once about Jimmy, the greengrocer of my childhood with his horse and cart—same name, same occupation—but my Greek wasn't up to the anecdote and he just smiled at me as if I was half-witted and said he had never owned a horse. Wendy liked to carry Nibby up the road to look at the vegetables, and we would spread a blanket in the great brass weigh scales that hung above the zucchini and lay him upon it to see how much he had grown since the week before. He was certainly putting on weight—a proper little bruiser with the merriest temperament in the world.

In the spirit of scientific enquiry, I often quizzed Dimitri about his produce, and the ladies of Zervou would listen until they could bear it no longer, all chiming in at once with criticisms and recommendations, testimonials to the usefulness of rock celery in a soup or the superior quality of pears from their own garden. Meanwhile Dimitri's pretty red-haired wife sat in the cab of the van, totally indifferent to the hubbub.

No doubt the grocer's good offices were partly responsible, but word of our book was spreading. Shopping one day in Spiro's store in Peritheia, on the way home from the beach, we were waylaid by his mother, who came bustling out of the kitchen at the back of the shop when she heard our voices. Was it true we had been writing down a recipe for rabbit stifado from a woman in Aghios Ilias—a woman notorious for using far too many pearl onions and far too little vinegar whenever she prepared the dish? Come by tomorrow and taste a stifado as God intended it to be cooked, properly seasoned with all ingredients in a most righteous balance. We promised we would.

The mothers and grandmothers of our own village were just as eager to assist in our education, though they wanted nothing to do with me. Propriety insisted that it was Wendy who went up to Koula's house on the day she made salt cod with garlic sauce or to another kitchen farther up the village where a cook famous for her quince jam and sour cherry spoon sweets was about to embark on the new vintage. Wendy's Greek was so much better than mine that she soon took on almost all of the research, sometimes giving Michelle money to translate when the subject matter was particularly arcane or the interviewee in need of reassurance.

My contribution centred more on the men of the village. At first, this had seemed likely to prove a most daunting task, since every one of them was quick to imply that he had the skills and experience to open a Michelin-starred restaurant if only he weren't quite so busy. I soon discovered, however, that only those who had actually cooked professionally were prepared to discuss anything more esoteric than the barbecue. Philip, of course, had been a steward on a ship. So had two other men—Christos and Spiro—and this year, with a bumper crop of our *Sunday Times* tourists expected in the village, both had decided the time had come to turn their experience into money.

We had known Christos by sight long before we discovered his name. He was a friend of Philip's and had a thick black Pancho Villa moustache. Back from the merchant navy and a stint as a caterer in Athens, he had formed a consortium with Tasso the electrician and a couple of other men and had bought the old police station on the main street of the village. They intended to turn it into a restaurant of such irresistible quality that every tourist from Roda to Kassiopi would have no choice but to make their way up the smooth new road into the mountains and dine there seven times a week.

Spiro was more of an unknown quantity. He had inherited a large house on Zervou where his wife and infant children lived while he was at sea, protected by his mother, a six-foot-high chicken-wire fence and a dog of noisy ferocity. During the winter, Georgie had decided to retire from the taverna business, and Spiro had rented the property, intending to give Christos a run for his money.

The two enterprises could not have been more different. Working all winter long, the Christos group had transformed the police station, drawing deeply on Tasso's considerable expertise and connections in the building trade. A handsome marble-topped patio thrust out into the street with room for half a dozen tables, each demurely dressed in a red-and-white gingham cloth. The dining room was immaculate and dominated by a long bar of glossy, richly stained wood. On the wall behind it, hidden lights gleamed off rows of imported liqueurs. The kitchen was brand new and featured ten of the latest high-tech stainless steel rotisseries and a massive, properly ventilated charcoal brazier.

A hundred yards away but on the opposite side of the street, Spiro relied on Georgie's lean-to souvlaki grill and a nervous optimism. The rickety old tables now had a firmer footing, for he had cemented over the old dirt garden where we had danced at Joe's christening. A heavy coat of whitewash had been splashed over the outside of the building, smothering detail, navy style, and the ancient blue jukebox was gone, replaced by a powerful hi-fi system, the speakers concealed in the trees.

Both tavernas chose the same weekend in May to open. Friends and relatives of the rival parties came from various parts of the island, and the main street was choked with cars. It was understood that this was not the occasion to sit down and order a formal meal. Instead, the relative merits of the two kitchens could be judged by the dishes of mezethes that accompanied the beer, ouzo, retsina or whatever other drink the customer ordered.

Spiro, looking simultaneously flustered and exhilarated, was relying heavily on souvlakia—foolproof and always delicious—while his wife and a team of volunteers worked in the kitchen, cooking french fries, slicing cucumbers and dressing plates of feta cheese with olive oil and oregano. Each morsel was speared with a toothpick for the sake of daintiness.

Christos had decided more elaborate fare was in order. There were tiny tyropittakia of soft, sweet cheese folded inside triangular envelopes of crisp phyllo pastry, all made by Tasso's wife, Dimita. There were fried sardines and slivers of grilled calamari surrounded by a salad of grated, vinegar-dressed white cabbage. Little mounds of white tzatziki and beige-brown mashed eggplant were ringed with juicy black olives. Saganaki—slices of firm kephalotyri cheese heated to sizzling point under the broiler—appeared in their small, piping hot saganaki pans, handled by the waiters with as much care as if they were plutonium rods. The dish that drew most praise, however, was a black ragout of chicken giblets, seethed for hours with vinegar, brandy and garlic, full of soft textures and gamy flavours.

I imagined that Christos had won the battle hands-down, but the villagers soon corrected me. Wait and see, they said. We have all summer to make up our minds. Yes, Christos's place is smarter and the food more elaborate, but Spiro's prices are lower and the feel of the place more relaxed.

I wasn't the only curious gourmet wandering back and forth between the two establishments that night, picking my way through the throng of giggling children in the middle of the street. They had found the one spot where the sound systems of both restaurants were equally loud (just outside Stamati's shop) and danced in circles, revelling in the cacophony. The music could probably be heard in Corfu Town.

CORFU TOWN . . . Over the years, the name, even the thought of the place had meant little to us but chores. The gynecologist, the pediatrician, the tool shop, the tinsmith, the lawyer, the airport, the bank, the customs house, the notary public all demanded a trip *sti' boli*—to town. None of these associations had actually disappeared, but they had dwindled steadily in importance—or was it that we had grown more used to their ways, more adept at coping with inefficiency and delay, more patient?

"We should all go in some day and simply enjoy it," announced Wendy one morning as she set out a breakfast of ripe, super-juicy, grapefruit-sized peaches and yoghurt—mashed for Nibby, unmashed for the rest of us. The night before, we had entertained a family of tourists for drinks—a straitlaced quartet from Scotland who were renting Maro's house, opposite Spiro's taverna. Decibels had settled down in the village as the novelty of the duelling restaurateurs wore off, but you never knew with tourists. This family had decided to take the experience in their stride, putting it down to local colour. The father did most of the talking. He clearly fancied himself an amateur historian and had done his research before coming on holiday. We swapped trivia about the island—increasingly competitively—until our wives skilfully but firmly distracted us. He had been most enthusiastic about the delights of Corfu Town and was genuinely shocked that in all our years on the island we had never even visited the archaeological museum.

"We could just act like tourists," continued Wendy. "Stroll around, duck into a church or two, have a coffee on the 'Spianada, have lunch somewhere . . ."

"Sounds great."

"Buy a newspaper."

"Just relax!"

"And we could stop at the pediatrician on the way in."

"And then pick up that guttering."

No! Not this time! No duties. No lists. An outing purely for pleasure.

We dressed up for the occasion, me in white trousers (which would have been destroyed by the merest suggestion of building supplies) and a clean striped shirt, the boys in T-shirts, shorts and tiny sun bonnets. Wendy looked absolutely gorgeous in pink culottes, a white top, sunglasses and a straw hat—like some French movie star on the beach at Cannes, on holiday but not quite *inconnue.*

For once, the drive into town was a delight—no buses or gear-grinding trucks labouring down out of the mountains keeping us trapped in the shadow of their diesel exhaust. The winding coast road gave up its usual succession of heart-stoppingly beautiful views, and even the straight mile of Ipsos, where the beach had been ruined by a strip of night-clubs beloved of drunken English tourists, seemed possessed of a raffish charm.

We pulled into the car park beside the cricket pitch in the centre of town before nine o'clock. Out in the suburbs, no doubt, our usual ports of call were already well into the working day—trucks loading up with sand and cement, marble, timber and tiles. Here, the elegant cafés along the 'Spianada were barely awake. Waiters were hosing down the promenade in front of the Liston, the arched stone colonnade built long ago by Napoleon's occupying army and modelled on the rue de Rivoli in Paris. Tables and chairs were still stacked under the trees. No matter. We strolled across to the old Venetian citadel and peered down over the wall at the little boats far below. A fisherman was working out in Gouvia bay, a silhouette against the glittering water, standing up in his shallow skiff to throw a small round net into the sea—a technique as old as time.

The determination to do nothing at all that day did not include shopping. At the newspaper kiosk, I bought a copy of the *Times* (only two days old) for the crossword and a *Herald Tribune* for the baseball scores, then we made our slow way through the maze of lanes to the market in the fosse of the other Venetian fortress.

Joe loved the market. He had reached the vocabulary-gathering stage in his development, constantly pointing at things and asking their name, absorbing the information like a small blond sponge. So we paused before the pyramids of glossy purple eggplant, the boxes of zucchini with their orange flowers, the early tomatoes and artichokes, the mounds of delicate green lettuces. The old ladies sitting on stools in their layers of black, herbs and horta spread out on newspapers before them, cackled with laughter at Nibby's smiling face, and one of them placed a tiny bouquet of sweet basil in the pushchair. Fishmongers held up crabs for the children to see, their claws still waving, signalling frantically for rescue. Only the man who sold caged songbirds, farther into the market among the basket shops, met with Joe's disapproval. He thought it cruel to keep birds in a cage and stood and stared in solemn reproach.

On the way back to the 'Spianada, we paused at the yoghurt shop, a small, dark, cool emporium run by a young man so pale and fat we imagined he never ventured into the sunshine. "Is the man made of yoghurt?" asked Joe. We bought two tubs of the strained ewe's milk variety, thick and rich as clotted cream under its sweet yellow crust, and watched while the youth slowly turned them into a parcel with squares of cardboard, white paper and yards of string.

Next to the cathedral of St. Spiridon was the vintner's, a dark, tiled cavern of a place where someone was always splashing water into a barrel and the sharp smell of new wine hung in the air. Townspeople came by daily with their empty plastic 7-Up bottles, choosing red, white, dry rosé or retsina straight from the barrel. We always chose the rosé because it tasted faintly of wild strawberries, but I had left our big glass demijohn back at the house and I didn't feel like guzzling two litres of pop just to get a container. The vintner grudgingly retrieved an empty glass bottle from the back of the store, wedging in an old cork as a stopper, and we slipped it tidily under the pushchair. By now, the cafés along the Liston were open, and we sat and ate slender toasted ham and cheese sandwiches while some sipped Greek coffee or a cup of the local cappuccino and others drank orangeade through a straw or sucked on a bottle of milk.

No doubt we passed for tourists, but neither Wendy nor I felt we were. This was our island and this was our town. Though we had not been born here, we had chosen it as our home, were Corfiots by an act of will, not an accident of birth. Whenever a waiter struck up a conversation we soon brought it round to the fact that we lived here, in Loutses, year round, in a house that we owned. A small house, to be sure, with many idiosyncrasies—but ours.

Detail by detail, life in the village was getting easier. The paved road up to Loutses seemed to inspire the local politicians (both those who actually held office and those who only played poker at Philip's bar), and before the season was over plastic garbage boxes had been installed at key points all the way down to the coast, emptied once a week by a noisy municipal truck. They were hideous and filled up rather too quickly, but everybody agreed they were an amazing improvement on back-yard incineration or the random abandonment of plastic bags.

Burning anything in the back yard was forbidden by law that summer with so many wildfires burning around the northern Mediterranean. The village had its share. One night we were woken by the church bells, and I was surprised to see Wendy clamber out of bed and start pulling on her jeans and cowboy boots.

"I'm actually going to do it this time."

She had often declared her intention to join the firefighters—bringing an annoying smile of disbelief to Philip's lips—and that night she would not be dissuaded.

"Don't worry," she said with a broad, excited smile on her face and she was gone, leaving me holding the baby. She came back four hours later, full of stories of beating out embers with a bough cut from a wild olive tree, her clothes smelling faintly of woodsmoke.

Now that her Greek was so good, Wendy's friendship deepened with Koula and Renna, the two young mothers up on Zervou. In their teens they had married a pair of brothers and lived in neighbouring houses, looking after their in-laws and their own small daughters and working hard in the olive groves. It was the late-night custom, during the summer, for some of the men of the village to head down to the coast once Philip's had closed. Wendy or I had often noticed their familiar trucks parked outside certain discos and bars as we drove back from a jaunt to the casino. But their wives were not invited.

"Do you know Koula and Renna have *never* been down there to have their own night on the town?" said Wendy one day. "It's so incredibly unfair!"

"They probably don't want to go," I suggested, instantly regretting the remark. Next morning Wendy climbed

Zervou to Koula's house and made her proposal—a girls' night out, that very week. Koula laughed and pretended to fan herself at the boldness of the notion. Renna smiled in her quiet way and asked what they would do.

"Whatever we want," said Wendy.

So the three women drove down to Kassiopi and strolled about the harbour for a while. They went into a bar and had a beer. They ate souvlakia at a restaurant and generally had a hilarious time, telling mildly scurrilous stories and paying little attention to anyone but themselves. If news of their escapade inspired the other women of Loutses to start a domestic uprising, no word of it ever reached our ears.

But the outing further solidified Wendy's friendship with the pair, especially Koula. She was fifteen years old when she married Haridimos, a man twice her age, and sixteen when she gave birth to her daughter, Antigone. Nothing strange about that—it was the way things were in the countryside. Still, it struck us as a young age to leave home and to enter into the responsibilities of a triple role as mother, wife and dutiful daughter-in-law. Renna's story was similar, but while she never lost her shyness around Wendy, Koula was more forthcoming. When she came down to visit—always bearing a small gift of oil or olives or pomegranates from the magnificent bush that grew beside her house—she and Wendy could talk for hours. Joe and Antigone (everyone except the village priest called her Andy) sat beside them at the table, drawing; Nibby and I took the hint and wandered upstairs or out into the courtyard to play, listening to the gales of laughter from the kitchen.

With Michelle, Wendy's conversations usually centred on nostalgia for the luxuries of life in their homelands—washing machines, central heating, videos and cinemas, supermarkets and Mothercare stores, reliable babysitting. With Koula, strangely enough, the bond seemed more primal. Wendy never mentioned to me how suddenly she had felt dragged into adulthood when Joe was born—the momentous and unsupported change from a privileged girl to a responsible woman. But she discussed it with Koula, at our dining-room table or up on Zervou or down at Kalamaki on a Sunday afternoon, standing hip-deep in the sea.

"What were you talking about?" I asked.

"Nothing." By which she meant everything.

"Please tell me."

"Oh, we talked about our periods, and how difficult it is for her to lose weight when she loves bread so much and how hard it is for me to gain weight, and about how tired we get, and how neither of us has particularly nice clothes, and how life is good all the same. You know, she thinks we live like paupers."

"What!"

"That's what they all think. They pity us."

"I thought we lived like kings!"

"Apparently not."

I envied Wendy her close relationship with the other young mothers of Loutses. I could see no equivalent for myself. My Greek wasn't good enough to inveigle myself into the poker circles up at the bar, and besides, the games they played, rotten with wild cards and obscure house rules, made a mockery of the science of gambling. Philip and I were friends, but that meant swapping stories and discussing sports and olive trees and politics. Man's deeper emotional landscape was not on the itinerary, though he had no trouble journeying there in his conversations with Wendy. Perhaps the problem lay in my English reserve, a buttoned-down reticence that some might have seen as a weakness but which I took for granted and of which I was even a little proud.

It was Renna, not Koula, who took Wendy down with her into the olive groves early one cool October morning, to spend the day together and give us material for the book. The land beneath the olive-laden trees was already cleared, but the black plastic nets had still to be spread beneath them. Walking in from the road to the particular hillside that needed work took a good twenty minutes, far enough that the rolled-up nets had been slung over low-hanging branches for the summer without fear of theft. Now they had to be hauled down and flattened around the trees, weighted with stones and laced together with twigs. Wendy and Renna left Loutses at dawn and worked hard all morning, stopping around eleven o'clock for the *marenda,* a fortifying little meal of bread, Spam, feta cheese and olives, washed down with water. The afternoon brought more of the same—back-breaking work, devoid of romance. They toiled on when the rain started to fall, filtered into heavy drops by the trees until Wendy felt she was standing beneath a leaky shower. Renna called a halt only when the twilight crept in under the canopy of leaves, wincing as she straightened her back.

"I have to go home, Wendimou. I have to get dinner ready."

"This is such hard work!"

Renna just shrugged. "Ti na kame? What can one do?"

When Wendy came home, sodden and aching, she was in no mood for banter.

"Renna knows a couple in the village. He has to get up at six every morning to get down to the building site. She gets up before him, makes him coffee, fixes his lunch, lays out his clothes. She even buckles his belt for him, just like his mother used to do before he was married."

"They're not all like that," I pointed out—meaning *we're* not all like that. "And things will change. The next generation . . ."

We were beginning to see beneath the surface of Loutses, to notice the undercurrents of the traditional rural way. We caught a glimpse of them from a different perspective on the autumnal afternoon we spent interviewing the wisewoman from Zervou. She, it turned out, was a rather sophisticated lady who had spent much of her married life in Athens, and she sat with us out in the courtyard wearing a grey cardigan and an Hermès scarf over her hair. Michelle translated while I dutifully wrote down the dozens of remedies she knew for everyday ailments, everything from a decoction of camomile tea for sore eyes to a complicated embrocation of oleander leaves, chili pepper, white paraffin and olive oil to ease the ache of rheumatism.

"And if you ever want to know if someone has put the evil eye on you," she remarked after we had finished, "hold three cloves in a candle's flame. If they all shatter, the curse was indeed upon you but now is gone. If they just blacken, it is still upon you. To find out who gave you the evil eye, drop grains of charcoal into a glass of water and say the names of those you suspect. The charcoal will sink when you guess correctly."

Her words came back to me in November. I had driven the boys down to a remote beach to play, but the surf was thundering, each heavy breaker thick with dark brown seaweed.

Then the grey sky opened and we scampered back to the car, sitting there singing songs until it was clear the rain had set in for the rest of the day. By the time we reached the coast road, they were both asleep.

I thought I'd give Wendy an extension on her time alone and drove slowly and aimlessly up into the mountains along lanes I didn't recognize. The olive trees loomed black and dripping over the road. I approached a man trudging uphill, and he held out his hand to wave me down for a lift. I should have stopped, but to do so would have woken the children. I saw him in the rearview mirror, his face angry, his hand jabbing at us, giving the evil eye.

December 13, 1985

Dear Ros,

Today is Nibby's birthday and we had a little party with Michelle, Louisa and the girls from Zervou. Jim baked a chocolate cake with a soft chocolate and hazelnut frosting and we let your grandson make as much of a mess with it as he wanted. His first chocolate experience! He absolutely loved it and the other children thought it was the funniest thing in the world to see half his face covered in cake and brown goo. Thank you for the gorgeous clothes you sent him—he looks like a little cherub in the yellow sweater—and he LOVES the toy with the wooden cogs and wheels. We've attached it to the inside of his cot and he plays with it as soon as he wakes up.

Sorry we haven't phoned in a while but a storm knocked

the line out for days and also we're trying to save money—not that there's anything to worry about! It's more a matter of pride in our own self-sufficiency. Our living expenses are about 80 pounds a month, though that's bound to go up now that we've bought a second heater for our bedroom. Everyone says it's going to be a very cold winter and the valiant little wood stove downstairs can only do so much. Still, the house is very cosy, especially at night when the wind howls outside and the rain drums down on the roof. Joe is worried about the ants in the courtyard drowning. Even the little house is cosy. We move the radiator out there for an hour and it seems to keep the heat very well and is dry as a bone. Jim types out there late into the night after the rest of us have gone to sleep and picks up the midnight news from the BBC World Service on the tiny shortwave radio. The static's awful but he can usually make out what they're saying (they do enunciate beautifully) and in the morning tells Joe and me what's going on in the outside world. It all seems a very long way away. Far more important is the fact that there isn't a single onion left on the island. The rain ruined the entire crop so Jim can't test the recipe for onion pie until next spring! Never mind. Siga siga, as everyone says here all the time—take things easy, slowly but surely. It used to infuriate us when we needed something done in a hurry, but I guess we've become more philosophical over the years.

Apart from the onion recipe, the book research is going well. We finally interviewed Old Tomas. He's well into his nineties but he only stopped helping out his daughter-in-law, Maro, last year because his knees started to ache. Until then he had gone down to the olive groves every day, bringing back wood and bundles of forage for the family goat. He drinks a glass of fresh goat's milk every day and eats nothing but bean soup, horta and yoghurt. He says that's what has kept him healthy and made him live so long, but Philip says it's actually because he's never done a real day's work in his life.

Talking of P, I surprised him the other night by talking quite fluently in Greek with someone at the bar. Later on he said, "You know, man, your Greek is getting okay." Praise indeed. Of course he still refuses to talk to me in Greek, just like he insists on calling your son James, not Dzimi or Dmitri like everyone else does.

We really feel part of the community now, and the more research we do for the book, the better we understand how things work here—the way the big extended families interact and their complicated system of loyalties. Because Philip is our koumparos, we're kind of attached to the Parginoses—also because of our old association with Kostantes, I suppose. It's very casual, but it gives us a sort of discreet identity. I was shopping in Peritheia the other day and heard someone ask who I was, and Spiro explained we were from Loutses and that Philip was our koumparos. We're local now—not foreigners—and it's a good feeling. When we're in Corfu Town and we see someone else from Loutses we smile and shake hands—there's a definite bond between us—as if we're all travellers in the world outside our village. I'm not explaining this very well. I suppose I just mean that Loutses is our home now. The days are long and busy, full of a thousand small things that have to be done, a thousand small problems that have to be solved, but it's real life—much more so than life in a city—and we are very, very happy.

Love,

Wendy

P.S. Joe drew this picture for you. It's a kind of South American monkey called a red-faced wakari that he saw in his big wildlife book and it's currently his favourite animal.

Chapter Nine

The most charming legacy of Venice's four-hundred-year occupation of Corfu was the carnival held in Corfu Town every February on the last weekend before Lent. It had once been an excuse for a universal party, but these days only young children dressed up in costumes and masks to be led through the streets by their proud parents. We had told my mother about the tradition, and in February of 1986 a parcel arrived containing outfits for the boys. Joe was almost three; Nibby was fourteen months old: both took a keen delight in their matching costumes—baggy white cotton romper suits covered in tiny brown hearts. I was out working on the herb garden in the cold sunshine when they came toddling around the corner of the house to show me their finery—two tiny, gleeful blond harlequins. They wore the outfits every day, and though the carnival itself was a tad disappointing—it poured with rain and there were hardly any other children out on the streets of Corfu Town—they were far too happy to care.

That winter and spring, life seemed like one long children's party. On sunny days we drove down to a deserted beach, and the boys built castles of cold, fudge-coloured sand while Wendy and I took it in turns to gather driftwood for the stove. There were jaunts into Kassiopi, which regained much of its charm in the off-season when the clubs and discos were closed, the harbour peaceful and the streets empty. Joe loved the children's playground that had been erected in a vacant lot and spent hours on the rusty swings and the slide. Then we would walk up the street to the only restaurant that stayed open during the winter and have pizza for lunch while the owner's grey parrot clucked and fretted in its cage.

But most of the fun was had at home. The previous summer, my mother had sent down the kit for a plastic playhouse, big enough to accommodate one child and one adult if the grown-up sat cross-legged and hunched over. It had almost melted outside in the August sun but it was perfect when set up in our bedroom and lined with pillows and stuffed animals. The boys never tired of hiding inside it, shrieking with laughter while Wendy or I growled outside like the big bad wolf.

Under the sofa downstairs, we kept a suitcase filled with crayons and paints, brushes, Plasticine, paper and coloured pens, and the dining-room table became an arts workshop on wet afternoons. The group consisted of Michelle's three-year-old daughter, Louisa; Koula's daughter, Andy, and Renna's daughters Mary and Vasso, all of them now six or seven; and twelve-year-old Ranya and her five-year-old sister, Letta. The number of drawings and paintings produced soon ran into the thousands. Everyone—even Nibby—helped decorate the puppet theatre I made out of a big cardboard box. Propped up behind the sofa, it worked like a Punch and Judy show with me crouching underneath using teddy bears and glove puppets as actors. One very old puppet from my own childhood, a bizarre brown animal with no eyes and pointed batlike ears, was renowned as a mathematician. His name was Zoltan and he had his own showcase, a shoebox covered with numbers. The children would call out sums, and Zoltan, using a magic wand as a pointer, would provide the answer, to the wonder of all.

"You should open a school," Michelle often said to Wendy. "You'd get all the English women's kids from here to Kassiopi." And for a while she thought seriously about the idea. Wendy had started teaching Joe to read when he was six months old. A Canadian friend had sent her a book that outlined a simple and eminently logical phonetic system for encouraging literacy in babies. The idea excited her, and she had adapted the system into a brilliant game that delighted Joe, writing individual letters on cards and sticking them up in prominent places around the house, endlessly repeating the sound of each letter until he began to repeat it, too. Her patience and persistence paid off. At eighteen months, Joe could make the sound of every letter in the alphabet. Before he was two, he could read simple words like *cat* and *man*. After that, there was no stopping him. "No good will come of it," warned many of our Canadian friends. They seemed to think it unnatural, implied we were robbing him of his childhood and hinted that he would be shunned as a freak by normal boys and girls if we ever went back to Toronto. But Joe loved his books.

Eventually, however, Joe and Nibby would have to go to school. The schoolhouse in the village, right beside Philip's bar, was one possibility. There were a dozen students at the time, ranging in age from five to twelve, who worked in the single room. The new teacher, drafted by the municipality, was as bitter about such a remote posting as his predecessors had been, and his classroom was a joyless place. Once, in exasperation, he wrote all over a child's face in red ballpoint pen—or so the girls from Zervou told us, whispering at such a scandal. Wendy began to toy with the idea of volunteering as his assistant. She could teach English, keep an eye on Joe and make sure discipline was handled in a more humane way.

"We'll see when the time comes," I suggested, and we left it at that. Our days were so absorbingly busy we had little time or reason to think much about the future.

March brought our fourth spring on the island, and the sudden warmth spurred the need in me to do something new with stone and cement. The courtyard between the two houses was the obvious project. It had always been something of an obstacle course, its large, flat-sided stones protruding from the impacted earth at all angles, each one fringed by vigorous weeds. How long could it take to dig them up and reset them, firmly mortared with cement? I could leave a ring of earth around the oak tree where we could plant some more geraniums. It would all look very elegant.

The work soon became a compulsion, filling every spare moment, especially when it became apparent that we would need a great many flatter, larger stones than the current cobbles. We had built a low wooden gate across the front doors so we could leave them open without worrying about the children tumbling down the steps. The boys loved to stand there and watch me crawling about with a trowel and spirit level. Some nights I mixed cement by moonlight, and when there was no moon I brought out my desk lamp and plugged it into an extension cord, working deep into the night. Gradually the island of perfectly horizontal, immobile pavement spread across the courtyard. By the end of April it was half finished.

ONE AFTERNOON, at about five o'clock, Joe and the girls from Zervou were happily painting at the table. Wendy was in the kitchen, wondering what we would have for dinner; Nibby was sitting on the rug with his toys, looking forward to his bath. I filled the plastic tub with warm water and set it in the shower stall, then called Nibby in. He toddled happily across the marble floor, always eager for the splashy fun. But in the doorway he suddenly sat down heavily and started to whimper. I stood him back up, but his legs seemed to have no strength in them. Wendy came over to help. He still did not want to stand and now the tears were in earnest.

"Never mind the bath," said Wendy. We carried Nibby upstairs and got him into his pyjamas. He was happier lying in the cot with his teddy bear beside him.

Next day, when Nibby was still unable to stand, we drove down to the clinic in Kassiopi. The doctor was a smooth, confident young man with a penchant for prescribing antibiotics, but for once he did not conclude the examination by reaching for his pen. "There is nothing wrong," he announced. "The child is simply being naughty. If I were you, I wouldn't stand for such nonsense."

Wendy and I both found the diagnosis preposterous. Sturdy little boys like Nibby who loved walking and laughed out loud for the sheer joy of running across a garden or a beach did not suddenly go off the idea. Nor had we ever known him to look so pale, to seem so uninterested in his surroundings or to turn away from a cookie. That afternoon, Nibby's temperature started to climb, and thoughts of the baby who had died of meningitis the previous summer loomed in our minds. We packed the boys into the car and headed to the hospital in Corfu Town.

The emergency room was a grim and medieval place. In the summer, it was largely populated by young English tourists who rented motorbikes for the first time in their lives and then went drinking, only to find that a T-shirt and swimming trunks gave little protection against a hard tarmac road. This early in the year, however, the locals had it to themselves: a man with his elderly mother who moaned as she rocked slowly back and forth, another man who scowled at his shoes and fingered a loop of worry beads, several grandfathers with persistent smoker's coughs. We sat down, Joe uncharacteristically silent between us, Nibby in Wendy's arms. When the nurse came in all the patients insisted that we should be seen first. A woman doctor with an efficient manner led us away to an examining room. She listened patiently to our explanation, manipulated Nibby's legs and found nothing wrong, took blood samples and administered a lumbar puncture to check for meningitis. Quite rightly, I suppose, she refused to prescribe any medicine until the results were returned in a couple of days. "If you want to bring his temperature down," she suggested, "hold him under a cold shower for five minutes."

From the day Joe was born, Wendy and I had promised each other that if any one of us ever fell seriously ill we would hightail it back to England for treatment, whether or not we could afford the airfare. Without saying so, both of us knew that the time had come. So we didn't drive back to Loutses that night. We took a room in a hotel in Corfu Town and I booked Nibby and myself onto next morning's flight to London.

His fever was down as we boarded the plane and he sat quietly on my lap the whole way, smiling politely at the doting stewardesses. My mother met us at Heathrow and whisked us to her house, where a doctor was summoned. He in turn recommended that we see a specialist the following day at the Westminster Children's Hospital. More tests, more examinations, and Nibby was admitted overnight until the lab work came back. We did not have to wait that long. A different doctor, no older than me, with an oddly intense bedside manner, took me into a private office where a sister and the registrar were waiting. There, very gently, they led me into the knowledge that Nibby had leukemia.

That evening I called Philip's kafeneion at the prearranged time and spoke to Wendy. I didn't know how to break the news. In the end I just blurted it out and then stood there in the hallway of the hospital listening to her sobbing.

They let me stay with Nibby that night, though neither of us slept much. The young oncologist had lingered by the bedside explaining what lay ahead—that Nibby would remain in the hospital for the next six months, to be followed by two years as an outpatient. Two or three years after that they would be sure that the cancer had been checked. More immediately, he would undergo an operation in the morning to have an intravenous line inserted into his chest. Chemotherapy would begin as soon as it was in place. Nibby, he told me, had acute myeloid leukemia, not nearly as serious as acute lymphoblastic leukemia, but it was important to start the chemo as soon as possible.

A new sister came in and introduced herself. We would be moving up to her ward tomorrow. She seemed reluctant when I asked that a bed be put into the new cubicle so that Wendy or I could sleep beside Nibby. She explained that there might be times in the months ahead when we wouldn't be allowed to stay for fear of infection and she did not want him to be reliant on our presence. I told her that we would be there with or without a bed, in a sleeping bag on the floor, if need be. She did not argue, though I sensed the matter had been postponed rather than resolved.

When they had all gone, I sat down and looked at Nibby. His face was pale and there was swelling around his eyes, but for now he was peacefully asleep. A voice in my head kept reminding me that this was the last time his perfect little body would be whole and unscarred. Then another voice pointed out that his body wasn't perfect at all—not with blast cells burgeoning in his blood and bone marrow. He was too young to understand what was going on, which was good in some ways. He would be spared the dread of the idea of cancer, the anticipation of the ordeal that lay ahead. On the other hand, how could we explain to him that the pain and the indignities he was about to experience were intended to cure him? Instead of the world he was used to—his beloved cot, the room he shared with Joe, the garden, the village, the beach, the idyllic childhood we had planned for him on our beautiful island—he would grow up in a hospital, never knowing why his life had changed or where this regime of suffering had come from.

The incomprehension began the next day when he woke up thirsty and was denied anything to drink for four hours. I tried to distract him, cuddled him and instigated a hundred stupid little games, but his thirst was real and insistent and would not be denied. His angry glare accused me of treason for withholding his juice, until the premedication finally sent him drifting off to sleep.

He came back from the operation with his upper body painted brown with iodine under a transparent plastic dressing and a thick tube taped into a wound in his chest. It seemed a hideous intrusion but the sight of his wrist, bruised and tender from the IV, reminded me why he needed it. And I couldn't deny it was effective. When the time came to begin chemotherapy the nurse was able to disconnect the bag of saline, syringe out the contents of the line, draw all the blood that was required for a dozen different tests, wash the tube with saline, return its original contents and connect it to the box-like mechanical pump that delivered the chemo without waking Nibby up. He rubbed his nose and frowned in his sleep but seemed far more comfortable than he had with the wrist catheter.

Wendy and Joe reached London that afternoon. My mother met them at the airport and took Joe back to her house while Wendy came straight to the hospital. We barely had time to speak before the oncologist arrived with another doctor in tow, the senior hematologist from the Westminster Hospital. Their news was not good. The initial diagnosis had been wrong: Nibby had acute lymphoblastic leukemia after all. The chances of the chemotherapy working were no better than 50 percent, and even if it did, there was only a 25 percent chance of achieving total remission. A 12.5 percent survival rate, in other words.

"But how? How did he get it?" Wendy pleaded.

The hematologist spread his hands in a gesture of helplessness. No one yet knew what caused leukemia.

"I had German measles when I was pregnant with him."

The doctor shook his head. "Who knows?" Then the two men hurried away.

"He's going to die, isn't he," Wendy said.

"We can't think that."

"One of us has to be here every second."

"Definitely."

"And the other one has to be with Joe."

So that was decided. Wendy wanted to spend Nibby's days with him; I would spend the nights.

My mother, in her wisdom, had realized that we would not want to live in her house, where we would never be alone and friends were always coming and going. Her business partner and his family were at their home in the country and kindly lent us their London house, close to Hyde Park and a short taxi ride from the hospital. Audy was flying over from Canada to stay with us for a fortnight and get us settled.

So the vigil began. By day, Joe and I sought whatever distractions we could, exploring the zoo and every museum in London and spending endless hours in the park. For him it was an adventure, but he was too much in tune with his parents' emotions not to know that we were desperately, constantly worried about his brother.

In the evening I would go to the hospital to relieve Wendy. Sometimes I caught a faint memory of her perfume on Nibby's hair, she had been kissing and cuddling him so much. The sisters and nurses—wonderful, remarkable women—became our friends and doted on Nibby. They had told us there would be good days and bad days, and so it proved. When his temperature dropped he would sit up and play with his toys and books, though he quickly became bored with them. It frustrated him that his legs were still so weak and his clever fingers less dextrous than they had been. In Corfu, he had just started to speak—a few cherished words among the happy babble—but he had regressed in that, too. If he wanted something and we were too slow to guess what it might be he shouted with anger.

We dwelt on small triumphs, making him smile by tickling him, watching him eat a banana, seeing the pleasure he took in his two favourite cartoon videotapes, a haunting song called "The Snowman" and Paul McCartney's extended opus about Joe's favourite character, Rupert Bear, called "Rupert and the Frog Song." Very occasionally, he would be deliberately naughty, dropping toys out of his cot, and we prized such moments as signs of his old spirit. He woke often in the night, sometimes traumatically if his fever suddenly soared, sometimes just stirring and then lying calm and quiet for half an hour while I stroked him and whispered to him until he went back to sleep. Then I would sit and watch him, listening to the rhythmic tick of the chemotherapy machine as it trickled the poison into his body. Eleven days earlier we had been a carefree little family on our warm Greek island. Now all that seemed like somebody else's life.

Wendy and I rarely met, and when we did we were abrupt and intolerant of each other. I was too much alone, but she never had a moment to herself with friends and well-wishers visiting the hospital so frequently. One evening Nibby was still awake when I came to relieve her and she was reluctant to leave. We bickered about the best way to give him his oral syringe of antibiotics—we had each developed a different technique. Nibby lay watching us, making the little kissing sound that meant he wanted a cuddle, looking first at me, then at Wendy. We kissed him of course, from the soul, but I later realized he wanted to see us kissing each other as well. We were both so tense and emotionally drained we had nothing left for each other and no way of coping with even the most trivial irritation. We were no longer a team but more like competitors, each feeling he or she had to be the complete parent.

The effort of continually summoning hope was as exhausting as anything else, particularly when the daily reports from the lab showed that the chemotherapy was not working. There were still blast cells in Nibby's blood. Good days and bad days. The cocktail of antibiotics was making small progress against the various viral and bacterial infections that had taken root in his frail little body. When they tried different ones he had an allergic reaction, turning crimson and developing a rash within minutes. He would cough and vomit for hours in the night while I held him, his once chubby limbs just skin and bone, his neck so tiny now, his eyes sunken and shadowed.

Then there were afternoons when he was calm and even jolly. One evening I went in and Wendy's eyes were shining. She had coaxed him into taking a few steps and had carried him up and down the corridor. When he saw the balloon I had brought him he smiled and said "Balloon" and we all laughed.

During the second week of chemotherapy we were allowed to take Nibby home at night. His line was flushed out and sealed and we bundled him up in a taxi and carried him back to the house. We sat him on a rug, propped up with cushions, and Joe brought him every toy in the house, one by one. That Sunday the doctors said he could have an outing, and we all went rowing on the lake in Battersea Park. Nibby was happier than he had been in a long time, but so quiet and weak. We had cut off his mop of blond hair when it had started to fall out, saving every precious strand in an envelope. Bundled up in scarves with a close-fitting woollen hat on his head, he never took his eyes off Joe.

The third week brought more good news. The chemo had finally worked. His bone marrow was clear, purged of everything, good and bad. He must stay in the hospital now. The days ahead would show what they would show as new cells formed in his bones, cells that might be healthy or might not. Someone had thrown us a tiny thread of hope and I clung to it desperately.

My mother had found us a new place to live—a smart little house close to the hospital. She refused to say how much she was paying in rent but it must have been astronomical. Joe liked his new domain. There was a small yard—just a square of cement surrounded by the backs of other houses, like the bottom of a well—where he could trundle his toy cars with the intense concentration that was already part of his character. Many of his games involved make-believe, attempts to find resolution in the current confusion. "You be Mummy," he would suggest to me, "and Uncle Danny be Grandma." Joe himself was Nibby, quiet as a mouse and moving in slow motion until a sudden cure restored him to health and the game ended.

Pretending kept Joe's spirits up and the hospital psychiatrist, who had become a good friend to Wendy, approved. I sought more practical distraction, keeping detailed records of Nibby's treatment, learning everything I could about the pernicious disease, its side effects and the arsenal of drugs being pumped into my son. The desire to understand what was happening became obsessive. Doing anything else with my mind seemed irresponsible—or worse, a betrayal of hope. A friend suggested placing a healing crystal under the hospital bed, but I had no time for such gibberish now. Instead, I was filled with an unexpressed but roiling, unquenchable anger. One night I awoke and lay in the darkness clenched with fury at every novelist who ever manipulated the emotions of the reader, every peddler of fiction who ever invented scenes of sorrow and conjured up artificial misery, as if there weren't enough real despair in the world without their generating more. I vowed that I would never write fiction again.

On another occasion, an Anglican vicar poked his head into the cubicle, just to introduce himself and invite me to come by for a chat if I ever wished to. We talked for a while about the routines of treatment on the ward until Nibby started to cough—the bitter, dry, relentless coughing that left his back trembling and his withered muscles aching.

"Poor old chap," said the vicar. "But you know, he's got the best father there is."

"Thank you," I muttered, not knowing what else to say.

The vicar smiled. "I mean he has a loving father in heaven watching over him."

I thought of asking what kind of obscene sadist of an omnipotent deity would put a child through such torment, but there was no need to articulate the question. The vicar saw it in my expression and his face turned suddenly pale. He backed into the corridor, closing the door behind him.

Next day, at Wendy's prompting, I spent an hour with the hospital psychiatrist. She was good at her job and soon had me talking. I tried to explain how being polite—making small talk in social situations—had become an impossible effort. I felt as if I had been skinned alive—the slightest touch an agony against which I had no defences. I told her what had happened when I was driving home the previous day. A car behind me had sounded its horn when I made a right turn too slowly, and it seemed such an aggressive act that I burst into tears. The only time I had nothing to say was when she asked me to describe my emotional responses to Nibby's illness. I just sat and looked at her, unable to speak. After a while she changed the subject, but she must have found a more subtle path into my feelings, for I ended up venting my spleen in an anti-clerical diatribe of great length and vehemence. It was all extempore and not even true—I was surprised to sit there and listen to myself ranting away, all the time aware that the unfortunate vicar was no more than a scapegoat. That night, back in the dimly lit cubicle, I repeatedly went over the conversation until it occurred to me that

I was wasting valuable time. Nibby was the one to worry about, not my emotional well-being. Self-pity or self-analysis was intolerably self-indulgent. If I let my concentration waver for an instant I might miss something essential. So I consciously closed the door the psychiatrist had opened and dived back into the business of drugs and treatments, charts and protocols. It was the same on the couple of afternoons when Joe and I accepted the invitation to have tea at the home of some kindly friend. I sat there aching to be back at the hospital.

May slipped onwards through good days and bad, and Nibby grew weaker rather than stronger. The doctors described the results of his bone marrow tests as satisfactory: no sign yet of red or white cells generating, but no blast cells either. Sometimes in the night, his bacterial infections would erupt and send his temperature spiking, once even breaking the thermometer. Then the night nurse would take blood samples to see if the bacteria could be identified once and for all and therefore treated more effectively. Very occasionally, Nibby would manage to keep down a dose of oral analgesic and his fever would plummet, calming the trembling shivers that racked him, smoothing the frown from his brow and letting him sleep calmly for a while. At such times he looked fantastically beautiful, his white skin almost translucent in the dim light that filtered through the curtains from the corridor.

But Nibby's body, stripped of its defences by the chemotherapy, was beginning to fail. One morning, a month after he first came to live in the hospital, he awoke with a painfully stiff neck and more trouble than usual in breathing. The doctors suspected meningitis, but an X-ray showed fungal pneumonia in one of his lungs. Dark lesions began to appear on his face and under his fingernails, growing extraordinarily quickly. He no longer had the strength to cough up the phlegm that clogged his throat, and so a physiotherapist was summoned to pound his back and then suction the sputum out through a tube inserted down Nibby's nose. It made him scream, and we had no way of explaining why we simply stood by and allowed it to happen. The first time, however, it did bring a little relief and for most of the afternoon he sat up and silently watched his favourite videos over and over again. He even ate two teaspoons of applesauce at dinnertime.

It was watching the torment of the physiotherapy that finally broke Wendy's spirit. We agreed to trade places so that she would be with Nibby during the nights. I still believed there was reason to hope. If only his body would start to make white blood cells again, they would surely take care of the infections in short order. But his breathing was so fast and shallow and crackly, he was having problems getting enough oxygen. One afternoon, the distress this caused him proved too much. The room was suddenly full of nurses and doctors. Hypoxia was diagnosed and an ambulance called. Acting on a plan they had devised the day before, they transferred Nibby to another hospital where better ventilation equipment was available.

Nibby was sedated and a tube fed down into his lung, oxygen pumped in and out by a nurse squeezing a black rubber ball on the end of the tube. He was wrapped in a foil blanket, all his lines and intravenous tubes taped securely, and moved down to the ambulance. A nurse picked up his favourite toys, put them into a bag and handed it to me.

So we found ourselves back in the Westminster Hospital, where Nibby had been born, sixteen months earlier. He had a large room to himself in the intensive care unit and constant monitoring of the lines that now ran into his chest, neck, nose, foot and rectum. The ventilator gave him seventeen breaths a minute.

Wendy and I sat beside him, talking to him, playing his favourite songs quietly on a portable cassette player, touching him in one of the few places where he wasn't bruised or connected to a machine. Total anaesthesia was not possible, and though the doctors assured us he would remember none of this, they admitted they did not know exactly what he was aware of as he lay there. To us, he seemed to be sleeping.

Visitors came by—every one of the sisters and nurses from the children's hospital, our friends, my family. On the second morning the oncologist appeared with amazing news: the previous day's blood tests showed "occasional neutrophils," a sign that perhaps Nibby's bone marrow was finally beginning to recover. It was hard to respond with any enthusiasm. "There's still hope," he said, his voice suddenly husky. But the next day's tests showed the hope had been false. There had been no change in his bone marrow after all.

At the suggestion of the psychiatrist from the children's hospital, we brought Joe in to see his brother. The nurses had covered most of the tubes and lines with a blanket, and Wendy had explained to him that he shouldn't be worried by the hose going into Nibby's nose—it was giving him special baby air. Joe's eyes were huge and serious; Wendy's and mine were full of tears we could scarcely hide. After five minutes Joe made no protest when we asked if he wanted to leave.

That night Wendy and I sat together with Nibby. She was convinced now that he was not going to live. She had hoped that his body might be used for organ donations, that some good might come of this situation, but the doctors had explained that was not possible. For the first time in weeks, she and I seemed to be close, even though I still found it impossible to concede that all hope was gone. Emotionally, we were in the same condition, drained and exhausted, all control over the processes of our lives long since vanished. Even our own responses to events seemed mysterious. We talked, both aware that we hadn't talked to each other for a long, long time. I tried to ask myself what would become of us. Would we emerge from this forever embittered and fatalistic, or would it be possible to find some sort of reconciliation with life? We had to, if only for Joe's sake, but neither of us could imagine how that sort of peace could be achieved. On one point Wendy was obdurate.

"Nothing matters more than us as a family," she said. "We have to cling to that. We must be good people. We must have been doing something right to have made two such wonderful children."

We took it in turns to stay beside Nibby, the other one sleeping or trying to sleep in a room set aside for relatives of those in intensive care. Early next morning, the telephone rang and called me back. Things were not going well. Wendy and I sat and held Nibby's hands, stroking his brow. A male nurse was busy checking the monitors and drips, the tubes and lines. Then we saw his shoulders sag.

"Any moment now," he said.

We asked for the equipment to be disconnected. Both of us began to sob. The nurse lifted Nibby off the bed and laid him in Wendy's arms. Kissing him and cradling him, she held him as he died.

"You must leave him now," said the nurse eventually. "Come back at ten. Come to the chapel."

We brought Joe with us—necessary closure, said the wise psychiatrist—and explained that Nibby's pain was over. They had laid out his tiny body, a sheet drawn up to his neck. Then Wendy took Joe back to the house.

I crossed the road, as instructed by the hospital administrators, for an interview with the funeral director who would organize Nibby's cremation. The man's jovial grin and clumsy attempts at humour seemed profoundly offensive. He did not approve of our decision to do without a funeral service, suggesting that it was a useful way to let the mourning process begin. I assured him we were mourning already.

Wendy couldn't bear to be present at the cremation. I understood, but I felt the reverse. The thought of none of us being there seemed intolerably lonely.

It might have been next day or maybe two days later—I can't remember. While Wendy and Joe packed up our things and arranged for a swift return to Corfu, my brother drove me down to Mortlake Crematorium. It stands right beside the river, near where the Oxford and Cambridge boat race ends, a broad stretch of the Thames that I had rowed countless times in my schooldays. I walked a little way up the muddy gravel towpath. No one was in sight; there was no sense of the vast city that crowded around this extraordinarily peaceful place. The water was high, slipping quickly past with the tide. Tall poplars swayed and sighed in the breeze, bright green leaves shimmering in the sunlight.

Outside the chapel, Daniel pointed to the sea of wreaths and flowers sent by our friends, by my mother's friends, by the nurses, then we went inside and sat down in one of the pews. There was nobody else there. The sun streamed in through the high windows, its presence more comforting than any liturgy. Two of the undertaker's men appeared carrying a very small white coffin, which they set down carefully on a table at the top of the aisle. Then they left us alone.

The dogged clinging to hope that had carried me through recent weeks had prevented any mental preparation for this moment and I lacked the strength to organize my mind. All the rage and pity and disbelief that had stormed about in my subconscious had been suddenly arrested the moment Nibby died, petrified, frozen into numb and passive grief. I do remember a vision of a silver road winding away into the future—the long, happy life we had planned for our son—a road he would never walk now. And I could look back, past his illness, past the dark landscape we had stumbled into, and see him playing on the beach or peeping around the corner of the patio in his carnival costume, laughing and laughing. I could cling to the one sure truth: how lucky we were to have had such a beautiful boy in our lives, for even a little while.

Chapter Ten

As I sit here in this sleeping house, twenty years later, the silence closes about my ears as if I were down a mine. In the blackness, I tap with my hammer, looking for another seam of memory to follow. But so much has been forgotten. And so many tunnels were carefully and deliberately sealed. In the dust at my feet, I find no more than a handful of grains of any value, turning them over in the palm of my hand, bringing them into the light.

There, far below, a blue car climbs a ribbon of road in the mountains. Turquoise sea, olive-green trees, white rock. In the other direction comes a beaten-up yellow flatbed truck, loaded with blue metal gas cylinders, driven by Erakles, who owns the valuable propane concession down in Peritheia. The two vehicles converge, slowing to edge past each other, stopping. Erakles is laughing.

"Yassu, Dzimi! Ti kanis?" He leans out to peer into our car, grinning at Wendy. "Yassas! Hey, Dzimi, I thought you had two kids! Did you leave one behind?"

I turn to Wendy. "What's the Greek word . . . ?"

Her face is stricken. "Pethane. Pethane, to pethi." He died.

After a while, the cars slowly pull away, Erakles going downhill, us going up towards Loutses.

We had been desperate to leave England. The wary, restrained, inquisitive sympathy of our friends seemed like medical fingers probing a gaping wound—well intentioned but impossible to bear. My mother found us a flight as soon as possible.

The house was fine. Philip had filled the fridge with basic supplies; Koula had aired the rooms, made the beds and watered the flowers and the herbs. The half-paved patio had been swept.

But certain things needed to be done. Wendy took Nibby's clothes from the shelves in the boys' room and folded them carefully into a suitcase. I dismantled his cot and carried the pieces down to the apothiki. Neither of us could bear to take his high chair away from the dining table.

At six o'clock that evening, the first visitors came to the door. They bore gifts of oil or wine or fruit or eggs wrapped in paper napkins. They hugged and patted us and made much of Joe. They sat for a moment but would take no refreshment, not wanting to put us to the trouble. When the subject inevitably turned to Nibby, they lifted their hands. "Ti na kame. What can one do." It wasn't a question; it was a philosophical statement. Life brought such things. There was no question of justice or injustice. To me and to Wendy, it seemed the only possible response to what had happened. We were as grateful for such stoic practicality as we were for the shining kindness in their eyes.

Joe was our main concern and our solace. He would wake in the night and call out to us, worried that he had been left alone or that we were all going to die. We took him into our bed or sat on the edge of his in the dim amber glow of the night light, talking through his anxieties, explaining as best we could. After a couple of weeks he slept as soundly as he had ever done. He was also our hinge, for Wendy and I still felt isolated by our separate sorrows. In London, I had failed to provide the emotional support she had needed. I hadn't known how. That opportunity was gone and neither of us wanted to revisit it. We made an effort to communicate more, allowing ourselves to get tearful or angry whenever we felt like it, recovering quickly from the outbursts. But each of us had our own road to travel.

I felt like a hollow man filled with darkness—so brim-full that sometimes it welled up into my field of vision and I found myself looking at the world through a black frame, as if I were working in the darkness of the apothiki and had glanced up to see the dazzling sunlit garden outside the door. People in England had told us to give it time, that the bitter sense of waste would eventually fade. Perhaps that was true, but Wendy and I found the sentiment deeply insulting.

There was still work to be done, and I was grateful for the dogged repetition of it. Flat stones were needed for the patio, and we discovered them in the mountains beside the track up to Ano Peritheia. In the middle of the afternoon, when the villagers were asleep, we drove through the village and up into the silent clarity of the high places. Wendy and Joe went looking for plants and insects and animals and talked about all the peoples who had lived on Corfu since earliest times; I clambered up off the track, looking for rock. Levering away with the pick, I could pry great slabs of white limestone from the hillside, hefting them up like a weightlifter, my shirtless back shining with sweat. The heat and the exertion were a kind of balm, and when I paused to stretch, the faint breath of a breeze was delectably cool. Above all, I craved the searing light of the sun, almost violent in its intensity, that seemed to soak right through me until I was as transparent as glass. When the car could hold no more rock we crawled back to Loutses, shock absorbers groaning, back to our courtyard where the sunlight was more humane, dappled by the leaves of the oak and the vine.

So the patio grew, stone by stone. Down in the apothiki stood three pieces of strawberry pink marble, left over from the floor of the house. Each one was about six feet long and cut like a plank of wood. I had cherished them for years, imagining they might one day be useful for shelves or windowsills. Now Wendy suggested we could set them into the patio in the shape of a giant letter *N*. I had thought of placing the little bronze box containing Nibby's ashes beneath it, but Wendy had a better idea. One peaceful evening, she and Joe and I went down into the garden and dug a hole beneath one of the olive trees, close to the cherry sapling we had planted in Nibby's memory. We buried the box there. Then we all stood and held hands for a while before going back to the house.

"IT'S A PLUM SUMMER," said Joe.

We were working among the slender damson trees, harvesting the purple fruit for the year's supply of jam, our fingers and lips sticky with juice.

It was indeed turning into the most fecund summer yet. We had come back to find the oregano that grew wild beneath our olive trees just ready to bloom, each plant capped with a staff of buds but only one or two tiny white flowers. We gathered armfuls, pulling the long wiry stalks through our fingers to rub off the coarse lower leaves, tying them into bundles and hanging them upside down to dry for a week in the shade. The almond trees, carefully pruned the year before, had been smothered in April blossom. There would be sacks of nuts in the autumn, to crack with the hammer on the front step, and gallons of sweet blackberries from the impenetrable thicket that choked the derelict garden on the next property. They made fabulous jam when cooked with the furry yellow quinces from the tree that grew close to the path through the olive groves. But right now it was the turn of the plums, picked with the help of a stepladder and Joe on the ground below to point out any we missed. The twelve Mason jars would not be nearly enough.

Life had begun to creep about us again, filling in the edges of the days. We greeted it cautiously, more for Joe's sake than our own. The evening litany of visitors had finally ceased, though Michelle's daughter, Louisa, and the little girls from Zervou often came by in the mornings. It was good to hear Joe's laughter as they played in the garden, stirring an old metal pot filled with mud and gravel, then mischievously inviting us to sample the soup they had made.

When friends from England came out to stay—their children more company for Joe—playing host and showing them the island was usefully distracting. We spent days at the beach and nights, after the offspring were asleep, playing poker, bridge and Trivial Pursuit and drinking too much. The lure of cement making proved irresistible, and our friends helped valiantly with the last few yards of the patio. By the time they went home to England, it was complete.

Completion: such a strange and unexpected feeling. Sweeping up the last of the sand. Rinsing out the wheelbarrow. Putting the tools away in the apothiki. No doubt, there would be many repairs in the future, but suddenly, for the first time we could remember, there was nothing left to do. Nothing was broken; nothing leaked. The house—the whole property—was functional. The two upstairs bedrooms were cosy and comfortable; the downstairs room cool and, to our eyes, elegant. The little house across the courtyard doubled as a guest room and a perfect study, especially now that the rats were gone from its roof. The paved vista of the courtyard was smooth enough for toy cars to use, fringed with geraniums, jasmine, roses, gourd vines and various anonymous tumbling succulents. Our herb beds flourished (the sage bush, grown from seed, was a particular triumph). The state of the drystone walls down in the garden would have earned a thumbs-up from a Yorkshireman. Even the grass was cropped now that our neighbour had started bringing his donkey down and tethering it under the olive trees.

"There's really no excuse not to go back to the book," said Wendy one day, as much to herself as to me. "We really ought to get on with it."

Out in the study, tucked into the desk, was a box of notes and the first half of a chapter about the sea, dashed off immediately after the octopus hunt. I hadn't written a word since Nibby fell ill. Going back to it was difficult—reading the conversations, hearing the jaunty self-confidence of the voice on the tapes. It would be a different book now—cool and objective. Impersonal.

So the research began again, the long conversations with the ladies of the village, the late evenings with Philip filling gaps in our understanding. I pried recipes out of Christos and hung out in the kitchen of his taverna to see how he cooked, spent time with Kosta in Ano Peritheia and watched Chrisoula make her marvellous rockfish stew in the little shack among the bamboo behind Kalamaki. Wendy learned Koula's repertoire and spent mornings in the Kassiopi bakery where the brick ovens were still fuelled by the mash from the olive press. It gave us things to talk about—a mutual project—and encouraged us to leave the house. Therapy as much as work.

The villagers sensed it and welcomed us most generously. We had grown used to the initial expression of sympathy every time we met someone new, the frank acknowledgement of our loss, and had memorized the right replies—ways to say thank you and then move on to other, lighter topics. *Ti na kame* . . . In England, the death of a child felt horrific, unheard of. Here, it was less unusual. Life, people understood and gently insisted, must eventually go on.

But oh, it was hard. An amputee doesn't ever forget that something is missing. The structure of our lives had been built on the sure foundation of our tight little family unit, solid and elemental, a square, not a triangle. Everything in our small world reminded us of Nibby. We were grateful for that—not to remember him, even for a moment, seemed unthinkable. But it was emotionally exhausting. I saw it in Wendy's eyes. She probably saw it in mine. Joe was aware of it.

Which one of us first had the courage to mention that there were alternatives? That it might be permissible, and ultimately the best thing for all of us, if we left our island for a while? To start again, back in Canada maybe, for six months or a year. Realignment. Recovery.

"Did we really think we could live here for ever?" whispered Wendy as we lay on our bed in the moonlight.

"I never thought that far ahead."

"We could work hard. Make enough money to spend months every summer here. We will always come back."

"I suppose we should at least think about it."

"I'm afraid this house might become a shrine. Like the ones on the roadside. Full of sadness."

"Is that how you feel about it?"

"Sometimes."

She reached out and stroked my shoulder.

"These years have not been a failure. Never think that."

"YOU SHOULD go down and talk to Christos again, man," Philip suggested one morning when I had gone up to the kafeneion to try to telephone my mother.

"Oh yes?"

"They're having a bouzouki night in August. You can write about it in our book."

"What's a bouzouki night?"

Philip leaned back, striking a comical pose as if I had asked him what two plus two might add up to.

"Come on, man. It's like a big party." When he was a child,

he explained, people had bouzouki nights all the time. During the summer they held them outside, sometimes during the afternoon, sometimes late into the night. In the winter, they could be anywhere—in the shop, in someone's home, wherever there was a place for the musicians to play and room to dance. Everybody came from miles around. The best cooks provided the food and there were barrels of wine.

But there hadn't been a bouzouki night in Loutses for many years. Now there were going to be two. Apparently Spiro had thought his taverna could benefit from such an affair: it would be sure to bring tourists up from the coast. He decided on a certain Saturday in August and drove down to the police station in Kassiopi to get permission to extend his opening hours. The sergeant roared with laughter. Tasso and Christos had been in the day before on exactly the same mission and with the same date in mind. Spiro was not amused, but there was nothing to be done. He reluctantly agreed to postpone his own bouzouki night until the following Saturday.

Meanwhile, Tasso and Christos set to work. The paddock across the road from their restaurant was levelled and paved with cement to make a dance floor. Poles were erected at the four corners with lines of coloured light bulbs strung between them. A small wooden stage was built for the band. While Spiro was planning to bring a well-known group from Karousades for his evening, Tasso was relying on local talent. His apprentice played in a band with five other teenagers, backing their high-school music teacher, who was the singer and bouzouki player. It was widely understood that the group would soon turn professional.

Joe's four little girlfriends from Zervou were also involved. Wide-eyed and breathless at the scariness of it all, they explained to us that they would be performing traditional dances, part of a troupe of a dozen girls from the village. They had to wear puffy white blouses, headscarves and long skirts and carry a red handkerchief in each hand. Their mothers were making the costumes and they had to rehearse every day. We asked to see their steps, but they were too shy to show us.

"It's a shame Chris will miss the bouzouki," said Wendy.

Her friend was coming from Toronto on his annual visit, flying first class via Frankfurt, where he would plunder the duty-free stores for caviar and liqueurs, arcane toiletries unavailable at the shop in Peritheia and bizarre executive toys. One year there had been Canada Day fireworks in his luggage, which I had forbidden him to ignite on our tinder-dry island. Another time it was a litre of vodka bottled like an intravenous drip with a wire frame and a tube. An enormous African scorpion sealed in a solid acrylic dome. Twenty tins of smoked oysters. A mail-order book with a new and infallible system for winning at roulette.

Chris disliked being met at the airport. He preferred to rent a fast, air-conditioned car and make his own way up to Loutses. He and Wendy went to Tasso's restaurant for dinner and to catch up on news while I stayed at home with Joe. When they came back, Wendy took me aside.

"I told Chris we were considering moving back to Canada. He asked how we would live."

"Well, if we ever do decide to do that, I'll get a job, of course."

"Yes, but you wouldn't be allowed to work, he thinks, until you got your landed immigrant status—and that can take a year. But he had an idea. He said he'd been thinking about it for some time. He says he would be prepared to buy this house from us—and everything in it. We needn't tell anyone or go through the law or anything. He'd pay all the bills. He'd give us a lump sum up front and then the rest of the money in bits as we needed it. He would come here every year for his vacation—on his own, so he could relax—and we could come back and stay whenever we wanted to."

Wendy knew my first reaction would be one of total dismay. That was how I greeted every suggestion of change. A voice in my head was screaming that this was disaster and betrayal—everything we had worked so hard for could not simply be abandoned. But another, more reasonable part of me was already acknowledging that Chris's generous solution might be the best thing for Wendy and Joe. And for me.

"What if he sells it?"

"He won't. But we can make him promise to offer it back to us first."

"I don't want to leave. Not now that we've finally finished it."

"I know. I don't want to either. Except that I also do. And Joe really should go to school."

Chris had come for a fortnight. There was time to consider things, to explore all hypotheses. But a day or two later, standing on the new patio, looking out at the garden, I realized I was already starting to say goodbye.

The evening of the first bouzouki finally arrived. Wendy and Joe went down to see Michelle, sitting on the balcony above Stamati's shop, next door to the restaurant, to watch the final preparations. Hundreds of people were expected. Kosta had driven down from Ano Peritheia, the tables from his own taverna piled high on the back of his truck. Spiro the baker arrived from Kassiopi with two enormous panniers filled with loaves of bread. The street was already lined with cars—relatives from Corfu Town here for the festivities.

The kitchen was a scene of intense activity. Christos had a whole lamb, a whole kid and several long kokoretsi turning on spits above an inferno of charcoal. The aroma of meat and herbs was heavenly. A mountain of souvlakia had been prepared, pails full of squid already cut into rings and floured, buckets of french fries ready for the deep fryer, great bowls of cucumber, tomato and lettuce, green pepper and carrots cut into ribbons and freshened with vinegar, troughs of feta keeping moist in its briny whey. Tasso's wife, Dimita, had been making her small, triangular cheese pies for days.

"Yassu, Wendy! Hallo!"

It was Ilias—we hadn't seen him for years. After university and national service he had gone to work in a bank on another island.

"Are you coming to the bouzouki?"

"Of course!"

"Oh God! What's that?"

All eyes turned to the steep hillside across the valley. Smoke was rising behind the ridge, white against the blue of the sky.

The kitchen emptied, everyone standing on the patio among the tables, discussing the fire. The final consensus was that on such a hot day, with no wind at all, there was little danger. Even Kosta, who had more reason than anyone to be concerned, agreed it would burn itself out long before it threatened Ano Peritheia. But I couldn't help feeling a twinge of relief half an hour later when the fire truck from the coast rumbled by and disappeared up the road.

Up at Philip's bar, the tables and chairs along the edge of the vine-covered patio were already occupied—a great vantage point for looking down on the party and across at the fire.

And now people were starting to stroll in from other parts of the village, family groups, taking their time, the adults pausing to greet friends, the children racing off in all directions. I wondered if we shouldn't go down and find somewhere to sit, for the paddock seemed to be filling up rapidly though there was still an hour to go before darkness fell. But we lingered and lost our opportunity until Ilias saw us and beckoned us over to share his table.

No one was ordering food yet, though the friends of the management who had been drafted as waiters were busy enough bringing beer and wine. The musicians had taken their places on the stage—except for the music teacher himself, who was nowhere to be seen. The boys began to warm up by improvising some simple jazz.

Joe sat on my lap, taking it all in while we talked to Ilias about Nibby and our book and listened to his news about life on Cephalonia. He was married now, to his university sweetheart, and they had a baby daughter. And still the people were coming—the tourists from the rented houses, every one of our friends from the village. The strings of lights were switched on, deepening the shadows of dusk beyond their circle. We could see the fire on the hillside behind us, a broken red line creeping harmlessly over the ridge. The fire truck had returned and parked up the street, and the firemen were mingling with the crowd.

Food began to appear, though I had heard no one ordering any—plates of salad, squid and souvlaki to share, french fries and cheese pies. The lamb and the kid would come later. And now, at last, the music teacher took the stage, looking very Las Vegas in tight black trousers and a crimson shirt, sitting on a stool with the band behind him. The music began, a rousing bouzouki instrumental with a lively beat, and those who had been standing on the dance floor slowly moved back among the tables, not yet ready to dance.

The band was well rehearsed and skilful. Their first number drew appreciative applause, but the musicians did not acknowledge it, gliding into a slower, more measured melody.

"Are you going to dance?" we asked Ilias. He laughed and shook his head, indicating another man who had stepped out into the empty area—one of the regular poker players from Philip's bar. Quite unselfconsciously, he crouched, straightened, twisted around and crouched again, his arms stretched out for balance. Was it the same dance we had seen Ilias perform years ago? Something like it—the same intensity—head lowered as if he were watching his own movements. Murmurs of approval came from some of the men; the tourists' cameras flashed.

"He's very good," whispered Ilias.

Another man joined him for the second dance, which was a great deal faster and more carefree. A hand on each other's shoulder, they skipped from one side of the circle to the other, and this time the crowd was clapping, urging them on with shouts and laughter.

The girls appeared, much to Joe's excitement, lining up during a pause in the music, looking very demure in their traditional costumes. There was quite a disparity in height and age, but when the music began they all moved perfectly in sync, forming a circle, breaking it again, swaying from side to side. They might have been in a trance, their concentration was so deep. When their turn was finished, they curtseyed low and walked swiftly out of the circle, grinning and blushing at the cheers.

Now the crowd moved in, forming a circle of fifty people, hands on shoulders, stepping sideways, dipping and rising. We lifted Joe and stood him on the table to see, then I swung him up onto my shoulders, holding hard to his ankles. Koula was waving us into the ever-expanding circle, and we made our way to her, Joe clinging tight to my head. Wendy and I were laughing. Everyone was laughing, the rhythm of the insistent music growing faster and faster. It seemed as if the whole village were pressing around us in one huge affectionate embrace.

Long after we had walked home up Zervou and gone to bed we could still hear the band playing, electric bouzouki and "Roll Out the Barrel" bouncing about the smouldering hills.

SEPTEMBER BROUGHT little respite from the heat of that spectacular summer. The blackberries ripened early, but we made no jam. We picked our few bunches of grapes and carried them up to the old house on Zervou where Philip made and stored his wine, treading the fruit in a vast wooden tub until his legs were purple. There had been no rain since May—not a drop—and we awoke one morning to find a fine film of red dust over everything, Sahara sand blown clean across the Mediterranean by the sirocco. The long afternoons had a strange dry, oppressive weight. Sunsets were violently beautiful, as scarlet as a slap in the face.

Wendy's portfolio of lists waxed and waned. According to the private contract we had signed with Chris, almost all our belongings were to be left behind. In Canada, we would start again. This house, this life would not be dismantled. We were stepping away from it for a while but leaving it whole—a significant consolation. Joe had apparently inherited his mother's taste for adventure, and the idea of Toronto intrigued him. He would miss the ants that had already found chinks in the courtyard. He would miss Nibby's owl, peeping each night in the oak tree outside his window, answered by its brethren across the valley, endlessly reiterating the claim to their moonlit territories.

Like the nocturnal seas in which Philip swam, summer nights in the mountains were vibrant with activity. The sheep in the paddock on the other side of our northern fence wandered and stirred, the bells around their necks clanking like wind chimes. A dog on Zervou barked at a bat and another dog took up the cry, and another—all the way down to Aghios Ilias. One could hear the progress of a single motorbike struggling with the gradient from the coast to the village as a waiter made his way home at three o'clock in the morning. Somewhere an old man had left his radio on to scare off the Moro before it scared him. And behind it all was the nighttime chorus of the insects—a tireless rhythm section of maraca players concealed in the trees. The noise never stopped as the stars wheeled overhead until an hour before dawn, when suddenly silence fell.

It was the quiet that woke me. I climbed out of bed, pulled on a pair of shorts and tiptoed downstairs in the pitch darkness, bare feet feeling the familiar nuances of each wooden stair, and out into the cool air of the courtyard. I made my way to the new patio and sat on the wall, legs dangling over the invisible garden. The moon had set and the stars shone in all their glory—the Milky Way a brush stroke of light from horizon to horizon, the Great Bear high over Albania and close to it Cassiopeia, like a *W* for Wendy. One star was moving—a satellite of the technological age drawing a line across the sky, part of the world we were returning to, but no part of this farewell.

Silence is always relative, but that night it seemed almost absolute. Not a whisper of a breeze. When the ferry from Brindisi passed, far below and two miles away, lit up like a floating apartment building, I could hear the low throb of its engines.

I had built this wall I was sitting on, just as other men had built the house behind me, had planted those olive trees and marked out the hillside with drystone walls, dividing it up, rearranging the surface of things into areas where they could work and live and fail and triumph. The starlight was too faint to see any of our endeavours—just a glimmer in the sky, reflected in the sea, divided by the black bulk of the mountains. But the wall beneath me was real and tangible. It would outlast me, and one day Joe would bring his children here and show them the house where he grew up, the patio where he watched the ants and played with his cars, the small rhombus of land with its eleven olive trees where his brother's ashes are buried.

A shift in the air, a momentary stirring. The sky in the east was starting to lighten—still darkest indigo but not so dark as the valley below me. Stars fading. How long have I been sitting here?

The sky is decidedly lighter now, passing through the spectrum from blue to purple to brown to improbable pink, a Homeric cliché. Down in the olive grove, a single cicada wakes up with a rasp, like a football fan with a rattle alone on the terraces, whirrs for a moment, then goes back to sleep. My eyes are beginning to function, suddenly aware of the drop down into the garden—a sleepy vertigo that brings no panic. I climb off the wall and move to the steps. Same view. Same silence, but now the hush is expectant, gravid with all the life that is poised to awake for another day.

The birds are the first to appear. The house martins from the neighbouring ruins, diving out through the glassless windows, chattering in their flight. Then the crows, leaving their rookery in the mountains, huddling low over the garden en route to the coast. The sky is orange in the east, the sun imminent. Here and there, the cicadas are stirring. For a minute or two I can hear individuals to the left, to the right—then there are too many and the aural background is filled in.

Something stirs at my feet—a delicate snake coming up from the garden, a species I have never seen before. Slim as a pencil, a foot long, with a reddish body, pale belly, its head an iridescent turquoise with fine black markings. It is looking for water, gliding gracefully up the flower bed's retaining wall, tasting the morning with its tongue.

Up on Zervou, a neighbour opens his door, greeting the day with a coughing fit that echoes around the valley.

This time tomorrow we will be gone. We will carry our suitcases to the taxi that Philip has organized. We will leave our house and the memories of three and three-quarter years. Our books will remain on the shelves, for Chris to read, if he wishes. Our linen and pillows and rugs, sealed inside sturdy plastic bags, will be safe in the boys' room. In the winter, Koula will come and open the windows for an hour or two and turn on the new radiators Chris has bought to drive away the damp. The contact points of the water pump will rust with the first November rains as they always do. One day in January a storm will loosen the roof tiles around Kostantes's trap door and a rat will find its way into the loft and be grateful for the spacious apartment. Opportunistic neighbours will uproot the jasmine for its own good, transplanting it to a better-tended garden. Spiro's donkey will be passing on a winter morning and will kick out, breaking the great clay pot that cradles the roots of the gardenia. Sun and rain will work away at the front doors made by Dmitri the carpenter, warping and slowly dissolving the wood from the bottom up. The great brass knobs my mother sent us from England will blacken.

This house will always be our only real home, and we will come back one summer, two or three years from now, when the pain of losing our son has settled into a different, more manageable corner of our minds. We want Joe to grow up knowing this place, to remember his childhood here.

We will remember. Every stone, every board and tile, every plant. Wherever else we live will only be a temporary place to stay, the postponement of an eventual return.

Epilogue

August 2004

TODAY WE WENT INTO CORFU Town to visit George Kaloudis, our lawyer. His secretary chatted with us in perfect English, then showed us into his elegant office. We had not seen him for fifteen years but he greeted us with the same familiar affection and we all smiled and lied bravely about how the years had not changed us at all. George is now a power in the land, a leading barrister and former deputy mayor of Corfu Town. He talks international politics, municipal affairs and old times with equal ease, but there is an unspoken subtext to our conversation. We both make self-deprecating remarks about our thinning hair but take pains to imply that we are just as fit and active and physically capable as we were when we were young. We allude to our successful careers but make it clear that we are still loyal to the socialist principles of our youth. I congratulate him on the changes that he and his colleagues have wrought upon Corfu Town—and I do it sincerely, for the town has never looked smarter or more beautiful—but a small, sentimental part of me misses the way things were.

Here in the port, where Stephen and I stayed awake all night, waiting for the five a.m. bus after losing our pittance at the casino, fending off a pack of feral dogs, praying for dawn, there is now a tree-shaded piazza. The alleys and lanes behind the 'Spianada have become a pedestrian precinct, scrubbed clean, repaired, the quaint streets lined with chic boutiques and elegant little restaurants charging Athenian prices. A tinsmith still works behind the building where Kostantes once owned an apartment, but most of the other dimly lit emporiums are gone. So are the old toothless women selling bunches of herbs on the curb. So is the yoghurt shop with the twin icons of Saint Spiridon and King Constantine above the softly buzzing fuse box and the albino boy with the skin like buttermilk. The citizens now shop at supermarkets on the outskirts of town and the yoghurt they buy comes from France. I even miss the bank, where every transaction took the best part of a morning while the clerk wrote out details of our account in a massive, leather-bound ledger and where Wendy once fainted in the heat. Now we can slide our Canadian plastic through an anglophone ATM—in and out in an air-conditioned minute.

Wendy and I stroll hand-in-hand through the fashionable town, as we did the first time we saw it, so long ago, yesterday, so long ago. It's just the two of us again, with Joe completing a second archaeology degree in London and our daughter, Mae Pearl, back in Toronto. I feel younger than I have felt in years, and I buy a foolish shirt in one of the new boutiques, wearing it out of the shop, walking back to the rented car that we parked by the 'Spianada.

We drive home along the coast road, recognizing certain

houses that once stood in isolation surrounded by olive groves and orchards of lemon trees, now hemmed in by hotels and hypermarkets. Kalamaki beach, where we wandered alone and naked, is ringed by villas and restaurants. Yanni and Chrisoula's shack is not one of them. More powerful concerns closed him down, and these days he makes a small living renting out beach chairs and umbrellas. Garbage bins and portable toilets bake in the heat where the bamboo once grew. There's a car park on the sand and a jetty stretching far out to sea where the caiques from Kassiopi disgorge their holidaymakers for a barbecue lunch with disco and rowdy games of pass-the-orange. In Peritheia, Spiro has expanded his store into new premises across the road, his prices in euros now, the drachma entirely forgotten.

Peritheia has become quite the hub, with a modern butcher, a nightclub and a gelateria on the coast road. New houses peep out behind bushes, climbing a little way up the hill towards Aghios Ilias. The road is sleek and painted with white lines, its surface smoother than any street in Toronto. Close to each hairpin bend is a stripe of cement where the great pipe is buried, a pipe that brings mains water to Loutses, pumped from a spring on the coast—pure drinkable water, as virtuous as any Alpine mineral source. The pipe follows the old shortcut up the mountain, above ground most of the way, and the sun heats it in its progress so that a cold shower after the beach is perfectly warm. When the mains water was connected to our house, the pressure burst the pipes under our kitchen sink.

The road climbs on, winding into the mountains, into the village, into our past. Loutses is quiet these days. The young men and women have moved to the coast, no longer interested in farming olives. They drive German cars and talk constantly into cellphones. Ilias has a successful accountancy firm on Cephalonia and also owns a radio station and a popular hotel on Corfu. We see him occasionally—a prosperous man. Up here, the old people who remain grow more somnolent every year. Stamati's shop has closed. So have the two tavernas. Christos sold his to an Austrian woman who turned it into a private house, stayed a year or two, then left the island. The lean-to over Spiro's souvlaki grill rotted and was taken away. Someone cut down the trees that had shaded Joe's christening party. Only the fig tree remains, larger than ever, the unpicked fruit bursting with juice to intoxicate wasps.

In the peaceful, deeply cleft valley above the village, below the road to Ano Peritheia, the Loutses cemetery holds many old friends. Old Tomas. Panayotis and Elpitha, who sold us the house. Georgie. Tasso. Stamati. Ilias's father, Petros. Philip's father, our koumparos Leonidas. Cancer took Renna, tragically young, and Koula's husband, Haridimos. We were back in the village for a summer vacation when Kostantes died, fifteen years ago. I went down to offer my condolences to Alexandra. His body had been laid out in the bedroom, and I spent some minutes alone with him, remembering the old rogue's many kindnesses to us. He was our first friend in Loutses, and we miss him.

Philip still tends his kafeneion, though half a dozen customers gathered around the poker table now constitutes a busy night. Ten years ago, driving back from Corfu Town at three o'clock in the morning, his car went over a cliff. If he had been wearing a seat belt, he often tells us, he would be dead, but he crawled back up to the road, losing blood from a broken arm and shattered leg, his scalp draped over his face. Endless operations and physiotherapy have allowed him to bend his knee an inch or two.

The schoolhouse next to the kafeneion is also closed. There are too few children in the village to justify the expense of a teacher, but those who are left still make use of the schoolyard. Some months after we moved to Canada, my mother organized a fundraising tribute to Nibby, gathering all her famous friends and clients into a theatre in London's West End on Valentine's Day. It was a theatrical who's who of unprecedented proportions, with songs, poems, sketches and short plays written and performed by dozens of stars. The substantial amount of money raised was donated to hospitals to improve the daily lives of children with cancer, but a little was set aside for Loutses to buy swings and a roundabout, see-saws and basketball nets for the schoolyard. A plaque on the wall informs those who glance up that the playground was built for the village children in memory of Ford Lightfoot Martin.

Loutses is falling asleep, would be sleeping now if it weren't for the dozens of Europeans who have bought houses in the valley. Many of those from England trace their lineage to the tourists we lured to the village twenty years ago. A small part of me regrets the fact that Loutses has become such an international community, but these adventurous English families love the place as much as Wendy and I do. They understand its ways and cherish its idiosyncrasies, and we are happy to count them as friends.

Up Zervou and a short walk down on the other side of the ridge, in the little valley that few now remember is called

Koulouri, our house has survived. The *N* in the courtyard is still pink against the grey stones, the broad steps down to the borthro satisfyingly intact. The cherry tree we planted for Nibby among the olives withered soon after we left and the lone cypress was cut down and stolen for timber, but the garden is green and vigorous. Fireflies still blink beneath the olive trees on warm nights in May and snakes and tortoises go about their business in the neglected grass. For the last few years it has rained in July—a side effect of global warming. Or perhaps the unnatural fecundity comes from the mains water that our neighbours up on Zervou use to hose down their gardens every morning and evening until a small flood, rich with topsoil, sluices down the driveway onto our flower beds.

Two summers after Nibby died, Wendy and I came back to Corfu, bringing Joe and our beautiful one-year-old daughter, Mae Pearl. We threw open the shutters and let in the breeze, brought up the trunks from the apothiki and unwrapped the bundles of linen from the shelves in the boys' room and the plastic bag full of stuffed toys. In the evening, Koula came down, bringing much gossip and a two-litre bottle of oil pressed from our olive trees. Hard on her heels came the girls from Zervou, leading Joe out into the garden to play.

Chris had paid builders to add a vast new bathroom onto the northern side of the house, complete with a bidet, an actual bath, a state-of-the-art washing machine and a wall-mounted boiler three times the size of our old one. He was using the old bathroom as a cupboard—however had we managed with such a small space?—to store the trunks full of his summer wardrobe and beach toys. There was a telephone in the house and Chris's pictures hung on the walls; the kitchen shelves under the stairs held his bread-making machine, his electric juicer, his electric waffle maker and hibachi.

But they were just things. None of his changes had altered the spiritual identity of the place. We spent our precious weeks laughing with pleasure, rediscovering innumerable details, as if we had picked up a favourite old book and found we remembered every word.

Nibby never had a Greek baptism, but Mae was christened that summer with a party to rival her brother's. Koula stood as her godmother and gave her the Greek name of Antigone (this time with our blessing).

In the years that followed, we returned almost every summer, sometimes for a couple of weeks, sometimes for months, staying as long as our increasingly busy lives in Canada permitted. In Toronto, we moved from one place to another, putting down only the shallowest of roots. Here on Corfu, the connection was never severed. Our children have their own layered, transparent memories of hot mornings on the beach and endless, silent afternoons under the olive trees.

This house on its steep patch of land is our home and will always remain so. And now it is once again ours. In April, in Toronto, we gave Chris the last of many payments, then we all went out to celebrate. He hasn't been here in years and there is a long list of work to be done. We have also bought the ruin next door, complete with its ancient oven. The Vlahos brothers had lost interest in renovating it and eventually agreed to sell. Yesterday our neighbour, Yorgos the carpenter, mentioned that it was built as a monastery, three hundred years ago—twice the age of our own house. No one had ever thought to tell us. In summers to come we will link the two properties, extending the patio, adding a roof and floor to the ruin, fitting doors and windows, recycling every sound beam and plank, every single old stone. Our driveway will once again be a construction site, piled high with sacks of cement and mountains of sand. For now, I must be content with a small hill—just enough to let me mix up a batch of mortar to repair the roof tiles on the little house across the courtyard. The wooden handle of the spade feels smooth in my hands.

Wendy has taken the shutters off the downstairs windows and carried them out to the patio. She is busy with sandpaper—intent—her long auburn hair tied back in a pony tail. Straightening to inspect her work, she looks exactly as beautiful as she did the first time she painted them, twenty-one years ago.

In the evening we walk up Zervou and down into the village, pausing at Dee's rock to admire the sunset over the distant promontories. On the terrace outside Philip's bar, three elderly men are sitting, each nursing a beer. We knew them in the swaggering prime of their lives but they are calmer now, their voices softer, their gestures more cautious and curtailed. They have grown into the gracious good manners we always noticed in the old people of the village. I have forgotten most of the Greek I once knew, but Wendy has been improving hers and sets them all chuckling, describing the night she and they fought the fire on the hillside across the road.

Philip comes out and sits down with us, propping up his leg on a chair. In no time at all he is arguing about those global leaders whose policies displease him, giving his own forthright perspective, cursing and laughing in a single breath. His new dog, Prudhomme, named for the philosopher, wakes up as the twilight deepens and lopes off into the village, looking for action.

Wendy and I stroll home in the darkness, my arm around her slender waist, her hand on my shoulder. The lights of Albania glimmer under the sky. In our oak tree an owl is calling.

A NOTE ON THE TYPE

The Greek for Love is set in Monotype Dante, a font family originally designed by Giovanni Mardersteig in the late 1940s. Derived from classic book faces such as Bembo and Centaur, Dante features an elegant italic well suited to its roman sibling. The digital version of Dante was issued in 1993, in three weights and including a set of titling capitals.

ABOUT THE AUTHOR

James Chatto's award-winning writing on food, wine and travel appears frequently in leading magazines and newspapers in Canada, the U.S. and England. He is the author of four cookbooks and a contributor to many others. His nonfiction book, *The Man Who Ate Toronto* (1998), was nominated for the City of Toronto Book Award and won awards from Cuisine Canada and Heritage Toronto. In an earlier incarnation, Chatto was an actor, a singer and a saxophonist with a single that reached number two on the British Northern Soul charts.